To a v ... riend,
♡ C

Treasures of a Woman's Heart

A DAYBOOK OF
STORIES AND INSPIRATION

EDITED BY

Lynn D. Morrissey

STARBURST PUBLISHERS®
Lancaster, Pennsylvania

To schedule author appearances, write: Author Appearances, Starburst Promotions, P.O. Box 4123, Lancaster, Pennsylvania 17604 or call (717) 293-0939. Website: www.starburstpublishers.com.

CREDITS:
Cover design by Richmond & Williams
Text design and composition by John Reinhardt Book Design

Scripture taken from the HOLY BIBLE: NEW INTERNATIONAL VERSION®. NIV®. Copyright © 1973, 1978, 1984 by International Bible Society. Used by permission of Zondervan Publishing House. The "NIV" and "New International Version" trademarks are registered in the United States Patent and Trademark Office by International Bible Society.

To the best of its ability, Starburst Publishers® has strived to find the source of all material. If there has been an oversight, please contact us and we will make any correction deemed necessary in future printings. We also declare that to the best of our knowledge all material (quoted or not) contained herein is accurate, and we shall not be held liable for the same.

First Printing, April, 2000

ISBN: 1-892016-25-7
Library of Congress Catalog Number: 99-69034
Printed in the United States of America

With devotion to the Lord . . .
  Soli Gloria Deo

With deep gratitude to the women who comprise my rich heritage—each a unique treasure, herself . . .

My mother Fern Morrissey, my sister Carol Gonzalez, my great-grandmother Enola (MaMa) Ayers[†]; my grandmothers Clara Ayers[†] and Nina Morrissey[†]; my great-aunts Marie Gemmer[†], Frances Reiman, Hazel Bretsnyder[†], Marie (Kewpie) Feiler[†], Martha Bretsnyder, Esther Bretsnyder[†], and Bernice (Bee) Bretsnyder[†], and my aunts Wanda Iola Jones, Elizabeth (Nancy) Ayers, Ruth Ayers[†], and Jeannette Marshall[†].

. . . and my daughter, Sheridan Suzanne, my precious treasure, bestowed by God as my fortieth birthday "surprise package"!

With appreciation for their assistance . . .

My *Lifeliner Prayer Partners* for *LifeWords Ministries©*, my treasured husband, Michael, my publisher Sharon Hanby-Robie, Ruth Alfeld, Chad Allen, Gail Boutelle, Connie Joy Caruso, Rose Violet Flowers, Armené Humber, Jo Manwarren, Sharon Neal, JoAnn Rosa-Hanes, John Reinhardt, and Rachel St. John-Gilbert.

[†] At home with the Lord.

Contents

Introduction

One of my most treasured possessions is a calico quilt, as worn now as the loving hands that painstakingly fashioned it. I still see vividly the large, lined hands of my great-grandmother, Enola "MaMa" Ayers—hands that could animate conversation with broad, sweeping gestures or guide a needle with a surgeon's precision. Mama cut each scrap from her colorful dresses, from her colorful life. At times, the pieces unraveled, and she sutured them together with the same love that stayed my childhood fears and mended my heart into wholeness.

And now, many years after MaMa's death, my heart is being torn again. At this writing, I am packing to leave my home of twenty-four years, Linden Cottage. Developers are preparing to raze our treasured 1912 Arts and Crafts bungalow. We sold it to accommodate our growing family and home business responsibilities. The house will be destroyed, as land value exceeds that of the structure.

Yet no price tag can be placed on our experiences here. This is where my young husband, Michael, whisked me over the threshold; where Grandma Nina rippled ivory keys in tuneful serenade; where extended family said grace around the Thanksgiving table, or implored grace as death began emptying our dining room chairs; where we picnicked under umbrageous oaks in summer and under white-saucered dogwoods in spring; where, on our sprawling porch, I rocked my infant daughter, Sheridan, wrapped in MaMa's frayed quilt.

One day I will give the quilt to Sheridan, and it will be her treasure. For now, I box it up to be delivered to the new house.

As I fill box after box with memory after memory, I realize the essence of Linden Cottage—its beauty, its warmth, its love—cannot be destroyed. It will be forever treasured in my heart.

Mary listened to the wisdom of her young son, Jesus, and she "treasured all these things in her heart."[1] Women instinctively know what has value—those timeless intangibles—those vital "invisibles," unseen, yet *real* and crucial to living a meaningful life. Women esteem God's touchstone testaments of grace—love, laughter, faith, family, comfort, courage, wisdom, wonder, relationships, remembrances . . . the joy . . . the journey . . . We understand it's not only the destination that counts, but the lessons learned, the joy shared along the way.

In this devotional, join your sisters of faith as we "set [our] hearts on pilgrimage,"[2] journeying to the very heart of God. In our materialistic world, we have learned to acquire excess baggage that weighs us down—possessions, power, prestige. As you read these true stories you'll see how women razed visible pretense and raised up the invisible platform of Christ—a heart-place from which to adopt His virtues, His values. Jesus spoke of value when He said, "For where your treasure is, there your heart will be also."[3] Treasures in Heaven are laid up only as treasures on earth are laid down. It will not always be easy to relinquish earthly treasures, but with Jesus it will always be possible. "If in utter helplessness we cast our all on Christ, He will be to us the whole treasury of God."[4]

Lynn D. Morrissey
Saint Louis, Missouri

---

[1] Luke 2:51
[2] Psalm 84:5
[3] Matthew 6:21
[4] Henry Benjamin Whipple

Relationships

Treasure in Sacrifice

BY ELISABETH ELLIOT

Do little things as if they were great because of the majesty of Jesus
Christ Who dwells in you; and do great things as if they were little
and easy because of His omnipotence.

—BLAISE PASCAL

When I was a student at Wheaton College, I was greatly blessed
in having as my dormitory "housemother," a dear Southern gentle-
woman, Miss Cumming, whose extremely wealthy family had
disinherited her for becoming a Christian. Because of her devotion to Christ, she had sacrificed all her worldly possessions.

A gracious, petite lady with an eternal southern drawl, she
had a charming way of clasping her bosom and pouring out her
soul—especially if there were a sad story to relay.

On one occasion she said, "Oh, Betty, I came to Wheaton to
be a spiritual counselor; but here I am carrying mops and toilet
paper across campus!" But she wasn't complaining. Although she
had been raised in an elegant mansion staffed with servants, she,
herself, possessed a servant's heart, willing to offer to God any
job that needed doing, no matter how seemingly menial. That
greatly impressed me.

Years later, when my husband and I visited her at a retirement
center, I reminded her of the day that she had toted mops, and
of what she had said. Once more, clasping her now less than
ample bosom, she exclaimed, "Oh Betty, just think . . . the Lord
allowed me to carry mops and toilet paper for His glory!"

Miss Cumming's comment underscored for me, once more,
that true treasure lies not in our earthly possessions—in the good
material gifts that God bestows, but in those gifts that we sacrifice and offer back to Him—out of our obedience. In the sacrifice lies immeasurable reward—an opportunity to see His glory.

". . . You have been faithful with a few things; I will put you
in charge of many things. Come and share your master's
happiness!"

—MATTHEW 25:21

Thought . . . Do you long to do great things for God?
Don't "despise the day of small things" because they
are humbling. Tackle them by the Spirit's power.

A Few Good Hens

BY REBECCA BARLOW JORDAN

When a friend laughs, it is for him to disclose the subject of his joy;
when he weeps, it is for me to discover the cause of his sorrow.

—JOSEPH FRANÇOIS DESMAHIS

Just before we moved from the Dallas metroplex to the laid-back
town of Greenville, Texas, Becky, a new writing friend, called
ahead to welcome me. Would I like to join their "hen" gathering
as soon as I got settled? I had just said good-bye to my old writers' group, and I welcomed the thought of a new one. But as
soon as I hung up the phone, I remembered the old seminary
warning: "Ministers' wives shouldn't have close friends." Old fears
fueled my timidity as a newcomer. Will they like me? Can a city
chick make it in a country coop?

I joined their group and, gradually, my walls of timidity
tumbled down. Still, moments of self-doubt lingered, like one
particularly tiring Sunday at our church. Afterwards, I pulled
into the driveway of our home, feeling exhausted from greeting
and running, smiling and singing, teaching and hugging. I was
in desperate need of encouragement when I noticed something
strange about my front door. A foreign object was hanging from
my welcome wreath. Something dead? A harassment? Had I
ruffled someone's feathers? As I tentatively approached, I realized that someone had hung a scraggly, rubber chicken on my
front door. I let out a long series of belly laughs. I knew exactly
who had done it—Gracie, one of my new "Hens with Pens"
friends. Gracie's deed was more than ludicrous. It was *medicine*.
My new friend had reminded me of the simple treasure of friendship—and that life is much easier—and better—when we laugh
together.

> Two are better than one, . . . If one falls down, his friend
> can help him up. But pity the man who falls and has no
> one to help him up!
>
> —ECCLESIASTES 4:9–10

Thought . . . Do you and your friends enjoy the treasure
of laughter? One way to begin is to have the ability to
laugh at yourself, first; then laugh *with* each other and
never *at* each other.

I Can Do This!

BY LYNN WORLEY KUNTZ

People who say they sleep like a baby haven't got one.

—ANONYMOUS

Artis, our oldest, recently moved into an apartment and is working for her dad. "Working with him is much easier than living with him," she says. It seems a short time since she sprouted her first tooth.

Our high school daughter and middle school son are first up, last to bed—both so busy I sometimes wonder if they still live here. (One glance into their bedrooms makes it abundantly clear that they do!) Wasn't it only yesterday when Piper took her first steps and Nick pronounced his first words?

Seven candles topped Quinn's recent birthday cake. "Do horses drool?" he asked. "What's behind brains? Do ears sleep? How many cats are having babies right now? Is there a law against doctors giving kids shots in the head? How far up are clouds? Are we on top or bottom of the world? How many crumbs are in a chocolate chip cookie? Do fish get thirsty?"

Quinn, fourth and last, recently entered first grade. After twenty years (we could have planned better!), I'm home alone a few hours each day. I'll always treasure those years with my preschool children. We had such fun, and I'm a far better person because of them. However, I also treasure the new directions my relationships with my growing-up kids are taking. I'd be fibbing if I said that I was inconsolably lonely now! Assuming that Quinn leaves home at eighteen, it will be twelve more years before my husband, Darryl, and I experience an empty nest—the same year we start collecting Social Security! I can't imagine it. But I have fun trying!

Sons are a heritage from the Lord, children a reward from Him.

—PSALM 127:3

Thought . . . Are you ill at ease in your "empty nest" or dreading the thought of having one? Instead of lamenting the loss of your babies, treasure the friendships that you can develop with your adult children.

Treasured Tea and Sympathy

BY MARILYN WILLETT HEAVILIN

Somehow, taking tea together encourages an atmosphere of intimacy when you slip off the timepiece in your mind and cast your fate to a delight of tasty tea, tiny foods, and thoughtful conversation.

—GAIL GRECO

My friend, Diana, had been through a very rough year. Her husband had had a stroke at the age of forty-seven which had forced him into retirement. Diana was caring for him as well as working full time at an outside job.

She loved to attend the outdoor concerts in the summertime at the Redlands Bowl. We arranged for a night that she could have someone else stay with her husband. We told her we would go early and save seats so she could come as late as she needed. When she arrived, I opened my picnic basket and we had a tea party. Diana is from England and loves tea and teatime. I had hot tea in a thermos, and I served it in my most delicate china cups. I had bought yummy desserts from a deli . . . and served them on china plates. I used my best silverware and linen napkins. I also gave Diana a beautiful picture book about English teatime. We had a crowd watching us and drooling! The setting was perfect, the music was inspiring, the sky was filled with stars, and my friend Diana felt loved and pampered. She will never forget that night, nor will I.

". . . He has filled the hungry with good things . . ."

—LUKE 1:53

Thought . . . How can you pamper a weary friend? Handle one of life's "necessities" for her—such as cooking, cleaning, or grocery shopping. Then give her your time and your listening ear.

Evie's Joy

BY KATHLEEN DALE WRIGHT

The humblest Christians are the best Christians, and most like to Christ and highest in His favor.

—MATTHEW HENRY

A young woman named Evie regularly attended the Bible study which met at our house. She was about thirty at the time, and had a mental age of six or seven. Her mother had not been able to take her to services at their church because of Evie's disruptive behavior.

It was not long after she and her mother started attending the Bible study that Evie, in her childlike way, came to know the Lord as her Savior. After that, she listened quietly to the Bible teaching, and she entered happily into the singing. Often she clapped her hands softly in time to the music, holding them just beneath her chin. Sometimes her joy overflowed in soft, rippling laughter as she lifted her face heavenward, her eyes sparkling. No matter how discouraged or out of sorts I felt when the group came together, Evie's joy lifted me into a spirit of genuine praise.

"Evie is always telling people about coming to Bible study at your house," her mother told us one day. She says, "I like to go there. They have such joy." Child-woman that she was, she didn't realize that it was her joy that lifted us.

Some people just saw Evie as a retarded woman. But to us she was a pure treasure, a pearl of great value. And I hope someday to join with her, making the courts of heaven ring with praise.

"See that you do not look down on one of these little ones. For I tell you that their angels in heaven always see the face of my Father in heaven . . ."

—MATTHEW 18:10

Thought . . . Do you have a childlike joy in Jesus or do you insist on solving the complexities of life? When you have a childlike faith, trusting Him without question, your joy will return.

Taking Time for Friendship

BY ANN HIBBARD

. . . the only way to have a friend is to be one.

—RALPH WALDO EMERSON

Debbie and I settled in with our cups of steaming coffee for our oasis of conversation. We rendezvous at the bookstore's espresso bar every couple of weeks. Our different lifestyles work against our spending time together. We consider these espresso bar moments a major triumph for our friendship.

Today Debbie began, "Ann, I need to ask you a question. Have I offended you?"

"Of course not, Debbie! What have I done that gave you that idea?" I asked.

"You haven't been calling me. That's not like you, not to be in touch."

I reflected over the past six weeks. It was true. I had picked up the phone to call my dear friend only once or twice. The reason was not hurt feelings, but a busy schedule. The first thing to go was my time on the telephone keeping in touch with my closest friends. Relieved she was not at fault, Debbie understood my reasons, forgave my neglect, and moved on to our next topic of conversation. Yet, I was saddened that in my flurry of activity, I had disregarded one of my most precious treasures—my true friend.

Time is an essential ingredient in cultivating true friendship. If we are not available when our friend needs us, we communicate that we do not really care. A true friend takes time for friendship, especially when she is needed.

Dear friend, I pray that you may enjoy good health and that all may go well with you, even as your soul is getting along well.

—III JOHN 2

Thought . . . Has your friend hurt you? Take time to explain your feelings. Chances are she may be unaware of her offense. She can't correct a situation about which she knows nothing.

The Tenderizer

BY ELIZABETH M. WILT

Hardening of the heart ages people more quickly than hardening of the arteries.

—E. C. McKensie

No doubt about it. Dads are treasures. As I watch my husband tuck our three-year-old daughter in bed, I am reminded of those nostalgic bedtime moments when I was a kid. Bedtime with my Dad was fun time. After he pulled the covers up to my chin and gave me a kiss, I was given the choice of two bedtime tucks— the "Tenderizer" or the "Steamroller." Each was guaranteed to keep me tucked securely under those covers through the night.

My least favorite tuck was the Steamroller. As Dad said, "Only the rough and tough order the Steamroller." (It deserved its name as it flattened anyone in its path.) Dad would lie down on the bed and roll right over me. Of course, Mom had more than two cents to say about that tuck.

I loved the Tenderizer. Dad could tenderize better than anyone else. He used the sides of his hands to "chop" faster than a drum roll from my head to my toes, and back again. The Tenderizer seemed to vibrate every last giggle from my tired little body.

Twenty-five years ago, I thought that no one could top my father at tenderizing. But now I understand that my Heavenly Father is the best Tenderizer in the business! He can soften the hardest of hearts, break through the toughest of barriers. He can speak such tender, treasured words that we are forever changed, tucked securely in His love.

And be kind to one another, tender-hearted . . .
—Ephesians 4:32 (NASB)

Thought . . . Do you fear God as an angry, Heavenly Steamroller? Knowing that He gave His precious Son, Jesus, to die for you in an agonizing death, you can never again question His tender love nor His desire to have a personal relationship with you.

Recovery Room

BY PAT DEVINE

Sorrows remembered sweeten present joy.

—ROBERT POLLOK

For years I had been praying for healing of memories and reconciliation between my youngest daughter and me. She had overcome a childhood tragedy to become a successful professional woman, wife and mother, but her wounds had not healed. My sorrow at failing to save her from harm was a burden that I carried in my heart. Never did I dream that the time and the place for resolution would be a hospital room.

I was filling the role of chauffeur/hand-holder/pray-er. We had progressed from registration to pre-op holding, where she was probed and prepped. She was to undergo a bronchoscopy to see if a persistent cough indicated some lung damage. It was a time of worry—a time for prayer.

At last, a nurse came to take her to surgery, and I was directed to another waiting room. Forty-five minutes later I rejoined my daughter, still coughing, face pale and swollen. The recovery room was small, but private. I sat holding her hand, giving silent thanks to God for her safe return. As our hands joined, our hearts began to overflow, and we spoke of old wounds and new joys. We laughed and cried for three hours until the doctor came to say, "Good news! Nothing to write home about. She's all yours now."

Little did he realize how good the news was. The operation was a blessed event. Mother and daughter are doing fine!

". . . You will grieve, but your grief will turn to joy . . ."

—JOHN 16:20

Thought . . . Is there someone with whom you have some misunderstanding? Don't wait until an emergency to reconcile. It might be too late. Swallow your pride and start over. Likely, neither of you will recall how the problem started.

Jesus, My Friend
BY JONI EARECKSON TADA

The dearest friend on earth is a mere shadow compared with Jesus Christ.

—OSWALD CHAMBERS

A friend loves at all times (Proverbs 17:17). If you have a friend like that, you have a treasure—someone with whom you can peel back the layers of your heart, knowing that he or she will handle tenderly and loyally everything that's revealed.

That's why I consider Jesus to be my friend. Of course, there used to be times in prayer when I would get tongue-tied over whether or not I was praising Him properly. I would measure far too carefully my words, wondering if my prayer was progressing the way it should in a tidy order of adoration, confession, thanksgiving, and supplication. Sometimes I just gave up in frustration.

All the while, Jesus must have been waiting for me to simply peel back the layers of my heart and openly share a tumble of thoughts and confessions, like chaff and grain. He wanted to assure me that with His faithful hand He would keep what was worth keeping in my prayer and gently blow the rest away.

Jesus is a friend with whom you can feel safe.

". . . Greater love has no one than this, that he lay down his life for his friends . . ."

—JOHN 15:13

Thought . . . Is Jesus your friend? Don't be afraid. Share with Him *anything* on your heart. Amazingly, He, too, considers you His friend and promises to reveal to you the things of God (John 15:15). Most astonishing of all, He's the friend Who gave His life for you! How can you not feel safe in a personal relationship like that?

Hats Off!

BY BONNIE WATKINS

Thank you, Father, for these tears that have carried me to the depth of Your love. How could I have known Your fullness without the emptiness, Your acceptance without the rejection? You have brought me to Gethsemane and oh, the joy of finding You already there!

—BONNIE BARROWS THOMAS

Tilting the bright red hat rakishly onto my ten-year-old head, I was having the time of my life. My beloved Aunt Annie had taken me downtown for a special shopping trip. Next I chose a multi-flowered creation to model.

All efficiency, the prim saleslady swished over in her navy dress. "Children aren't allowed to try on the hats!" she snapped.

"Well, she's not hurting anything," my aunt suggested.

Yet "store policy" prevailed. I was crushed. The sting of rejection was so strong that the saleslady might as well have slapped me in the face. I turned just as red as the hat I'd enjoyed moments before.

Back at home, Aunt Annie grabbed a hatbox from her closet. She lifted out a soft, furry hat and rubbed it against my cheek. "It's mink. There's a muff, too." She put them in my lap. I just sat there, incredulous. "You put your hands inside the muff to warm them," she explained. Afterward, she allowed me to try on *every* hat in her sizeable collection! It was a day that I shall never forget. Her love salved the wound and warmed my heart.

I treasure this memory. When I recall that day now and remember the pain of rejection, I realize how often Jesus was rejected—ultimately, on the cruel Cross. My pain was only a fraction of His. I never want to be the one to cause rejection, but hope to be the one, like Aunt Annie, to heal it—to mend relationships.

. . . And they took offense at Him.

—MARK 6:3

Thought . . . How can you minister to those whom others reject? A kind smile, a loving touch, gracious words, a patient attitude are ways to apply the balm of Christ's love to wounded souls.

Love Taps on the Wall

BY DORIS C. CRANDALL

There is no surprise more magical than the surprise of being loved. It is the finger of God on a [person's] shoulder.

—CHARLES MORGAN

Every day my strong, healthy daddy worked in the fields from sunup until sundown to make a living for Mother, my sisters, and me on a rented cotton farm in the Texas Panhandle. At times, his voice became gruff as if he were aggravated with me. I felt he didn't love me.

One day Daddy had a fever. He stayed in bed in his room. The next day I contracted the same thing and stayed home from school. Mother put me to bed in my room which was next to Daddy's. We had no radio, and my eyes hurt too much to read, so I whiled away the long hours by mentally drawing circles and squares on the ceiling. Mother, busy as usual, came upstairs only to bring medicine, but didn't stay long. I was so lonesome.

Presently, I heard a tap, tap, tap on the wall common to my room and Daddy's. I realized that Daddy was knocking for *me!* But what could three short raps mean? I thought about it as the sounds continued, always in sets of three. Then it hit me: "I LOVE YOU!" That's it. Daddy is lonely, too. He's thinking of me. At that moment I knew that Daddy loved me. I returned a message, tap, tap, tap—pause—tap. "I LOVE YOU, TOO."

Though I'm grown now and Daddy died long ago, I have always treasured that day—the day that Daddy so personally communicated his love.

Love never fails. . . .

—I CORINTHIANS 13:8

Thought . . . Have you listened for God's "love taps"? His "still, small voice" of love echoes through a whippoorwill's trill, rustling leaves, silver-splashing rain. They bid you "take notice" of His handiwork, created out of love, just for you.

12

Quality Time

BY JEAN FLEMING

We cannot put off living until we are ready. The most salient characteristic of life is its coerciveness: it is always urgent, "here and now" . . .

—JOSE ORGEGAY GASSET

I cringe when I hear, "It isn't how much time you spend with your children that matters, but whether the time is of high quality." High quality for whom? Quality time for a four-year-old may be having Mommie there to kiss a scrape and apply a bandage. A nine-year-old may consider it quality time if Mom is available to talk as soon as he bursts through the front door after school.

One morning our five-year-old, Matthew, ran into the house calling, "Mommie, Mommie, come quick!" Visions of an accident raced through my mind.

He put his finger to his mouth and pointed to the most wildly beautiful butterfly I've ever seen. Together we shared a magical moment. That was quality time.

We may fool ourselves to think that quality time is time scheduled for our convenience. But we won't fool our children.

In the midst of my writing, my daughter, Beth, came to talk. She had just watched an episode of "Little House on the Prairie" and wanted to talk about how the parents in the show handled an incident. So I set aside my writing and gave her my full attention. As we talked I sensed the richness of this time for Beth. After ten or fifteen minutes, I returned to my pen and paper wondering if our talk would have had the same quality if I had asked her to save it until bedtime. Would we have captured the same intensity?

And the child grew and became strong in spirit . . .

—LUKE 1:80

Thought . . . Do you spend *quality* time with your children? Give them *quantity* time, instead. Treasure every moment you can possibly spend with them. They won't be small forever.

Christ, Our Treasure

BY LIZ MOORE MEEKS

Wealth stays with us a little moment if at all; only our characters are steadfast, not our gold.

—EURIPIDES

My compelling urge to brush off the dirty chair was halted by an inner tug on my heart. *Don't! That will be offensive,* I thought.

I was attending a women's Bible study led by my daughter-in-law in one of the poorest sections of Buenos Aires, Argentina. The dingy one-room concrete home held all the family's meager belongings, including several wobbly stools and plastic chairs. A handwritten notice attached to the front door announced the Bible study and women were arriving with children in tow. *Lord,* I silently prayed, *I don't understand their language and I'm overwhelmed and burdened by their poverty. Please remove all hindrances from my heart and mind, and enable me to embrace them with Your love.*

As prayer groups were formed and hands were joined, we lifted praises and petitions to our Heavenly Father. My southern drawl mingled with their Spanish tongues as we gave glory and honor to God. Tears flowed freely as we were knitted together in the bond of love. These women were my sisters in Christ. Their poverty was not one of the heart, for they saw Christ as their Shepherd and nothing did they lack.

Thank you Lord, was my prayer now, *for this gripping, visible reminder that You are our All in all. Our hope is not in material wealth or tarnished earthen treasures, but in You, Lord Jesus Christ, Who alone provides everything that we need.*

> Listen, my dear brothers: Has not God chosen those who are poor in the eyes of the world to be rich in faith and to inherit the kingdom he promised those who love him?
>
> —JAMES 2:5

Thought . . . Are you rich in material possessions or in the treasures of Christ and the fellowship of the saints? His love and forgiveness are the only inheritance that will last eternally.

Loving Servant

BY LINDA J. HUCKABEE

It's so good.

—MR. FOOD ON TELEVISION

My mother, Gloria, was a treasure who changed my life. Mom loved to cook and to sing in the church choir—a perfect pairing, as the choir often provided meals for up to two weeks for people. The quintessential cook, Mom always kept chicken or roast in the freezer for just such emergencies, and took enormous pleasure in delivering meals, complete with veggies and homemade muffins. On her missions of mercy, she would also stop to pray with people, or just listen as they talked. This amazing lady also delivered Meals On Wheels lunches every Friday for twenty years, receiving no reimbursement or recognition; she simply loved doing what God had gifted her to do.

In 1995, she was diagnosed with a malignant brain tumor. After her surgery, the choir asked for volunteers to bring meals. A week later, the coordinator tearfully told me that they couldn't feed our family for two weeks. Then she brightened. "It looks as if we'll be able to feed you for more like two *months!*" In fact, there were so many volunteers, both inside and outside the choir, that the customary two-week period stretched to over six months! People brought food to Gloria and thanks to God for her quiet service to them in His name.

Until her death, Mom was a cheerful servant, who gave no thought of what she might gain. She was truly a woman after God's own heart—a shining example for her daughter. Thanks, Mom. It's so good.

> Whatever you do, work at it with all your heart, as working for the Lord, not for men, since you know that you will receive an inheritance from the Lord as a reward. It is the Lord Christ you are serving.
>
> —COLOSSIANS 3:23–24

Thought . . . Are you God's cheerful servant? The key to service is in discovering your spiritual gifts and employing them. When you operate according to your gifts, you do so effortlessly, bringing pleasure to others and enhancing your relationships.

Time to Waste

We all find time to do what we really want to do.

—WILLIAM FEATHER

Susan calls and says she's on her way to *Starbucks* for coffee. Will I join her? "No, no," I say. "I need to write."

I think, *My schedule is flexible. Why is it hard for me to say yes?* I think it's more virtuous to stick with work than to spend an hour with a friend. An inner voice says I'd be wasting time, but do these words speak truth? I don't believe that time spent cultivating a relationship is wasted.

I pull out the work. Two hours later I take stock: Have I written as fluently as I intended? Hardly. Sentences eke out like hardened molasses. In my mind, a puritanical voice recites: *Write every day. Write, write, write!*

Wrong, wrong, wrong, I answer back, startling myself. I've reached the law of diminishing returns. I need human contact. I need to drink coffee with Susan.

When I "waste" valuable time with Susan—if I listen to her life—I express my love. I show she's more valuable than a manuscript. I touch her soul and she reaches mine. Being together reignites my creativity. I return to my work recharged.

What stops me from buying that cup of coffee? I've developed a bad habit. I'm in the habit of saying no, thinking it more efficient to work and "not waste my time." But for the sake of my soul and its relationships, I need to develop the habit of "wasting time" on people, of throwing away a precious commodity to love them as Christ does, of refilling my cup when I'm empty.

Teach us to number our days aright, that we may gain a heart of wisdom.

—PSALM 90:12

Thought . . . Do you value "things" (even work) more than people? Your actions speak louder than words. Put down this book. Call a friend and *share* what you've read—share your life!

My Little Extra

BY BARBARA CURTIS

God's gifts put man's best dreams to shame.

—ELIZABETH BARRETT BROWNING

I call Jonathan my "little extra" because he has an extra chromosome—that extra one on the twenty-first pair that causes such panic in parents-to-be. Down's syndrome was what the doctor diagnosed when he was born. But Jonathan was what we named him—"Gift of God."

Though he was our eighth child, he took us into new territory. Once we had brought him home, visiting experts told us that we would need to work a little extra to help Jonathan realize his potential. What they didn't tell us was how Jonathan would help us realize our own.

Through Jonathan, we've learned so many things that we might not have otherwise: that life is about more than intelligence or appearance—that the greatest gifts are not the kind you can measure or quantify—that until our hearts are stretched and tenderized, there are truths we'll never know.

As my son, Matthew, once asked, "Wouldn't it be nice if every family had someone like Jonathan?" Wouldn't it indeed?

Jonathan was followed a year later by our daughter, Madeleine—then by Jesse and Daniel, two baby boys with Down's syndrome whom we adopted. When people express surprise that with our large family we would take on two more children with special needs, I tell them, "When we found out what a treasure we had in Jonny, we decided that we wanted more."

An extra chromosome, a little extra work, but so much more than a little extra benefit all around!

I praise you because I am fearfully and wonderfully made; your works are wonderful, I know that full well.

—PSALM 139:14

Thought . . . Have you avoided people who are different from you? There are no "accidents" of birth because God has uniquely fashioned everyone in His image. Delight in His infinite variety.

Moments Like These

BY NANCIE CARMICHAEL

It is not enough to be busy . . . the question is: what are we busy about?

—HENRY DAVID THOREAU

We were involved in a major remodeling of our house. I had resolved to paint the railing in the family room. I could get that job crossed off the list. Chris broke into my thoughts. "Mom, see those bluffs? I've heard that's a great hike. Let's pack our lunches and go."

"I was going to paint, but . . ." The eager look on his face weakened my resolve.

It was a spring afternoon, the sun warm and air sweet with the smell of wildflowers. We started off on a trail through the ponderosa pines, wending our way up the bluff. His slender form stooped with his backpack, [his] blond hair glinting in the sunlight. Fortunately the path was well defined, and before long we reached the top, breathless yet exhilarated. I caught my breath. Stretched far below was a vast green meadow with a stream winding through it. Towering above were glistening snowcapped mountains against the forever-blue sky. Hawks and eagles soared.

"Chris . . ."

"Yeah, Mom?" he inquired.

How do you tell your son how much you love him? How do you say, "My child, you are almost an adult, and you're wonderful!" Instead I said, "Thanks, honey, for bringing me here."

The memory of my son talking with me high on a rocky bluff that warm afternoon is one I will always cherish. In moments like these, time stands still. And each person, each interruption adds quality to my life—a gift from the Father's hand. A treasure that fills my [life] with beauty.

" . . . Do not work for food that spoils, but for food that endures to eternal life . . ."

—JOHN 6:27

Thought . . . How do you handle people's interruptions? They are divine interventions because, in reality, people (especially your children) are gifts from God with whom to enjoy life.

I Will Always Love You

BY REBECCA BARLOW JORDAN

There is nothing you can do to make God love you more! There is nothing you can do to make God love you less! His love is unconditional, impartial, infinite, perfect! God is love!

—ANONYMOUS

One evening, our girls refused to go to sleep. I scolded them and, during the course of our conversation, I said something like, "I love you anyway, even when you don't obey. But it makes me happier when you do."

Children seem to have a unique way of avoiding serious discussions, and this time was no exception. They asked questions like, "Would you still love me if I drew all over the walls?" I assured them that I would still love them, but I wouldn't want them to do that. Not satisfied, one fired another question: "Would you still love me if I ate all the pie myself?" "Yes, I will always love you, no matter what you do," I added. "Why?" she pressed. "Because you are my child." Some five or six ridiculous questions later, both girls ended in sidesplitting laughter. They soon tired, and after a warm hug from me, they finally settled down and closed their eyes.

As I was drifting off to sleep myself that night, my mind parked on all the weaknesses I'd displayed in the last week—unkind words, selfish deeds, thoughtless actions. But before I could confess my faults and voice the question, God seemed to answer in my spirit: "Yes, I will always love you—because you are my *child*." And, suddenly, I felt like a little girl again as I crawled up into my Heavenly Father's arms and basked in the treasure of His unconditional love and grace. I fell asleep—happy, forgiven, and eager again to obey.

We love because He first loved us.

—I JOHN 4:19

Thought . . . Do you doubt God's love? Remember that He gave His Son, Jesus Christ, to die for you so that you, too, could become His child. There is no greater proof of His love than that.

That's Worth Everything

Eternity is not something that begins after you are dead. It is going
on all the time.

—CHARLOTTE PERKINS GILMAN

Bill and I have never been attracted to "playing it safe" with life.
A life worth living should be one of reckless abandonment to
something worth abandoning oneself to. Perhaps the most important and all-encompassing words Jesus said are these: "Whoever would save his life will lose it, and whoever loses his life for
My sake will find it (Matthew 16:25 RSV)."

Not long ago we sat down to make a list of those things that
were, at this stage of our lives, worth everything. Our list was
very short.

We have discussed this list in our family and applied it in
many ways.

When trying to prioritize our time and energies, it has been
helpful for all of us to ask ourselves and each other, "Will it last
forever? Does it have any eternity in it?" Or the way I phrase it
for myself is: "Think 'forever!'" People are "forever." Relationships are "forever." God's Word will endure "forever." But the
"forever" list is short indeed.

When Bill and I breathe our last breath and leave behind
whatever we have done with our days, I hope this epitaph will
ring true: "They gave themselves away for things that last forever." If that could be the case, then the "eternity" we've recognized and embraced here will simply open into the eternity we
will embrace there, and we will be "at home" in the familiar presence of Him Who is Alpha and Omega, the Beginning and the
Ending, the First and the Last. And that will be worth everything.

Set your minds on things above, not on earthly things.

—COLOSSIANS 3:2

Thought . . . What do you value? Ask God to give you
"forever eyes," with the ability to see only those things
with eternal significance. Treasure those. Nothing else
really matters.

We Are Secure

BY MICHELE HOWE

But being absolutely confident and comforted in the fact that my salvation is secure, based on God's keeping power, not mine, all cause for anxiety is removed. I may tremble on the Rock, but the Rock never trembles under me!

—CHARLES R. SWINDOLL

A few years ago, my husband, Jim, and I sat with several hundred men, women, and children listening to the bereaved father of a young twenty-year-old man who had died of cancer. All around us, young girls cried softly, elderly adults wiped their eyes with their handkerchiefs, and families wept openly. This dad spoke about the importance of fathers bonding with their children—taking time to really know and love them. "For you never know," he reminded us all, "when God will take them home."

It was a frightening thought. Yet, at that sobering moment, I believe that husbands and wives, alike, were inexplicably united together in hope. Just as if a veil had been lifted, I recognized what a treasure simply *living* can be. God was giving us all another chance to make a real difference in our children's lives— to spend time loving them and teaching them about Christ's gift of salvation. God was reminding us that no matter what happened, if we have His greatest gift of all, eternal life, we have everything. We are secure.

I felt my husband's presence beside me and knew, without a doubt, that this grieving father's words would echo in both our hearts for a long time. God used this message to bring life from death. Together, my husband and I would make a difference in our family's life, both now and eternally.

". . . Blessed are those who mourn, for they will be comforted . . ."

—MATTHEW 5:4

Thought . . . Where is your security found? If you literally "stake your life" on the Lord Jesus Christ, you are promised abundant life now and in His presence eternally. Stand on Christ, the solid Rock. All other ground is sinking sand. (Paraphrased from hymn: "The Solid Rock.")

A House Brimming with Love

Deprive someone of love and you deprive him of the very core of
life itself.

—ANABEL GILLHAM

I knocked at the door and entered a big, friendly kitchen, eventually falling into a hug from Anabel, my dear friend, and a pretty
picture of a southern lady. She had soft peaks of white hair, tender blue eyes, and a drawl as low and soothing as a lullaby. But
before I could get to Anabel, I had to go through Bo.

Bo was quite possibly the ugliest dog I had ever laid eyes on.
He looked too big to be hovering so low to the ground, like a
dining room table cut off at the knees. He was the color of a
slightly rusted iron skillet. I couldn't begin to guess the mixture
of breeds from which he might have descended.

"I've never seen a dog like this," I offered as kindly as I could.

"And you never will," said Anabel's husband, Bill, laughing, as
he tugged the big lump of happy dog out of the way. "He's one
of a kind!"

"Love us, love our dog," Anabel chimed in, half laughing, half
apologizing.

And it was then that I knew, without doubt, that I'd come to
the right place. For as I glanced at poor ugly Bo, and back at the
sentimental look on Anabel's face as she stroked his old coat, I
knew I'd just entered a house of unconditional love.

For human and animal "strays," there's no treasure like finding
folks who accept us as we are, who even choose to love us.

My cup, and Bo's bowl, runneth over.

. . . "I have loved you with an everlasting love; I have drawn
you with loving-kindness . . ."

—JEREMIAH 31:3

Thought . . . Do you need unconditional love? Receive it
at the foot of the Cross, where Jesus offers the gift of
salvation and forgiveness for your sins. The only "condition" required is for you to admit your sin, ask His
forgiveness, and receive Him as Savior and Lord.

Blessings

 Flat Broke

BY EVELYN ANDERSON SHEETS

The tests of life are to make, not break us. . . .

—MALTBIE D. BABCOCK

Our world almost crashed that day. Millie, Harold, and I were weeding the garden while Arvid played nearby. I went inside to get a cooler blouse. That's when I heard the quarrel. Papa and Mama hadn't heard me come in. From the other bedroom came Mama's tearful voice:

"Well, I give up. I'm tired of being broke."

"Greta, I know it's hard. But we have nowhere else to go."

Curled up on the bed I prayed, "Please, God, don't let this happen to us. I'd rather *die*. I mean it, God." But He paid no attention.

"I'll take Arvid with me; he's only three. Stella will help me get a job." (Stella, her sister in New York, was two thousand miles away!)

"But, honey, we can't *make* it without you! Please don't leave." Mama started to sob.

They mustn't know I had heard. I tiptoed out the door, tear-and-perspiration soup dripping from my nose. Somehow I went back to weeding. Later I glanced at Papa, smoothing his mustache with a calloused hand. I searched Mama's face as she set the table. I stifled a scream inside me.

Mama *didn't* go. She must have known that she couldn't get far without money, and that her place was with us. Thank you, God, for stopping her from going. I understand now that her breaking point just caught up with her that day.

God *was* paying close attention. He gave our family a curious blessing, but one that worked—being flat broke.

[Love] always protects, always trusts, always hopes, always perseveres.

—I CORINTHIANS 13:7

Thought . . . Are you contemplating divorce? Don't voice the word. When considering divorce an *option*, you come closer to making it *reality*. Ask God to help you solve problems as they occur, strengthening your marriage and your resolve.

Fully Alive

BY GLORIA GAITHER

I asked God for all things so I could enjoy life. He gave me life so I could enjoy all things.

—ANONYMOUS

I stopped for breakfast and a cup of coffee at the pancake house. "Just an egg and homemade biscuit," I told the waitress, "and a coffee, please." I turned to the book I'd brought to jump-start my mind. I had barely finished the second page before she returned with my breakfast. She poured the coffee and asked if there'd be anything else. "No, I'm fine, thank you," I answered, my eyes really looking into hers for the first time. She smiled. "Enjoy!" she said, then hurried to deliver someone else's order. "Enjoy!"

Her final word hung in the air like a blessing. It was a sermon of sorts. The taste of a fresh egg and a warm biscuit. The warmth of a cup of hot coffee in my hands on this Winnie-the-Pooh blustery day. The colors, textures, aromas, voices, the morning music that surrounded me. "Enjoy!" It was a choice she had offered me. I could go through this day oblivious to the miracles all around me or I could tune in and "enjoy!" Her invitation returned again and again to bless my day.

"Mamaw!" Grandson Jesse's happy voice greeted me as I got out of the car. His strong little arms were already around my neck, and he was covering my face with kisses. I could hear, I could feel, I could see this precious child who blessed my days with the joy of being adored. I was his "mamaw"!

"Enjoy!" the waitress sang to my heart.

Rejoice in the Lord and be glad, you righteous; sing, all you who are upright in heart!

—PSALM 32:11

Thought . . . How can you enjoy life? By seeing it all as God's free gift—each new day, every breath you take, every thought you think, every sight, sound, and sense you experience.

Music That Ministers

Hymns contain the holiest thoughts of the holiest people at their holiest moments.

—SILAS PAYNE

One of the loveliest memories I have is of my mother sitting in the dark playing the piano. My father died when I was eight years old, and life for Mother after that became quite a struggle. We could not afford to waste kerosene to light more lamps than necessary. Nor could we afford to keep fire in all the stoves, so often the living room was cold as well as dark. But Mother's music warmed her; she needed it in order to survive. Because mother's favorite selections were hymns and gospel songs, I grew up with the blessing of hearing them over and over. When company came, we gathered around the piano and sang.

My own appreciation of this kind of music has increased tremendously over the years. When my children were growing up, and I worried about every problem that came along, I discovered that the best remedy for my spirits was to saturate my soul with gospel music. Even today, I read hymn lyrics like poetry, marveling at the insights of the hymn-writers and at their beautiful expression of thought.

My love of sacred music is one of the greatest treasures of my life—a blessing that cannot be taken from me. And when life's dark times overwhelm me, though I cannot actually *hear* them, I remember mother playing hymns in the dark. I am comforted by the warmth of their melodies, uplifted by the light of their words.

Speak to one another with psalms, hymns and spiritual songs. Sing and make music in your heart to the Lord.
—EPHESIANS 5:19

Thought . . . Do you read a hymnal devotionally? Not only do the lyrics express sweeping emotions, but they are a treasure chest of theology, adding insight to biblical knowledge.

Brother Lawrence . . . Sister Rachel

BY RACHEL ST. JOHN-GILBERT

Everything I really need to know, I learned in kindergarten.

—ROBERT FULGHUM

During college, I remember reading in a curious, but detached manner, the journals of Brother Lawrence. I can still picture the brown-clad monk contentedly peeling potatoes while communing with God. Little did I know that I'd need to rely on those images later in life. My husband lost his job and, as the financial pressures grew, my self-esteem shrunk. I began working as an aide in a kindergarten class and found myself wiping down paint-splotched easels, sweeping up cracker crumbs, and cleaning mud off waffle-soled sneakers. Oddly enough, these Lawrence-esque tasks became a welcome distraction and an impetus to pray. And even on my grayest days, I couldn't help but smile at the uninhibited innocence of my charming charges:

"Were Adam and Eve made out of mud?" questioned Adam. By the look on his face, it was clear that he was picturing God's first family as creatures from the Black Lagoon.

On a spring day, Daniel raced over to me, arm outstretched, palm cupped tightly, and grinning ear to ear. A slow-motion uncupping of his dirt-stained hand revealed the brownish-pink booty . . . "A wuhm!"

Later, the children were role-playing a *Leave It To Beaver* kind of family. I overheard a pint-sized Ward call to his child-bride, "Honey, come quick! A shark just bit our baby!"

As I laughed aloud, God's comfort began to reach me. I forgot about self-esteem and discovered the joy of losing myself and my troubles in the smiles, hugs, and enthusiasm of eleven earthly cherubs.

". . . He will yet fill your mouth with laughter and your lips with shouts of joy . . ."

—JOB 8:21

Thought . . . Do you possess a child's innocence and wonderment? Jesus asked that little children be brought to Him to show them tenderness. Maybe He needed their comfort, too.

Be Still and Know

BY KAY ARTHUR

Renewal and restoration are not luxuries. They are essentials. Being alone and resting for awhile is not selfish. It is Christlike.

—CHARLES R. SWINDOLL

I have been "shut up"—physically unable to teach. I have been so weak that I have had to be totally still as I recuperate. It has been wonderful! Taking me away from the distractions of life (many of them good things in themselves), our Lord has given me the opportunity to be still and know that He is God. In doing so, He has reminded me anew that only pleasing Him matters.

I've enjoyed the spring—reveled in the dogwood and azaleas we planted and delighted in the mass of color from tulips planted as a birthday surprise. I've eaten when I wanted, slept when I've wanted, and I've worked on a new *Precept* course on II Thessalonians. I've rented the movie series on Winston Churchill. I've turned on the stereo and listened to George Beverly Shea sing wonderful old hymns of faith.

I've listened to the Bible on tape, and I've prayed and read—especially the Psalms. I've noticed the gamut of emotions and situations David had to deal with; and I've seen how, through it all, even in failure and sin, David never let go of God. When his life was over, God called David a man after His own heart!

In all this, weak though I've been, often to the place of tears, I've found rest. Rest in the promises of our Father, rest in the assurance that nothing depends upon me. It all depends on Him. I'm simply to trust and obey, to be still and know He is God.

. . . "Come with me by yourselves to a quiet place and get some rest."

—MARK 6:31

Thought . . . How do you rest in the Lord despite inner and outer turmoil? Literally be *still* and read His Word. The more you come to know God's faithfulness, you can rest in His character.

I'm Rich? Wow!

BY MARGARET PRIMROSE

Content makes poor men rich; discontent makes rich men poor.

—BENJAMIN FRANKLIN

The students at the South American Bible school where I had begun teaching were curious about me and my family in the States. When they asked to see some pictures, I promised to show them some slides. I did not understand why they gasped in surprise when I came to one of my father in a Nebraska feed lot.

"Whose cattle are those?" a spokesman for the group asked.

"They're my dad's," I answered.

"Señorita, you're rich!" he exclaimed.

Rich? I asked myself, as I resolved never to show that slide again. Nor did I comment that Dad could not have made a living with just the six or eight cattle that they saw. What I had begun to hear is that all North Americans were rich.

Practically all of the students grew up in one- or two-room mud huts with grass or corrugated tin roofs. Probably not many of their families had even a pair of oxen to help them till their fields. Yet I do not remember that they ever complained about it. In a very real sense they were rich, indeed. They had trusted in Jesus as Savior and decided to serve God. That made them His children and heirs. They could look forward to golden streets, mansions in heaven, and an eternity to spend there.

So may all of us. The kids were right after all. I *am* rich!

Now if we are children, then we are heirs—heirs of God and co-heirs with Christ, if indeed we share in his sufferings in order that we may also share in his glory.

—ROMANS 8:17

Thought . . . Have you ever thought about what it means to be God's heir? You will enjoy the rewards of Heaven for eternity! No earthly treasures can compare with these.

Joy Beads

BY BARBARA JOHNSON

Christ's limitless resources meet our endless needs.

—CORRIE TEN BOOM

When I bought new makeup, the salesgirl told me if I dropped a BB in the bottle and shook it, the makeup wouldn't get gooey.

I told my husband I needed a BB. Bill had something wonderful to show me. He had a huge plastic carton. Inside were 10,000—that's ten thousand!—BBs. "BBs only come in tens of thousands," he told me proudly. I smiled appreciatively and took one.

Recently I saw that plastic carton full of 9,999 BBs in our garage. I got to thinking how much it's like the riches of God in Christ. We have much, much more than we'll ever be able to use: forgiveness, grace, mercy, love . . . God's riches are beyond anything we could imagine! If my life gets gooey and stale, I have no excuse.

[When I was] a child, my Sunday school teacher always told me, *"God's blessing bucket is bottomless."* Her favorite Bible story was about the widow of Zarephath. When you live in obedience to God, she would tell us, the jar of oil never runs dry; the bowl of flour never becomes empty.

God has never withheld resources from me, although I've gone through loss after loss. It takes just one BB to shake things up: the decision to be joyful. Life can't get thick and unmanageable if you drop joy beads in the jar. It puts worries in their place.

What is the treasure we have in earthly vessels? It is Jesus Christ and the precious Holy Spirit. It is the capacity to be divinely happy wherever we are, in whatever circumstances.

> . . . I have learned to be content whatever the circumstances.
>
> —PHILIPPIANS 4:11

Thought . . . Have you dipped into God's bottomless blessing bucket? Drink of Jesus' living water. He promises you a wellspring of joy, welling up to eternal life (John 4:14).

Mary at Prayer

BY HELENE C. KUONI

The purpose of prayer is that we get ahold of God, not of the answer.

—OSWALD CHAMBERS

"Can you come over?" she asked on the phone.

I couldn't refuse Mary. Our families were lifelong friends, and she was ill. I went immediately.

We chatted endlessly and reminisced about parents and siblings and the wonderful times our families had shared. We talked about my sister, Dorothy, and her sister, Pat—both had died in their forties. We talked about Christ and Heaven and being reunited someday with those we loved so much.

"Can we pray?" she asked hesitantly. "Like conversation with God? Aloud?" I took her hands into mine and silently planned how to begin, how to phrase each request, but she surprised me by starting first. "Heavenly Father," she prayed, "thank you for my friend and for her beauty."

It startled me. What was she saying? I thought we were to petition the Lord on her behalf. She continued her thanksgiving—for husband, children, doctors, parents, sisters, brothers. So caught up in counting her blessings, she asked for nothing—not health, not even relief from the pain.

We prayed every time I visited after that, and Mary always "entered His gates with thanksgiving." Her skin was pale and her strength ebbing, but as she approached the Lord, a brightness and beauty appeared on her face.

I treasure the memory of Mary at prayer. I know when the Lord took her home, her face must have shone with beauty, and as she had done so many times before, she "entered into His courts with praise."

> When Moses came down from Mount Sinai with the two tablets of the Testimony in his hands, he was not aware that his face was radiant because he had spoken with the Lord.
>
> —EXODUS 34:29

Thought . . . Are you transformed when you pray? When you look to God, for *Who* He is and not for *what* He gives, you become radiant (Psalm 34:5).

A Humorous Treasure of Humans

BY BECKY FREEMAN

Among those whom I like or admire, I can find no common denominator, but among those whom I love, I can: all of them make me laugh.

—W. H. AUDEN

I love to go and share stories at churches and retreats or the ever-popular "Ladies Night Out." Though most of the events are variations on a standard theme—decorations, door prizes, music, food, laughter, and spiritual lessons—each gathering is unique, each woman a blessing. I can't imagine meeting kinder, more loving and genuine hostesses and audiences. And funnnnnnnny—oh, my! Even without our trying, humor has a way of ping-ponging between me and my new found friends wherever I go.

At a recent banquet where I gave the keynote speech, a few men kindly offered to unload my suitcase of books for the table. Before long, the hostess came up to me. "Becky," she said, barely able to suppress her laughter, "I told everybody to be ready for *anything* when you arrived. The deacons just unloaded a bra with your books!" I blushed, but then relaxed—after all, I knew from experience, I was among friends.

It is just such experiences, unplanned and so human, that bond us together as sisters—with our feet firmly potted in clay.

I've discovered that behind the fru-fru-fiest of hair, beneath the lace and flowered-print dresses and broad-brimmed hats—lie women who love to laugh at themselves, with hearts that need and want to give love, and who ache when life hurts—women who struggle with doubt and failure, even as they reach out in faith to an all-loving, all-forgiving God. In a word, these women are real. What a treasure!

There is a time . . . to laugh . . .

—ECCLESIASTES 3:1, 4

Thought . . . Do you and your friends enjoy the gift of laughter? To best unwrap the gift, be willing first to laugh at yourself, and not take life so seriously. Feel free to "fru-fru"!

A Penny from Heaven

BY KATHLEEN HAGBERG

Love cannot be forced; love cannot be coaxed and tested. It comes out of Heaven, unmasked and unsought.

—PEARL BUCK

My daily visits with Susan would soon be ending. Her battle with cancer had taken its toll, and she was dying. "Lord," I cried, "what about me?" I had invested my heart into our relationship. Each day for the last several months of Susan's life, I would prepare meals and escort visitors to her room. Two by two, Susan's friends came each day to pray. One was Penny. One day after praying with Susan, she sought me out in the kitchen as I was preparing dinner.

"This must really be hard for you," Penny offered consolingly.

"When Susan dies it will feel like hitting a brick wall," I whispered.

Penny smiled, said good-bye and left. She was gone no more than a minute when she retraced her steps to the kitchen.

"Forget something?" I asked, continuing to scrub potatoes under the running faucet.

"I have something to say to you," she whispered. As I turned to face her, she placed her hands on my shoulders.

"I just want you to know that I'll be there for you when Susan dies."

Susan died a short time later and, just as she had promised, Penny was there. She phoned me frequently. She prayed with me, but mostly she listened. Like Job's friends she saw that my "grief was great." The long cold winter following Susan's death was easier to bear because of God's blessed promise . . . "I will give thee treasures of darkness." "A Penny from Heaven" was God's treasure in my darkness.

". . . I will go before you . . ."

—ISAIAH 45:2

Thought . . . Do you grieve the death of a loved one? Don't cover your emotions. Pour out your suffering to God—but also to a friend. You need someone to hold your hand and your heart.

Discover the Treasure of Parenting

BY JANEY L. DeMéo

The duties of home are discipline for the ministries of Heaven.

—ANONYMOUS

It was a deliciously scorching afternoon by the sea. The vibrant, turquoise water reflected the bright sun. But as I contemplated our family's morning ritual "battlefield," this picturesque paradise contradicted my inward struggle. Why did parenting seem so difficult at times? I glanced at my children, paradoxically now playing peacefully. Suddenly, Francesco interrupted my pondering, and plopped pretty stones on the sand.

"Look, Mama! I found some VERY treasure!" my five-year-old son proclaimed excitedly.

Remembering that I had taught the children the parable of the buried treasure that morning, I smiled at my son's interpretation. Francesco had heard "VERY treasure" rather than "BURIED treasure." He proceeded to categorically pile stones on my towel, pointing to explain their distinction. "Now here's the treasure; these are the VERY treasure, and these, the VERY, VERY treasure!" Not daring to offend my son, I retained my laughter. My spirit felt lighter, as I recognized my own little treasures—my children.

Like kings reigning over their household under the Great King, we parents are to seek the very treasure of godly parenting. It may be buried under layers of exhaustion or weaknesses. But the treasure is revealed to all who seek (Matthew 7:7). God's Word is an eternal source of wisdom waiting to be unveiled to strengthen us as parents. Discovering God's Word makes parenting a VERY treasure, our children God's VERY, VERY treasure, and His path for them, the "VERRIEST" treasure of all!

> "The kingdom of heaven is like treasure hidden in a field. When a man found it, he hid it again, and then in his joy went and sold all he had and bought that field . . ."
>
> —MATTHEW 13:44

Thought . . . Do you treasure your children? Teach them the *very* Word of God and they will be *very, very* blessed. God will be the *verriest* pleased by your obedience.

Green Pastures

BY LOIS WALFRID JOHNSON

It is impossible to have the feeling of peace and serenity without
being at rest with God.

—DOROTHY H. PENTECOST

As children, we liked to find a "country" spot and lie on our
backs in the long grass. With the scent of clover around us, we
looked up at clouds driven by the wind across a brilliant sky. We
imagined what those cloud shapes could be, and far-flung stories filled our mind.

Then we matured and decided we were too grown up for
such goings-on. But one day when my own children were married and gone, I felt a weariness deep in my soul. In the midst of
all I felt compelled to do, I longed for the simple pleasure of my
Shepherd's presence. I yearned for His whisper—the calling of
my name—the sense of His pleasure and peace.

Our country neighbors knew my love of the land and encouraged my wandering heart. That day I climbed our steep
hill, scrambled under the barbed wire fence into our neighbors'
pasture, and walked to the edge of their hill. Far away from their
horses and goats, far from the noise of the city, I sat down.

Looking out over woods and pond to distant hills, I enjoyed
the long view. I listened to the silence. I felt the whisper of my
name, the gentle touch of peace. And when the stillness had
crept into my spirit, I lay down, gazed up at the clouds, and fell
asleep.

Our Shepherd is a kind one. He tells us when to find a green
pasture, lie down, and rest.

The Lord is my shepherd, I shall not be in want. He makes
me lie down in green pastures . . .

—PSALM 23:1–2

Thought . . . Are you weary of soul? Ask your Shepherd
to lead you to green pastures. He'll show you if you
need a nap, a retreat, or the stillness of prayer. Enjoy
His blessings. Rest in His guidance and care.

The Mother's Day Note

BY JERI CHRYSONG

It is a greater compliment to be trusted than to be loved.

—GEORGE MACDONALD

As a single mom, my "treasures" consist of things my sons, Luc and Sam, have said or written. My most recent prize came from Luc on Mother's Day. I felt doubly blessed being sandwiched between both teenagers in church that morning, listening to our pastor speak about families, rather than just about mothers. His message was encouraging and uplifting, with instruction directed to both parents and children, alike.

During the sermon, Luc scribbled a note to me. I expected his written declaration to state that I was the best mom in the world, with whom none other could compare. Instead, I read, "Watch the *Laker* game today for me while I'm at work." I had to think of dying puppies to stifle an unladylike guffaw.

After the sermon, I greeted Pastor Paul and asked if I could share something my son had written to me during the sermon. He nodded, reflecting interest, possibly thinking his sermon had connected with a teenager. He read Luc's note, laughed out loud, then shared it with his wife and visiting grown children.

I said to him, "You know, Pastor, the silly thing is that now I probably will spend my Mother's Day watching the *Lakers* play basketball!"

Smiling, Pastor Paul took my hands and said, "Oh, but Mom, what a wonderful thing—Luc trusts you enough to watch the game through your eyes!"

I guess he does. And that, too, is a treasured blessing—my son's trust.

"Whoever can be trusted with very little can also be trusted with much . . ."

—LUKE 16:10

Thought . . . Do your children trust you? We, as parents, find it imperative to be able to trust our children. Can they trust *you* to set an example worthy of emulating?

Restoration

BY JAN KARON

The problem of restoring to the world original and eternal beauty is solved by the redemption of the soul.

—RALPH WALDO EMERSON

I found it at a favorite antique shop. It had come all the way from France and was very old. I loved it at once. It was a lamp. This little lamp, whose base was the hand-painted porcelain figure of a yellow bird, came home with me and sat on my mantle. When I switched on the light, . . . I always thought the little bird might sing. It was very delicate and lifelike, my favorite lamp in a lifetime of lamps.

A tile-setter was working in my house, and repositioned a chair so that the lamp cord went round the chair leg. When I moved the chair, unknowing, the lamp smashed onto the floor. I remember standing over it, frozen and unbelieving. . . . There were twelve fragments of porcelain, some very small. I put them in a box, chiding myself for being so fond of a created thing. I thought the little lamp was gone forever. But not so. . . . I discovered a one-hundred-year-old family-owned restoration company in Philadelphia. They said many of their restorations are nearly impossible to detect. . . .

Last week, my little bird returned to her perch on the mantle. And, needless to say, these human eyes can't detect where the breaks occurred.

The lamp reminds me daily how God is able to lovingly restore us through His Son. All we have to do is ask for restoration, for healing, for new life. . . . Christ was sent that we may be restored. When we offer Him a willing and contrite heart, we have only to ask, and He will make us brand-new.

And the God of all grace, who called you to his eternal glory in Christ . . . will himself restore you . . .

—I PETER 5:10

Thought . . . Does your past haunt you? Christ promises to restore you as a "new creature." Amazingly, He even promises to make past sins—*all* things—work out for your good (Romans 8:28). There is no greater blessing!

Rainmaker

BY MARCIA VAN'T LAND

It is not our trust that keeps us, but the God in Whom we trust Who keeps us.

—OSWALD CHAMBERS

The summer had been hot, dry, and dusty. We desperately needed rain for the crops. This was the fourth year in a row that my parents had hoped and prayed for rain that never came. Each year I'd watch my parents' disappointed, worried faces as the crops withered in the fields.

Trying to capitalize on the plight of the farmers, people came on the yard explaining that if they shot some chemicals into the clouds above our farm (for a stiff price, of course) rain would come. "Rainmakers," we called them.

My dad, usually an easygoing man, listened to a rainmaker's speech and then ordered him off the yard. "Men cannot make it rain. Only God can. Leave and don't come back!"

After supper that evening, my mom and dad went out to the fields and gave their future to the Lord—rain or shine. "Whatever You have in mind, Lord, we'll obey, and we know that You will provide for us in some way."

Two years later, my parents sold the farm machinery and livestock, and headed for California with three kids, a '56 Chevy, no job, no house, and, thankfully, no debts. God had arranged that.

Now, when I get into difficult circumstances, I picture my parents standing in the thirsty, wilting cornfield placing their trust in God. They had certainly shown us kids that treasures of faith in God were far superior to earthly riches, and that God would always provide blessings, come rain or shine.

. . . They are clouds without rain, blown along by the wind . . .

—JUDE 12

Thought . . . Do your children know that you depend upon God? Pray with your children in *every* life circumstance—whether in good times or bad. They'll know by experience that God is *real* and that He answers your prayers.

Put a Song in Your Heart

Let's go and wake up the universe . . . and sing His praises.

—MARIAM BAOUARDY

I can always tell if the birds are working on their nest outside my window by their songs in the early morning. Long before I can *see* them, I can *hear* their music. When I gently raise the blinds and sneak a peek outside, there is Mom tucked into her bird-house hole and Dad watching guard on a branch of a nearby tree. While she sits and he flies and brings food, they sing.

On occasion, the cheeriness is too much for me. I wonder what they have to be so *chirpy* about, and I walk back to my chores with disdain. But on other days, I pull up a chair, perch in observation, and lose myself in their happy antics. They are committed to each other, to their nest, and to the hopes of their brood. Not a bad lot in life. And I look back over my life with greater appreciation.

What do you have to sing about? If you had to come up with twenty items under the heading, "Thank you, God, for" could you? Put aside the things you would "die to have" and jot down a mental list of what you do have.

It changes the attitude, doesn't it? Now one more thing. Try a tune. Flip through your favorite songs about God and punch one into your own throat. You don't have to be an accomplished musician to hum a song of praise.

Give yourself something to sing about, and when you've finished the second verse, you'll probably have a song in your heart.

I will sing to the Lord all my life; I will sing praise to my God as long as I live.

—PSALM 104:33

Thought . . . Are you bugged by cheerful people—especially when they don't have anything to be cheerful about? Maybe they're just happy to be *alive*. Life really *is* a miracle, isn't it?

A Quarter for Your Thoughts

BY JAN BRUNETTE

Love is a fruit of all seasons at all times and within the reach of every hand.

—MOTHER TERESA

My day had gone utterly awry. My exhaustion had reached its peak. In order to regain my momentum, I would need a hand from Heaven if I were to complete the day without screaming. The children in the classroom squirmed and chattered. The science project spelled disaster, as anger spilled out from several cherubs during lunch and recess. My patience hung by a thread.

During a brief fifteen-minute break, I prayed, "Father, please send me a special touch of Your love. I can't handle this without help from You."

Later, after giving the class an assignment, I sat at my desk, musing over the day. Hearing someone clear his throat, I looked up and saw Sedric standing there. Shifting back and forth, hands behind his back, his face revealed a sheepish grin. Quietly I asked, "Sedric, what can I do for you?"

Calmly and slowly, he held out his palm and revealed a shiny quarter. Confused, I asked, "Did you find that somewhere?"

"No," he responded. "It's my quarter. I saw you thinking so hard that I thought you deserved a tip. Teachers never get tips, and I want you to have one."

With tears welling in my eyes, I said, "Thank you, Sedric, but I don't need your quarter. Your gift of love and generosity has blessed me with everything that I needed." Smiling from ear to ear, he returned to his seat. The treasure this special child offered with his gesture and words possessed much greater value than any amount of money I could have possibly received.

From the lips of children and infants you have ordained praise . . .

—PSALM 8:2

Thought . . . How might you "tip" someone needing encouragement? Make a phone call or send a cheery card to show her her specialness to God and to you.

Prayer for Annie

BY LINDA EVANS SHEPHERD

We cannot hold a torch to light another's path without brightening our own.

—BEN SWEETLAND

My severely handicapped daughter lay in ICU recovering from a severe bladder infection that had almost taken her life. I held her hand and rejoiced as her condition improved. One morning, I found another parent in the ICU hallway, weeping. I had seen her earlier in the unit, hovering over the limp body of her tiny daughter who was hooked to tubes and monitors.

I knelt beside her. "Can I pray for you?" She looked up through her tears. "Would you?" I put my arm around her. "What's your name?" "Annie." I could feel her body tremble as I prayed, "Lord, Annie's journey is so hard, yet I know You are with her. Let her know that You care."

I opened my eyes and gently asked, "What's wrong with your little girl?" "She's profoundly handicapped . . . " was all she could manage between sobs. I nodded with understanding. I bowed my head again. "God, Annie's handicapped daughter is such a special gift. May her life bring joy and blessings just as my handicapped daughter's life has brought me joy and blessings. In Jesus, name, Amen."

The young mother looked up. Her tears had stopped and joy lit her face. "Thank you so much for praying," she said. "I feel at peace now."

The funny thing was, I felt at peace, too. God had just revealed to me how blessed I truly was. When we reach out to others, the joy of encouragement always reflects into our own hearts. I am blessed, indeed.

You hear, O Lord, the desire of the afflicted; you encourage them, and you listen to their cry.

—PSALM 10:17

Thought . . . Have you been able to comfort others with the same comfort God has given you (II Corinthians 1:3–4)? It helps to make sense of your suffering and brings joy in your pain.

Everything's Free

BY KATHLEEN DALE WRIGHT

The cost of your sins is more than you can pay. The gift of your God is more than you can imagine.

—MAX LUCADO

My husband and I purchased an old, fifteen-bedroom hotel in a quiet Midwestern town. God had led us there to provide a haven for those in spiritual and physical need. And many people came.

One day a woman appeared at the door with two young boys. They lived with their grandmother who had just had a stroke. Now the mother, an airline stewardess, had no place to leave the boys. We gladly welcomed Joe, six, and Andy, nine. "There's no charge," we told her, "but we'd appreciate whatever you could give toward their care." Months later she had not given us anything. *Surely she could afford to contribute something*, I thought!

Then Andy showed me a picture he had drawn at school. "Heaven" was written across golden clouds. A narrow road led from a cross, in the center of the page, to "Heaven." "My teacher asked why I drew this," Andy said. "I told her about coming to stay with you and that everything here is free!" Andy pointed to the narrow road. "I told her that Jesus died for us and wants us to stay on the road that leads to Heaven. That's where I'm going to stay."

I prayed a special prayer of thanksgiving. Yes, we still needed money. But knowing that Andy understood what we'd told him about Christ's death on the cross was a blessing more precious than gold. And I was reminded that Christ had extended His gift of salvation at no cost to us.

"... Freely you have received, freely give ..."

—MATTHEW 10:8

Thought ... Do you share the treasure of your salvation with those who don't know Christ? He freely gave His life for you. Freely share the Good News. It doesn't cost a thing.

Dialogue with God

BY BECKY TIRABASSI

When you pray, things remain the same, but you begin to be different.

—OSWALD CHAMBERS

Because I had once viewed prayer as rehearsed, rote monologues for the spiritually elite, I was relieved to discover it to be passionate, thought-provoking, honest dialogue between two people who shared a mutual love and commitment. I had allowed everything else—work, friendships, workouts, television, extra sleep—to get in the way of my daily communication with God. Faith had become an isolated compartment of my life rather than the center of my existence.

I made a practical and purposeful decision to communicate daily with God. I chose to keep a daily one-hour "appointment" with Him, putting it on my calendar. To successfully avoid being distracted from concentrating, I made the experience both practical and powerful by writing down my thoughts.

Without fail, for the past thirteen years, I have recorded my words and God's responses in a three-ring binder, which has been a visual place for me to "meet" with God. When I put pen to the paper, I picture that I am writing to or speaking with Him and that He is listening to me and will respond! In addition to providing a tangible resource to express thoughts, hopes, dreams, and confessions to God, the method of journaling prayer has provided the accountability and excitement that I need to keep my appointment. I have more than 4,500 hours of recorded conversations with God, not only my words, but His responses! Written prayer has been the key to keeping my faith from becoming a compartment in my life and remaining a relationship with God.

My heart is stirred by a noble theme as I recite my verses for the king; my tongue is the pen of a skillful writer.

—PSALM 45:1

Thought . . . Does prayer intimidate you? Write "love letters" to God. *Writing* allows greater concentration. Your prayers will make sense and will comprise a virtual treasure chest—a written record of God's faithfulness and blessings.

What's for Dinner?

BY TERESA ARSENEAU

Anxiety is the natural result when our hopes are centered in anything short of God and His will for us.

—BILLY GRAHAM

I could fly around the kitchen naked in a hot air balloon and my teenage son would still ask me what was for dinner. He started asking after school, then at lunch time, then at breakfast, before breakfast, and the night before! *Why does he get onto me like this?* I wonder. I may not always decide far ahead of time what we're going to eat, but I know it's important that we do. I'm not going to forget.

God knows my needs are important, too, and He's not going to forget either. But time and again, I do the same thing to Him that my son does to me. He promises to bless me with my daily needs, but I want to know that tomorrow is taken care of, and also the next day, and the day after that. How will the bills be paid—groceries, gas for the car, clothing? There are so many things about which to worry when your bank account stares back at you with glaring red ink. I want a healthy bank account in which I can trust, but God wants me to trust in Him, alone. I want my needs met as far in advance as possible. God's provision is always there just when I need it.

So, what's for dinner? I have no idea, but that's okay. The real treasure is in learning to be content with the blessings of today, and leaving tomorrow to the One Who holds it in His Hand.

Keep your lives free from the love of money and be content with what you have, because God has said, "Never will I leave you; never will I forsake you."

—HEBREWS 13:5

Thought . . . Are you worried about today's struggles and frantic over tomorrow's? Recall the many times in which Christ has met your needs in the past. He is the same yesterday, today, and tomorrow (Hebrews 13:8). He will never fail you.

Traditions

Making a Christmas Memory

BY TWILA PARIS

When we honestly consider the well-being of others, we become truly rich in the deepest sense.

—DENIS WAITLEY

As a romantic gesture in honor of the first gift he gave her on their first date, my Grandfather Paris always gave my grandmother a box of chocolate-covered cherries for Christmas. And every year my grandmother would open her present and exclaim with joy that once again she had gotten exactly what she wanted.

My grandfather passed away before Christmas several years ago and in an effort to help ease my grandmother's sorrow, her sons bought her a box of chocolate-covered cherries. As she had done for so many years, my grandmother opened her gift and expressed sincere appreciation for this tasty reminder of her first date. This loving exchange went on for eight years, until one day my grandmother told my sister Starla in private that she had never really cared for chocolate-covered cherries but had eaten them so as not to hurt anyone's feelings! When my father and uncle heard this revelation, they did the only honorable thing good sons could do—continued to buy my grandmother her box of chocolate-covered cherries each Christmas.

We have since laughed many times about how my grandmother didn't express her love for her husband in such common ways as fixing grand meals or wearing his favorite perfume. Instead, she lovingly ate the one thing that made her tastebuds cringe: chocolate-covered cherries.

". . . But when you give to the needy, do not let your left hand know what your right hand is doing, so that your giving may be in secret . . ."

—MATTHEW 6:3–4A

Thought . . . What treasured traditions have you established with your spouse? Try creating some just for him, with no thought of yourself. He'll end up thinking the world of you!

Shall We Gather at the River?

BY JOANN L. ROSA-HANES

Shall we gather at the river, where bright angel feet have trod, with its crystal tide forever flowing from the throne of God?

—ROBERT LOWRY

I was saved when I was eight years old. And in the small church where I was raised, profession of faith in Christ meant subsequent immersion in Rock Creek. Because our church didn't house a baptistry, several times a year, on soft spring days or sultry summer ones, our congregation gathered at creek's edge to observe the tradition of old-fashioned baptism. (Although I knew of one man so eager for baptism that he couldn't wait the long winter, so they broke the ice to accommodate him.)

Sweet fellowship commenced with "dinner on the grounds." Rows of long tables, interlaced with folding chairs, were laden with overflowing casseroles, Mom's sumptuous chicken and dumplings among them. We sat, we ate, we talked, and sat some more. Oh how I loved those dinners! Then, at preacher's prompting, we'd sentinel the creek's banks in joyful anticipation. Hymns were sung. Prayers were uttered. And often someone cried. As many as twenty new believers waded into the water, our soft strains of *Shall We Gather at the River?* rippling over them.

The last time I went to Rock Creek, a bawdy group was already gathered. They had been drinking. We proceeded with our service despite their raucous jesting and mock baptizing.

Yet after that, the church installed a costly baptistry in the sanctuary. People still gather and sing and pray as saints are baptized into Christ's Body. But for me, it has never been the same. No baptistry can replace my memory of what it was like to gather at the river.

. . . they were baptized by him in the Jordan River.

—MARK 1:5

Thought . . . Have you joined God's family through salvation? When Christ returns for His Church, the whole family will join in celebration at the River of Life flowing through Heaven.

From the Lips of Children

BY GAIL GAYMER MARTIN

It is not a bad thing that children should occasionally, and politely,
put parents in their place.

—SIDONIE GABRIELLE COLETTE

Holiday family dinners can arouse wonderful memories, and I
treasure the recollection of one Thanksgiving dinner about five
years ago. The Thanksgiving table overflowed with turkey and
stuffing, a variety of vegetables, salads, and all the traditional
mouthwatering delicacies. The family crowded around the table,
pulling in chairs and strapping little ones into high chairs. This
year, Amanda was old enough to sit on a regular chair piled high
with telephone books, and she posed like a little lady as the
adults gathered around the table.

Before the entire family was seated, one eager diner reached
across Amanda's plate toward the turkey platter. She watched as
the meat-filled fork swept past her again and was deposited on a
dinner plate. Another adult grabbed a dinner roll and covered it
with butter. In silence, Amanda observed the activity. Then in a
gentle, lilting voice, like a mother who tenderly reminds her
child to be careful, she said, "Fold your hands."

The adults turned to her as she sat with her head bowed and
her tiny hands folded. Meekly, the over-eager adults placed their
forks down on their plates, and folded their hands and bowed
their heads for the mealtime prayer.

I thought of the Child Jesus in the temple speaking to the
learned men. We can learn a lesson from children. God's meth-
ods of guidance are awesome.

The wolf will live with the lamb, the leopard will lie down
with the goat, the calf and the lion and the yearling together; and a little child will lead them.

—ISAIAH 11:6

Thought . . . Does your family observe the tradition of
saying "grace" before meals? Thank God for His bounty
both at home and at restaurants. Your children will set
this example with their friends and their families.

The Wedding Gift

BY KATHY COLLARD MILLER

The word "grace" is unquestionably the most significant single word in the Bible.

—ILION T. JONES

My husband, Larry, and I attended the wedding of our friends, Rick and Fausta, several years ago. When it was time for us to leave the reception, Larry and I wished them the best in their marriage. Fausta said, "Kathy, I have a gift for you," and walked away. *Wait a minute,* I thought. *She's not supposed to give me a gift. I wasn't in her wedding so I don't deserve one.* I was amazed! Fausta returned and offered me a small white box. I wanted to say, "Fausta, I can't accept this," but realizing how rude that would be, I received the gift and thanked her.

As we drove home, I pulled off the box top, peeled away the layer of tissue paper, and stared at a beautiful sterling silver candy dish.

Just then a wonderful thought dawned on me. "Larry, this dish could symbolize the gift of salvation God gave you and me. Just as I didn't do anything to deserve this dish, I didn't do anything to earn or deserve His love. Isn't this just like His blessing of grace?"

I still don't know why Rick and Fausta gave me that beautiful gift. It must have been the tradition of Fausta's family's native Italy to give wedding guests a similar gift. But today that silver dish reminds me of God's wonderful treasure of grace: something I never could have been good enough to deserve.

He saved us, not because of righteous things we had done, but because of his mercy. He saved us through the washing of rebirth and renewal by the Holy Spirit.

—TITUS 3:5

Thought . . . What is grace? God's Riches At Christ's Expense. At the expense of His life, through nothing you deserved, Christ paid the penalty for your sins at the Cross. Now you are His joint-heir in glory (Romans 8:17).

In Eggshells Is Deum . . .

BY LYNN WORLEY KUNTZ

The best Christmas gift of all is a happy family all wrapped up with one another.

—ANONYMOUS

Although silent nights are virtually unknown at our house, and it's seldom that all is calm, no one enjoys Christmas more than we do! 'Tis the season again? Already? It must be, because Quinn is singing "Glo-oo-oo-oo-oo-oo-oo-ria, in eggshells is Deum . . ." And Artis, Piper, Nick, and Quinn are in the kitchen baking Christmas goodies. Sibling harmony never reigns for long, but what a blessing while it does!

As the Kuntz kids gain inches and pounds, they occupy more space around the holiday dinner table, but our family has grown smaller in number. We miss my husband Darryl's grandma, his mom and dad, my dad and, most recently, my grandmother, Gwynn. It was hard saying good-bye to Gwynnmother, who died at ninety-one. She loved us so unconditionally and egged us on in every endeavor. But she was ready. And I have no doubt we'll all be together again.

My mother, with no family now but for us, lives right next door. She's unfailingly supportive, with an ample and ready sense of humor. A superb audience for the wild, unending parade of Kuntz family activities, she stands at her door and shakes her head in amazement and amusement as we rush in and out of our shared driveway. ("Have we ever gotten ANYWHERE on time?" Piper recently asked.)

Soon Mother will be over to sample the Christmas baking. I'm reminded, especially now, in the midst of our favorite holiday traditions, of the treasure I have in my family, and how fleeting and precious our days together are.

One generation will commend your works to another; they will tell of your mighty acts.

—PSALM 145:4

Thought . . . Are there empty places at your holiday table? To overcome this loss, tell your children about loved ones now with the Lord; keeping their memories alive is the greatest family "heirloom" you can bestow.

Jar of Tears: a Gift from a Daughter's Heart

BY AMBERLY NEESE

A mother is a person who, seeing there are only four pieces of pie for five people, promptly announces she never did care for pie.

—TENNEVA JORDAN

My mom gave me a secular book that she had enjoyed reading, revolving around the story of the relationship between a mother and daughter. As I delved deeper into the story, I realized that this was a parallel to the relationship that my mother and I shared.

At the end of this emotional book, I discovered a wonderful treasured tradition. As a means of reconciliation, the daughter in the book presented a lachrymatory (holder of tears) to her mother. Victorian women would exchange such receptacles as symbols of their desire to support one another through life's circumstances—even painful, tear-provoking experiences. With the bestowing of the gift, each woman also understood that the past had been forgiven, and that the future was bright.

I decided to purchase a lachrymatory for my mother as a gesture of love at Christmas. I realized that the book was probably her way of trying to express remorse for past experiences, and I wanted to reciprocate.

As Christmas approached, I grew nervous. Had the book just been a good story to her? Would she misconstrue my gift as a declaration of guilt? I nervously awaited her phone call on Christmas morning. My husband and I decided to empty our stockings while we waited. As I unwrapped the last gift, a tiny box, everything changed. Tears flooded my eyes. My mom had sent me a lachrymatory!

". . . He will wipe every tear from their eyes. There will be no more death or mourning or crying or pain, for the old order of things has passed away."

—REVELATION 21:4

Thought . . . Do you and your mother enjoy a good relationship? Someone said that a mother is a girl's best friend. If that isn't the case, can you, as a daughter, reach out to become your mother's best friend? You will never regret it, and neither will she!

51

Thanksgiving in a Box

BY JEANNE ZORNES

Thanksgiving was never meant to be shut up in a single day.

—ROBERT CASPAR LINTNER

"Thanksgiving again," I muttered, as I turned the calendar over to November. Start checking the grocery ads for turkey prices. Don't forget the olives. Will the pumpkin pie overcook again? And—*ugh*—all those dishes and no dishwasher . . . except me!

Several years ago, Thanksgiving was becoming my least-favorite holiday. I would orchestrate a masterpiece turkey dinner. Then, while the rest of the family drifted back to the bowl games, I would single-handedly clean up.

Then one year my preteen daughter put a "Thankful Box" on the table. All through November each family member was to fill it with notes about things for which they were thankful. On Thanksgiving night, when we sampled the pies, we opened it and read the notes aloud. One note expressed thanks for the first snowfall. Another, for getting the car fixed after a rear-ender in which the driver wasn't hurt. Others were for hugs, good grades, our youth pastor, kids who liked to read, Dad's job, music and violin lessons, eternal life . . . because Grandpa had just died. This time of sharing "thanks" was so special that the "Thankful Box," a boutique tissue box covered with fall fabric, now has become a Thanksgiving tradition. It comes out every November in anticipation of our attitudes of gratitude.

I still fix the turkey dinner, but with more gratefulness for my treasures: We have money to buy a turkey. We have a home in which to gather. We have family to rim the table. And we have the love and blessings of God to acknowledge through our "thankful notes."

Give thanks to the Lord, for he is good; his love endures forever.

—PSALM 107:1

Thought . . . Are you bored or struggling with life? Every day write down even one of your blessings. At year's end, you'll discover *at least* 365 treasures for which to praise God. Your joy will be boundless.

No Solution in Sight

BY CAROL KENT

It is not difficult to be independent of human comfort when we have God's comfort.

—THOMAS À KEMPIS

Many time events have seemed out of my control and I feel powerless and upset.

One of these times occurred on my wedding day. Gene and I had spent hours memorizing special vows we were going to share as we exchanged rings. Our vows would be the most sacred part of the ceremony. Everything was progressing as planned. How could any event be more perfect? The music was inspiring. Significant people from our past had traveled vast distances to witness this merger of two people who had dedicated their lives to God and to each other. We had kept our relationship pure and desired to have this ceremony be a testimony of God's goodness and love.

But before Dad was to "give me away," I panicked as I realized something. "Dad, Dad," I whispered, "I've forgotten the ring!"

I had left it in the dressing room. I had *nothing* to give during the special vows we had memorized for the ring exchange. I was convinced I had ruined the entire ceremony!

Without hesitation, my father began removing his own wedding ring—the first time in twenty-three years he had taken the ring off. Dad tenderly took my hand, opened my nervous fingers, and placed his wedding ring in the palm of my hand. With a loving squeeze, I knew my father was telling me, *"Carol, everything is going to be okay!"*

That day my earthly father reminded me that I have a loving Heavenly Father Who has control of all the details of my life.

The Lord watches over you . . .

—PSALM 121:5

Thought . . . How do you handle anxiety? Realize that God is sovereignly in control, and that His Holy Spirit will give you self-control (Galatians 5:22) if you let Him.

Treasured Traditions

BY PATTY STUMP

Urgent things are seldom important; important things are seldom urgent.

—ANONYMOUS

Each year our family engages in an accelerated hustle-bustle, struggling to juggle the details of creating a Merry Christmas! While I would enjoy a silent night to roast chestnuts on an open fire, I find myself, instead, dashing to the mall in my dirty minivan, racing through each store, uptight all the way!! At home I've been known to ponder, "O Christmas tree, O Christmas tree, where did I store your branches?"

Amid parties, programs, and the pursuit of presents, our family treasures three traditions that remind us of the reason for the season. One brings us together each evening during Advent for reading a Scripture passage and sharing a familiar carol or two. The second tradition occurs one Sunday in December when we open our home for an annual neighborhood drop-in with cider and cookies. The third occurs Christmas morning. After the gifts are given and packages unveiled, we take a few private moments to write thank-you notes to God for what He has given to us throughout the year. After everyone has finished, we lay our handwritten letters in a straw-laden manger near our Christmas tree.

Each tradition reminds us to keep Christ in Christmas, drawing us closer to Him and, simultaneously, closer to one another. True treasures aren't always found inside pretty packages or captured in "Kodak moments." Often they're found when ordinary moments are spent focusing on God's extraordinary love for us.

". . . Blessed are the pure in heart, for they will see God . . ."
—MATTHEW 5:8

Thought . . . Have you a bah-humbug Christmas spirit? Avoid stress by buying presents gradually throughout the year. During Advent, relax and focus on Jesus. When Christmas day arrives, your *blahs* will have turned to *blessings*—your *humbugs* to *hymns* of praise!

Rise and Shine

BY DIANE SHIRLEY

Keep your face to the sunshine and you cannot see the shadows.

—HELEN KELLER

When I was a girl, Dad observed his own tradition and would come into my room every morning trumpeting, "Rise and shine!" It was time to get up and get going.

When I was little, it was a minor interruption to my sweet dreams. However, as I entered my teen years it became a major irritation as my hormones screamed, "You are very *sleeeppyy!*" I preferred the comfort of my nest under the covers to facing the glare of another challenging day. I would crawl out of bed, promising myself that I would never treat my children in such a way!

Years later, when I had children of my own, I would enter their room with a prayer for them on my heart and a declaration for them on my lips. You guessed it: "Rise and Shine!"

And, as the years pass, on those days when I have been dead tired and bone weary, I still remember my father's wake-up call, and unearth a deeper treasure. The Bible tells us that we are a reflection of our Maker and, like Zion, are to shine in a world growing increasingly dim. It's God's wake-up call. When you don't think you can face another day, know that because Jesus, your risen Savior, shines on you, He will help you to "rise and shine" in dark places.

My dad also used to say "bright-eyed and bushy-tailed," but that is a whole other story!

"Arise, shine, for your light has come, and the glory of the Lord rises upon you . . ."

—ISAIAH 60:1

Thought . . . Are you depressed, overcome by the world's darkness? Even a pinprick of light dispels darkness. Rise to the challenge. Fix your eyes on Jesus and His Sonlight will shine in your heart. Give God the glory!

A Christmas Blessing

BY EDWINA PATTERSON

Let us remember the foundation of this joy—the fear, the journey, the refuge, the birth, the revelation.

—WELLERAN POLTARNEES

The Christmas tradition that I treasure the most is our family sharing the Lord's Supper together. My husband, R. J., and I wanted a way to impress upon our children that Christmas is not simply the custom of "Santa Claus" and the gifts they receive, but it is receiving God's greatest gift to us, His Son, Jesus Christ. As we struggled to keep Christmas from becoming commercialized, our son suggested that we observe the Lord's Supper on Christmas Eve. What could be more perfect! Jesus came to this earth with a purpose—He was born to die for you and me.

At Christmas, teach your child that Jesus came to be born in a manger in Bethlehem, but don't stop there. Include Christ's death and resurrection in your Christmas story. Without His death and resurrection, we wouldn't have hope. The victory is not just in the fact He came to earth, but in that He died for us and He lives today.

On Christmas Eve, just before bed, our family gathers around the dining room table. We try to "shut out" the world by turning off all the lights. We each hold a candle and, by flickering light, R. J. reads the Christmas story from the Bible. Then he leads us in observing the Lord's Supper. We sing one verse of "Silent Night," blow out our candles, and quietly go to bed, cognizant of the truth that the real treasure of Christmas lies not in the world's trappings, but in Jesus' gift of eternal life.

And we have seen and testify that the Father has sent his Son to be the Savior of the world.

—I JOHN 4:14

Thought . . . What Christmas traditions does your family observe? Center them on the Treasure of Christ. The world's trappings will pale by comparison and yours will be a powerful witness to the world.

Little Things

BY BARBARA PERETTI

Life is a great bundle of little things.

—OLIVER WENDELL HOLMES

Married in 1944, Mom prayerfully entrusted her marriage to the Lord as Dad piloted bombing raids over northern Europe. After the war, they left the security of the Kentucky home for northern Idaho and struggled financially while raising their family. Life was strenuous at times but, like the lunches Mom made, it was the little things that became daily reminders of God's faithfulness to her and her childhood sweetheart. I was touched that twenty-five years later, as a vice president for Merrill Lynch, Dad still carried Mom's lunches to work. Perhaps he treasured what they represented—the faithfulness of God and that of his devoted bride.

Alone now, Mom still sits at the kitchen table meditating on God's Word and praying for her family. And though Dad has passed on, his thoughts still unite with hers when she ponders the notes he penned in his Bible.

As a little girl, I decided I wanted to have a marriage like the one my parents had modeled. I dreamed of being devoted to a godly husband just as Mom was devoted to Dad.

On June 24, 1972, that little girl's dream came true. I consecrated myself to Frank as we openly dedicated our marriage to the Lord.

In times of plenty and in times of want, I have carried on Mom's tradition. The lunches I now prepare for my childhood sweetheart have become our daily reminders of God's faithfulness. He's been faithful to direct our path. And when we've been weak, He's been strong.

He who finds a wife finds what is good and receives favor from the Lord.

—PROVERBS 18:22

Thought . . . Are you a successful wife, mother, Christian . . . ? Yes, if you have done the little things well, because they add up to a lifetime of godly service and surrender.

Our Thankful Tree

BY ELLIE KAY

Your friend is the one who knows all about you, and still likes you.

—ELBERT HUBBARD

As an "Air Force household," we have made ten moves in our first twelve years of marriage. As a family of seven, we make and leave many friends. That is why keeping in touch with these treasured people has become such a priceless undertaking.

In order to gather this "wealth" annually, we created a "Thankful Tree." *Woman's Day Magazine* liked our family tradition so much that they sent a photographer to shoot our active family around the Thankful Tree for their November issue. Four hours and eight rolls of film later, we survived, but the photographer resigned!

Every November, we make leaves from construction paper in an assortment of fall colors. The youngest child cuts with safety scissors while an older brother addresses the envelopes. Papa personalizes leaves for each of the families—"The Taylors are thankful for _____." We attach our bare Thankful Tree, made of laminated poster board, to the front door of our home. It awaits the arrival of its "foliage" from the four corners of the globe.

As each leaf is returned, we thank God for the family who sent it and add it to our treasured collection. By the middle of November, our tree is fully arrayed, its leaves taped in place by careful little fingers. The Taylors (North Dakota) are thankful for daughter Lauren. The Fahrenkrugs (Germany) are thankful for safety. The Thomas family (England) is thankful for *what?* Twins! And we are thankful to God Who has provided a creative way for us to establish "roots" while on the move.

Like cold water to a weary soul is good news from a distant land.

—PROVERBS 25:25

Thought . . . Do you dread an upcoming move? Look forward to making new friends. But never forget the "old" ones. Write letters. Place calls. And remember, you're only a prayer away!

The First Candle

BY SHIRLEY POPE WAITE

We must accept finite disappointment, but we must never lose infinite hope.

—MARTIN LUTHER KING

It was the first Sunday in Advent. One of our church families read Scripture and lit the first candle, explaining its symbolism. The pastor reminded us that many would reenact this simple, but meaningful ceremony in their homes later in the day.

How my heart ached as I thought ahead to the evening. We had always followed the Advent tradition of lighting candles, singing carols, and saying a prayer with our children. Now, for the first time, there would be only my husband and I. Would I break down as I looked at the old printed Advent service, wrinkled and worn with use, with the children's names penciled in? Was it worth the bother? No, we could forego it tonight. Why play the angel chimes and light the Christmas candles? Why go through a treasured family ritual for just the two of us?

About nine that evening, my husband turned from the television set and said, "Are we going to do our 'thing'?"

"I guess so," I responded weakly.

As we passed the printed service back and forth, a lump grew in my throat. However, as "Father" asked "Mother" to light the first candle, I felt an almost imperceptible quickening in my spirit, a growing sense of joy beyond the pain in my heart. *Why*, I thought, *the coming of Christ is not just a feeling. It's a certain knowing, no matter what our age or stage of life.* I smiled, and lit the first candle—the candle of HOPE.

May the God of hope fill you with all joy and peace . . .
—ROMANS 15:13

Thought . . . Have you lost hope because you have an "empty nest"? Recall treasured memories made with your children. Create new traditions with your spouse that revolve around Christ. When you have Jesus, you always have hope.

The Mulberry Tree

BY KATHRYN THOMPSON PRESLEY

> Any married couple who says they've never had a fight has either a
> poor memory or a very dull life to remember.
>
> —ANONYMOUS

All the sweet young things in my office showed me their Valentine flowers and candy. "What did your husband give you, Kathryn?" their fresh, young faces turned to me in guileless anticipation. "A fruitless mulberry tree." *Where did that come from?* I wondered. It was a bald-faced lie. I'd never cared for mulberry trees!

I fumed all day, and that evening my husband recognized "stormy weather."

"All right, what have I done *now?*" he questioned.

"It isn't what you did," I raged, "It's what you *never* do." And then I sobbed out the whole story. "Your selfish neglect has turned me into a liar, and I'm a Sunday school teacher! How can I go back tomorrow and tell those girls that I lied?"

His tired face was troubled as he left the room. In a little while, I heard his old pickup drive away. Much later, he sheepishly stuck his head in the back door. "Could you come help me with this?"

There in the chilly February darkness, lay an eight-foot fruitless mulberry tree, its roots encased in a burlap ball. It was nearly midnight before we had it installed in the corner of our backyard. If you drive through Bryan, Texas, you can see it today, towering over the other trees in the neighborhood.

Over the years, in every new home since then, my husband has kept the tradition of carefully planting a fruitless mulberry tree. I've come to adore them, as I treasure the thought of all those trees spread across the Texas prairies, standing sentinel to our love.

> Be kind and compassionate to one another, forgiving each
> other, just as in Christ God forgave you.
>
> —EPHESIANS 4:32

Thought . . . Do you resent something that your husband did—or hasn't done? Gently share your feelings, be forgiving, and give him a chance to rectify the situation.

It's Later Than You Think

BY LUCI SWINDOLL

Lost, yesterday, somewhere between sunrise and sunset, two golden hours, each set with sixty diamond minutes. No reward is offered for they are gone forever.

—HORACE MANN

When I was a child, our family had a chiming clock that had been handed down through the generations and was a well-loved treasure. On the hour, it would chime out the time, and by it we kept on schedule. Many nights, each of us would call out the number of chimes until the last one stopped.

One night, after we had all gone to bed about midnight, the clock began to gong and we started our audible ritual: "Nine . . . ten . . . eleven . . . twelve." As we closed our mouths after shouting out TWELVE! the clock struck thirteen. *Where did that come from?* I wondered, as we all laughed heartily from our beds. Almost in perfect unison, we called out: "It's later than you think!"

For most of us, that's the problem: our greatest fear is running out of time. So we hurry through life trying desperately to get everything done: working overtime, eating fast food in the car, racing down the freeway.

In our quest to save time, we're losing something. I thought about how my grandparents valued time. They always had time for my parents and my brothers and me; they emphasized beautifully served meals, family reunions, and long conversations. It seemed they had time for everything in life that was important, because they took time to live. They treasured the biblical injunction that proclaims, "This is the day the Lord has made; let us rejoice and be glad in it (Psalm 118:24)."

Don't wait for another time. Rejoice in *this* day and be glad! Tonight, your clock *could* strike thirteen.

> . . . What is your life? You are a mist that appears for a little while and then vanishes. Instead, you ought to say, "If it is the Lord's will, we will live and do this or that."
>
> —JAMES 4:14B–15

Thought . . . What's the key to time management? Doing God's will ensures doing what matters most. If traditional plans go awry, see disappointments as *His appointments.* Knowing He's in charge brings peace.

Piano Lessons

BY PAT DEVINE

Music gives form and voice to scrambled emotions without explanations and rational interpretations.

—THOMAS MOORE

When I was seven, a dear friend of the family, Miss Ella, gave me a piano. Even then, I liked the sound my little fingers made as I struggled through the piano primers and knee-quaking recitals. As I learned to read the music, the best times were spent when family and friends gathered around for sing-alongs.

My early married years in a small urban flat did not accommodate a piano, but when we built our home in the suburbs after the birth of our third child, we had room to spare and the ebony Steinway came our way. It was here many family traditions centered around the upright. Christmas carols and Girl Scout songs brought harmony to chilly winter evenings and summer camp plans.

Now in my solitude, I play with the passion of a Paderewski. Nothing eases strong emotions like a few hours at the piano. If I am feeling angry or sad, the strident fortissimo of a Tchaikovsky concerto relieves the tension, and after an hour I can cover the keys and walk away totally relaxed.

The piano I now play is a third generation of the original instrument, yet Miss Ella's gift to that little girl is one that keeps on giving. Piano lessons continue—not those learned from the stern old teachers of my youth, but from time spent with *Keyboard Praise* by Amy Grant or études by Bach, or Ragtime tunes by Scott Joplin—life lessons "in sunshine or in shadow"—at my treasured keyboard.

. . . the Lord's musical instruments, which King David had made for praising the Lord . . .

—II CHRONICLES 7:6

Thought . . . Do you wish you played the piano? It's not too late to try. But if you don't own one, realize that the true treasure is enjoying the *music,* itself. Listen to masters tickle the ivories on tape or CD. Your spirit will revive.

Wisdom

My Favorite Lunch with Mama

BY CYNTHIA CARPENTER THOMAS

My mother was the making of me. The memory of her will always
be a blessing to me.

—THOMAS EDISON

"Sis, do you remember the time we had cupcakes for lunch?"
Mama asked.

Quickly, the pages of my memory flipped back fifty years.
The same day that my parents' divorce was final, a devastating
tornado blew our house away. Mama was left with lots of bills to
pay. Housing was scarce. We lived in a small, dark apartment
above an old newspaper office—just Mama and I. We lived from
payday to payday, and we walked wherever we went.

Mama and I always met at the apartment for lunch. This particular day she didn't put any meat or vegetables on my plate—
just one chocolate cupcake! Better yet, there was one on Mama's
plate, too. I loved sweets—especially chocolate—especially
Hostess cupcakes! We had cake for lunch, and it wasn't even my
birthday! I felt like a princess.

Today, Mama decided to tell me the "rest of the story." That
morning, we had not a crumb left in the cupboard. We had no
money in the bank, but Mama did have ten cents in her pocket.
Knowing what a perceptive child I was, Mama thought all morning about how we could dine on a dime without my knowing
how hard times really were. Her choice was one of wisdom.

Since those days, Mama and I have cruised the Caribbean
and enjoyed scrumptious buffets of exotic fare. We have eaten
in fine restaurants and ordered from unpriced menus; but the
day we dined on cupcakes was my favorite lunch with Mama.

She watches over the affairs of her household and does
not eat the bread of idleness. Her children arise and call
her blessed.

—PROVERBS 31:27, 28A

Thought . . . Do you believe in telling children the truth?
Life is tough, and you can't always protect them. However, when you needn't tell *all* the heartbreak you know,
let them remain children . . . just a little longer.

Jenny's Gift

BY JEAN RODGERS

It is quite clear that I will not be alive in the spring. But I will soon experience new life in a different way.

—JOSEPH CARDINAL BERNARDIN

"Why didn't he fight harder?" For years, I'd groped for a reasonable response to this anguished lament of the grieving. Neither late night Scripture searches nor early morning prayers provided an answer. Finally, insight came through a special gift from Jenny, my treasured friend in Christ, as she confronted death.

As I kept a bedside vigil with Jenny, she offered humbling prayers for forgiveness, prayers of praise for those who ministered to her physical and spiritual needs, and prayers of thanksgiving for her good years as a treasured wife, mother, "Nana," and friend. In the final hours, Jenny and I simply held hands, bonding in silence, as God set the stage for a wonderful surprise. His Spirit broke through the quiet with a startling revelation. Softly He spoke to me: "There is no question that Jenny is fighting for life. But it is for her *eternal* life that she battles, armed with deep faith, persistent prayer, and a grateful, loving heart."

Amazing! I had received God's wisdom at last! Depending upon His will, dying can be as much a fight for eternal life as it is for life here on earth. Because of Jenny's faith, the Holy Spirit delivered the treasure of wisdom to discern the difference between a "fight for life as we now know it" and a "fight for life as we hope to know it." And Jenny's gift keeps on giving. Each time I share the Holy Spirit's insight, the grieving are released from the trap of doubt to the refuge of peace.

For to me, to live is Christ and to die is gain.

—PHILIPPIANS 1:21

Thought . . . Do you struggle over death, clinging to your life or that of a loved one? If Christ is *everything* to someone, there is victory in life *or* in death. Either way, one is with the Lord.

Timeless Treasures

BY BARBARA PERETTI

> The [woman] who has God for [her] treasure has all things in One. Many ordinary treasures may be denied [her], or if [she] is allowed to have them, the enjoyment of them will be so tempered that they will never be necessary to [her] happiness.
>
> —A. W. TOZER

Occasionally God tempers my enjoyment of ordinary treasures by reminding me that material wealth is susceptible to destruction. That's what He did with my Queen Anne furniture.

About the time Frank and I had the financial wherewithal to purchase some fine Queen Anne furniture, we also decided to add a Great Pyrenees puppy to our family.

One day while vacuuming I was horrified to discover deep teeth marks in the legs of my cherished wing chairs. I couldn't believe my eyes! Surely the sweet bundle of fur wouldn't do such a thing! But though the disfiguring evidence was merely circumstantial, I had to rule Reuben the guilty party.

I have never replaced the scarred chair legs. Instead, I allow the scratches to remind me that ordinary treasures are perishable; they cannot offer enduring enjoyment. Our furniture has since accumulated additional mars and scratches, [and] even our "puppy" has aged. The distinct pleasure each earthly thing brings to our lives is temporal; the joy it affords lasts but a season.

Limitless joy, on the other hand is found in God's immeasurable bounty. Pearls of wisdom that endure the test of time lie hidden in God's Word. Deep abiding peace comes when we apply God's principles to our lives; and for those who accept Christ's redeeming act of death on the cross, He extends the most valuable treasure of all—life eternal.

> So we fix our eyes not on what is seen, but on what is unseen. For what is seen is temporary, but what is unseen is eternal.
>
> —II CORINTHIANS 4:18

Thought . . . Do you suffer material loss? Fix your eyes on Jesus, and things of earth will "grow strangely dim in the light of His glory and grace." (Quote from hymn: "Turn Your Eyes Upon Jesus.").

A Treasured Kiss

BY KAREN H. WHITING

There is a wisdom of the head, . . . and a wisdom of the heart.

—CHARLES DICKENS

One morning I kissed my young son, then watched him turn, wipe off the kiss, and pat his chest. I felt sad, thinking he was growing up and feeling too old for kisses. Suddenly, he turned back to me, looked up, and said, "Do you know what I did?" I shook my head "no," not wanting to admit that he'd brushed off the kiss. Grinning, he said, "I took the kiss you gave me and put it in my heart. I won't get sad today 'cause it will be here where I can feel it." How his words lifted my spirits! My son treasured the kiss and wanted to keep it close to him all day.

It made me think of countless times when Scripture that I'd memorized flooded my heart, easing my sadness, helping my need. I thought of how God wants us to devour His words, locking them in our hearts like treasure. Whenever we need a word of encouragement, joy, or comfort, we can open up our heart's "treasure chest," knowing that God is with us. We can rejoice, even in our troubles, because of the bounty that we have stored.

When your words came, I ate them; they were my joy and my heart's delight, for I bear your name, O Lord God Almighty.

—JEREMIAH 15:16

Thought . . . How do you lock the treasure of God's Word in your heart? Well-known preacher John MacArthur suggests reading the same book of the Bible every day for a month. It is a painless way to memorize and to understand Scripture. The Holy Spirit will bring to your mind what you have stored in your heart when you need it most (John 14:26).

The Treasury

BY BETH MOORE

God's Book is packed full of overwhelming riches; they are
unsearchable—the more we have, the more there is to have.

—OSWALD CHAMBERS

We beg and plead and moan and cry
To make sense of this place.
We sweat and strive to fix it all
Then seek You just in case.
When will we learn to listen
To the Master clearly say,
"Seek treasures tucked into My Word . . .
It's there you'll see My face!"
Oh, hasten that sweet moment
When we'll know as we've been known.
Such secrets of Your glory
Cannot be grasped, they're shown!
This fleeting puzzle makes no sense
Except in You alone
And missing pieces swell our faith
And stretch us 'til we've grown.

I wait for the Lord, my soul waits, and in his word I put my
hope.

—PSALM 130:5

Thought . . . Are you puzzled by the complexities of life?
Search for the missing pieces of wisdom in God's Word,
just as you would dig for gold—with great delight and
diligence.

Relinquishing a Gem, Receiving a Treasure

BY CASSANDRA WOODS

In all affairs it's a healthy thing now and then to hang a question mark on the things you have taken for granted.

—BERTRAND RUSSELL

One day while driving, I used my thumb to rotate my ring around my ring finger as I'd done many times before. But this time was different. I felt for my diamond solitaire and it wasn't there! I drove into a parking lot and searched the car. My eyes suddenly confirmed what my heart already knew. The gem was gone. I gasped in disbelief. *Where could it be? When did I lose it?* I agonized.

Realizing that getting frantic wasn't going to bring it back, I made a conscious decision to calm down. I simply assumed the diamond would show up later as I retraced my steps. As I started driving again I prayed, "God, how can You make anything good from this?"

Days later, I was meditating on Scripture when my heart was wisely challenged: Was I placing enough focus on God in my daily life? I recalled when I had first become engaged and received my diamond. I was so excited that I talked about it all the time, cleaned it regularly, and lifted my hand for all to see. But as the years passed, I hardly ever focused on it anymore.

I made a connection: how often had I lived each day without focusing on God? Yes, I miss my ring. But right now every time I look at my ring finger, I'm reminded never to take my relationship with God for granted. And that's the real treasure.

But his delight is in the law of the Lord, and on his law he meditates day and night.

—PSALM 1:2

Thought . . . Have you taken your "first love" for Jesus for granted? Like a dull diamond, it can be polished like new. Remember how you loved Him, repent of negligence, and do what you did at first (Revelation 2:4–5). Watch your love sparkle!

Simplicity

BY MARY WHELCHEL

Materialism is organized emptiness of the spirit.

—FRANZ WERFEL

A wise saying states, "Someday, the things we own may end up owning us." It's easy to allow the accumulation of "stuff"—things we think we can't live without—to complicate our lives needlessly. Possessions meant to simplify our daily round, end up weighing us down as we spend time, energy, emotion, and money in maintaining them.

A friend of mine went to a foreign country for a two-year missionary assignment. At the end of her term, before returning home, she gave away everything she had accumulated while there, so that all that remained fit onto one shelf in her closet! She wrote me and said, "I can't tell you how freeing it is to know that all my earthly possessions can fit onto just one shelf. It makes life so simple."

I, too, felt the need to simplify my life by selling my home in order to find a smaller townhouse that was easier to maintain. While I loved my house and had enjoyed decorating it, living in a townhouse has eliminated many unnecessary responsibilities. I realize that *where* I live is not nearly as important as *how* I live.

Jesus warned, ". . . Be on guard against all kinds of greed: a man's life does not consist in the abundance of his possessions (Luke 12:15)." When we hold onto possessions, considering them *treasures*, we come dangerously close to being greedy. I have discovered that the key to abundant living is in holding onto the only *true treasure*, Jesus Christ, Himself. Because I have Him, I have everything!

For the love of money is a root of all kinds of evil.

—I TIMOTHY 6:10A

Thought . . . How can you simplify life? Try living simply—eliminate anything that weighs you down, including things, activities, and bad habits. Know when enough is enough!

Picture It!

BY HELENE C. KUONI

Life is the soul's nursery—its training place for the destinies of
eternity.

—WILLIAM MAKEPEACE THACKERAY

When my little fingers couldn't exercise any more, I'd put the
violin down, and my mom would encourage me to keep practicing—*in my mind*. "Picture yourself fingering the notes in your
head," she'd say. When I became discouraged with learning short-
hand in high school, she'd say, "Practice the outlines in your
mind while riding the bus to school." She offered the same advice for tennis and bowling: "Visualize! You don't have to be on
the court or at the lanes in order to practice."

Mom's counsel was wise and followed the Lord's pattern, for
didn't God *show* Abraham the stars and tell him to visualize the
future? It's how Mom taught me about the Lord, too. She showed
me His "picture" in the Bible, His "picture" in nature, and "picture" after "picture" of His working in people's lives.

Then one day, my turn came to return her advice. "When
you're resting, Mom, close your eyes; picture your last physical
therapy session. Master each technique in your mind. You'll walk
again."

She nodded. She wanted to leave the hospital so badly and
whispered, "I can picture myself walking home." "Good," I responded, "Visualize yourself using the hallway as an indoor track."

But Mom had meant something different and the next day,
when she "walked" home to God, I realized that she'd been visu-
alizing her walk into the arms of Jesus. Her whole life had been
her preparation, her practice runway to Him. I treasure the wisdom she shared, and I can picture her on her walk home.

He took him outside and said, "Look up at the heavens and
count the stars—if indeed you can count them." Then he
said to him, "So shall your offspring be."

—GENESIS 15:5

Thought . . . Are your worldly burdens too heavy to
bear? Focus on Heaven, the Christian's true home. In
light of Heaven's glory, earthly troubles pale by comparison.

Do you Know Who God Is?

BY VALERIE HOWE

We are told the average child asks 500,000 questions by the age of fifteen. That's half a million opportunities to teach. Many of these are "why" and "how" questions which take us right to the feet of God.

—JOHN M. DRESCHER

No theologian anywhere has a better definition of God's identity than my two-year-old daughter, Malorie. One day, as my two daughters and I were riding in our minivan, five-year-old Meagan kept badgering Malorie, strapped helplessly in her car seat, with this question: "Do you know Who God is, Malorie?" Malorie's silence frustrated Meagan, so she persistently and adamantly repeated the question.

Finally in desperation, Meagan, with an exasperated sigh, reluctantly sat back in her seat and looked out the window. It was then that Malorie began to sing, "The Bible tells me so." It was as if she were saying to Meagan, "This is the only answer I know."

What a priceless treasure it was to this mother's heart and to God's, I am sure, for a little child to respond with such a wise answer. I can imagine Him saying, "Yes, Malorie, you are right. You know Who I am for the Bible tells you so." And perhaps as she sang, all the hosts of heaven sang along with her.

". . . I tell you the truth, anyone who will not receive the kingdom of God like a little child will never enter it."
—LUKE 18:17

Thought . . . Do you believe that the Bible "tells you so" . . . tells you the very truth that was written by men, yet inspired by God, Himself, without error (II Timothy 3:16, II Peter 1:20–21)? Unless you settle it in your heart that God's Word is inerrant, you will never believe nor follow what it *tells* you to do.

A Wise Maneuver

BY CAROLE MAYHALL

Children learn what they observe . . . if children live with fairness, they learn justice. . . .

—DOROTHY KNOLTE

"Carole, I'm not going to tell you not to smoke." Mother's brown eyes looked serious as I glanced at her in surprise. A few of my girlfriends had begun to experiment with smoking "behind the barn," and Mother and I were discussing it. I knew my parents disapproved of smoking, so I was quite shocked by her initial statement.

She continued, "I cannot be either your judge or your keeper as you are growing up, so I'm not going to tell you that you must not smoke." She paused and then said, "But I am going to ask you to promise me that you will smoke your first cigarette in front of me."

In our household, a promise was not given lightly. It had the solemnity of a sacred oath sworn on the Bible. To my knowledge my parents had never broken a promise to me and we were expected to act just as honorably.

A wise woman, my mother. I didn't know it when I promised that day, but she had just taken all the wicked fun out of sneaking off somewhere to smoke with friends. To this day I have never had a cigarette in my lips, because who in her right mind would smoke her first in front of a mother she loved and respected, and whom she knew would be heartbroken to witness the event? Definitely not this kid!

The wise woman builds her house . . .

—PROVERBS 14:1

Thought . . . Do you always discipline your children with a lecture? Sometimes you make more impact by setting a good example and trusting them to make a wise choice.

How Much Do I Have?

BY JO HUDDLESTON

What is yours is mine, and all mine is yours.

—PLAUTUS

Nothing else in the house moved as I stumbled up the hall. I stood half asleep at my kitchen sink. Looking through half-closed blinds, I discovered what had interrupted my predawn sleep.

On the deck, several pesky blue jays perched atop the patio table, ready to welcome a new day. I rapped impatiently on a window pane. With much fluttering, the birds scattered to nearby trees—all but one.

Then the concert began, the bird's music as crisp and clear as the spring morning. Each time he chirped, the little bird quivered from the black collar across his throat to the trembling tip of his brilliant blue tail feathers. This little bird put all of his body behind each note—he gave it all he had.

I wondered, *Could I measure up to the blue jay? Am I as committed in my efforts of praise and worship? How much have I given God? How much do I have to give?*

This tiniest of life's circumstances surrounding the blue jay gave me a treasure of wisdom: God showed me through the blue jay that it makes no difference how much I have, as long as I give all that I have to loving and serving Him—whether in performing my job, raising my children, doing my church work, or enjoying my leisure time. Like the little blue jay on my deck with only one song to sing, I must give it all I've got.

Jesus replied: "'Love the Lord your God with all your heart and with all your soul and with all your mind. . . . '"
—MATTHEW 22:37

Thought . . . Do you give the Lord your all, no matter how seemingly insignificant . . . like the boy who gave his loaves and fishes to Jesus? God wants from you all that He asks. Watch Him multiply your small supply into a treasure chest of resources for others.

Inner Sunshine

BY DIANA L. JAMES

A Child's Prayer: God, make my life a little light, within the world to glow; a tiny flame that burneth bright wherever I may go.

—M. BENTHAM-EDWARDS

Heavy rain was falling on the morning of Lorinda's fifth birthday, dampening all hopes that the birthday party in the park her mom had planned could still take place. Lorinda's seven-year-old brother, Alan, munched his breakfast cereal and muttered, "Boy, what rotten weather for a birthday party!" Their mom nodded in agreement.

Just then, Lorinda bounced into the kitchen, sat down at the breakfast table and exclaimed brightly, "Wow, what a beautiful day!" Her mother and Alan looked at her with wide, surprised eyes. Her mother said, "But, honey, don't you see it's pouring down rain out there." Lorinda flashed a cheery smile and replied, "I know, Mom, but you can't tell a day by its weather!"

I have often thought of my granddaughter Lorinda's words of wisdom when I'm tempted to complain about the weather, traffic delays, and other trivial inconveniences of daily life. Lord, help me do what Lorinda does. Help me greet rainy days and discouraging moments with the contagious glow of Your inner sunshine.

"Do you hear what these children are saying?" they asked him. "Yes," replied Jesus, "have you never read, 'From the lips of children and infants you have ordained praise'?"

—MATTHEW 21:16

Thought . . . Do you see the glass half-empty or half-full? Attitude determines your "altitude." Despite your circumstance, rejoice in Jesus, Who is your hope. He will lift your spirits.

An Old Man's Wisdom

BY DONNA CLARK GOODRICH

Nobody ever outgrows Scripture.

—CHARLES SPURGEON

"Time to read the Bible, Clarence," I said to my seventy-two-year-old stepfather. My mother—and his wife for only ten years before her death—had recently passed away and he had come to spend the winter with us. Because the two of them had read from a devotional book and the Bible every morning, I tried to maintain the same routine. Although his senile mind did not understand much of what I read, I knew that he enjoyed it.

This morning's reading was from Romans 8:35–39, and the text was Romans 8:28. As I looked ahead to the verses, I saw all the difficult words: "Who shall separate us from the love of Christ? . . . tribulation . . . distress . . . persecution . . . famine . . . nakedness . . . peril . . . sword . . . death . . . life . . . angels . . . principalities . . . powers . . . things present . . . things to come . . . height . . . depth . . . nor any other creature."

There's no way he can understand that, I thought. *I'll just read Romans 8:28. He'll understand that. It's familiar.* "All things work together for good to them that love God." But I sensed God say, "No, read it *all.*" So I plunged in and read every verse.

When I finished, Clarence sat there with a pleased smile on his face. "Nothing can separate us from God," he repeated with childlike happiness. "Isn't that nice?" I then realized that nothing—not even his failing faculties—had separated him from his awareness of the Lord. I was bolstered by this treasured wisdom.

Even when I am old and gray, do not forsake me . . .

—PSALM 71:18

Thought . . . Do you know an elderly person who is unable to attend church? Visit him and read Scripture to him, or give him the Bible "on tape." If he's lonely, with nothing but time on his hands, bless him with the comfort of God's Word.

Jesus, My Treasure

BY JOYCE ROGERS

The Bible is alive, it speaks to me; it has feet, it runs after me; it has hands, it lays hold on me.

—MARTIN LUTHER

Because my college major was religion, I learned many facts about the Bible, but the emphasis was mainly historical—like a skeleton of "dead" facts to me. Because of this, I seldom studied the Old Testament.

And then, through a combination of factors, the Lord led me to an exciting new approach to studying Scripture—a way in which to breathe life into this "dead body" of information that I had stored in my mind for years. The major factor, however, was a deep need in my life that caused me to want to go deeper into Scripture.

This new approach totally transformed my study of the Bible. It was so simple that I can't imagine how I had missed it! I began to "look for Jesus" in every book of the Bible—whether in the Old or New Testaments. Exploring became so very exciting! Some precious treasure lay right on the surface, while other treasures were hidden in rocky crevices. I determined that all of the wealth and wisdom would be mine!

This precious treasure was Jesus, Himself, present throughout God's wonderful Book. You must constantly search there to find out Who He really is. I began to search for Him in the most unlikely place—the Old Testament. It was here that I discovered the most priceless art treasures of Jesus. I could see Him from every angle, for example, as my Passover Lamb and as my Tabernacle. He was represented literally everywhere, in every book!

But he was pierced for our transgressions, he was crushed for our iniquities . . .

—ISAIAH 53:5A

Thought . . . Do you look for Jesus throughout *all* Scripture? He is there, from Genesis (1:26) as part of the Trinity Who created man, to the Revelation (1) that He gave the apostle John. He was with God. He *is* God. Through Him all things were made (John 1).

His Wisdom

BY CELESTE DUCKWORTH

A bundle of sticks is always stronger than a single twig.

—ANONYMOUS

Kevin, our twelve-year-old, slammed into the den and threw his bulky frame onto the green couch, his lower lip quivering. When we asked what was wrong, with a jumble of words, he spun his tale of woe before my husband and me.

John slowly walked to Kevin and, in a strong authoritative voice, stated loudly, "The world owes you nothing, so quit expecting it to give you something! If you need something from those kids out there, you'll have to get it for yourself! Now, get back out there and quit your sniveling!"

My mouth hung open at the harshness of his words, but before I could put my jaw back in place, John winked at me. That was an odd thing to do at that moment. Suddenly, he'd opened my spiritual eyes. My husband often sees the world as a harsh and unforgiving place in which one must fight in order to survive. He was teaching Kevin survival skills. It was the most loving gesture I had ever witnessed from John.

The world isn't all cruel and harsh as John sees it, nor is it the utopia that I often picture it. When God put the two of us together, in His wisdom, He knew that we could bring a balance to our part of the globe. Now, as we go out together and conquer, John, courageous, and I, diplomatic, we own the treasure of a stronger and wiser marriage. And our son, too, has profited from this God-ordained balance.

And God is able to make all grace abound to you, so that in all things at all times, having all that you need, you will abound in every good work.

—II CORINTHIANS 9:8

Thought . . . Have you ever complained because your husband is so much different from you? How wonderful to know that where you are weak, he is strong. Viva la différence!

Get Wisdom

BY GAYLE CLOUD

Wisdom is the foremost key to having everything you need and desire in life.

—LARRY LEA

Many years ago, when I was a college student, I visited Old Jerusalem—a city filled with the sights and sounds of history. Walking through the narrow corridors and seeing the desert-weathered faces of long-robed merchants hawking their wares in open air markets, I could almost imagine Jesus walking alongside His disciples.

I went to see the wailing wall, which tradition says is a portion of Solomon's Temple. It is a literal wall for Jews to visit to mourn their people's suffering. Traditionally, they place a prayer-inscribed note in one of the wall's many chinks and crevices, as did I. That moment left a vivid memory. I thought about all the prayers I could have written—for a splendid husband, a good career, world peace. But the request I made was one I *knew* He'd answer. I prayed, as did Solomon, for wisdom.

Although I've not gained Solomon's wisdom, I've received my small portion: Wealth doesn't satisfy. Earthly life will end. Prestige is not enduring. Knowledge is "puffed up." Wisdom brings understanding.

I didn't understand all those years ago how that choice would affect my life and bring me back to my God. As a college student at the wailing wall, I had more knowledge than wisdom, and more of the world than of the kingdom. But God knew what He was doing. He was preparing my heart for His presence—and answering my prayer for wisdom.

Wisdom is supreme; therefore get wisdom. . . .

—PROVERBS 4:7

Thought . . . How important is wisdom to you? First seek God's wisdom in His Word, and you will find answers to any question or struggle you will ever face. Wisdom is treasure beyond compare.

Depending on Jesus

BY JENNIFER KENNEDY DEAN

Prayer is . . . the opening of a channel from your emptiness to God's fullness.

—E. STANLEY JONES

My son, Stinson, and I discussed over breakfast one morning the meaning of the word "trust." After much consideration, we settled on the phrase "depend on." "For example," I told Stinson, "you depend on me to fix dinner for you every night. You don't worry all day about whether or not you'll have dinner. You don't call and remind me through the day that I'm supposed to fix dinner. Because you trust me to prepare it for you, you don't even think about dinner until dinnertime."

Stinson and I decided to perform a "prayer experiment." Every time some problem arose that day, we agreed to say, "Jesus, I depend on You," then leave the solution to Him.

That day Stinson's kindergarten class played soccer at recess. Stinson kicked the ball with such gusto that his shoe flew off his foot, soared over the fence and into the private yard next door. Since he could not have permission to leave school grounds, he had to call me. I, however, was not home to receive his call. As he walked, one-shoed, out of the school office, he prayed, "Jesus, I depend on You." Proceeding down the hall toward his room, he was met by one of the school custodial staff. "Stinson," she said. "I was just looking for you. The woman next door saw a shoe fly over the fence and brought it to me. I think it's yours."

Stinson reported on our prayer experiment: "When I depended on Jesus, He found my shoe!"

And He found it in record time!

And he said: "I tell you the truth, unless you change and become like little children, you will never enter the king-dom of heaven. . . ."

—MATTHEW 18:3

Thought . . . To what extent do you depend upon Jesus? Remember that He is the "vine," and you are a "branch." Treasure this wisdom: you can do absolutely nothing without abiding in Him (John 15:1–10).

Honey, Did We Shrink-Wrap the Kids?

BY BARBARA JOHNSON

If a child is to keep alive his inborn sense of wonder, he needs the companionship of at least one adult who can share it.

—RACHEL CARSON

I think of kids as people who spread peanut butter, measles, and happiness. They start out as babies, totally dependent on you for everything from food to clothing. Then they end up as teenagers, old enough to dress themselves—if they could just remember where they dropped their clothes. How is a mom supposed to know how to relate to these fluctuating personalities?

We get best results when we smile. Grin more, not less. Lighten up. Don't be supermom. Do what you do well and leave the rest to God.

Hugs help, too. Seize the day, the hour, the moment—to tickle, cavort, and celebrate your children! After all, you have a treasure at your dining table, in front of the TV, out on the baseball field. Be your kids' biggest fan.

Kids grow up unpredictably. Sometimes they don't turn out like we expected. They may bring us shame. They may die before we do. All wrestle with tough issues. If we could shrink-wrap them to protect them, we would. Instead, we hope they find contentment and God's love. We let them go. When they fall back our way, we catch them and try not to act too surprised.

The psalmist reminds us that children are a reward from the Lord (Psalm 127:3). Let's not forget that for a moment!

Remember that kids are not yet what they should be. Nor are they yet what they are going to be. But then, they are not what they were. They are on their way—thanks to you, who touched their lives significantly.

". . . All your sons will be taught by the Lord, and great will be your children's peace. . . ."

—ISAIAH 54:13

Thought . . . Do you really want to shrink-wrap your kids? Isolation prevents their pain, but also their joy. Instead, wrap them in God's love and wisdom, and they can face anything.

81

Peaches

BY ESTHER BANDY

Give a little love to a child and you'll get a great deal back.

—JOHN RUSKIN

Children swarmed the camp nurse's station like bees around blossoms. I put Band-Aids on cuts, ice packs on swollen fingers, and poured God's love on lonely hearts. It was my first summer as a volunteer camp nurse and my husband was a camp counselor. I value those memories.

Peaches, a battered child from a broken home, often came to the nurse's station. She was like a wounded kitten, afraid to get close, but needing attention. Her eyes revealed more suffering than any eight-year-old should know. I asked God to change her life.

The last day of camp she didn't come to see me. "Why, God? Where is she?" I asked.

I prayed for wisdom, then searched until I found Peaches. I listened as she shared painful secrets. I knew that only God could heal her heart, so I shared His love and gift of salvation. Receiving Christ, she found eternal life and eternal love that day.

When camp ended, we didn't want to say good-bye. I reminded myself that although Peaches' earthly father was in prison, her Heavenly Father was watching over her. When she hugged me, the tears in her eyes matched the ones in my heart. I fingered the precious Cross necklace my husband had given me and searched his face for understanding. He nodded. I placed my gold necklace on Peaches and whispered, "God loves you and will never leave you. And I love you, too!"

Through Peaches, God showed me that the joy of touching the life of a child is treasure more precious than gold.

". . . For where your treasure is, there your heart will be also. . . ."

—LUKE 12:34

Thought . . . Do you share Christ's love with children other than your own? There are hurting, unwanted children waiting to hear about Jesus. Tell them by *showing* them. Spend time with them.

Grandma's Attic

Just a Plain Old Rolling Pin

BY DONNA OTTO

> The woman who creates and sustains a home and under whose
> hands children grow up to be strong and pure men and women, is a
> creator second only to God.
>
> —HELEN MARIA FISKE HUNT JACKSON

My grandmother was raised in an orphanage until she was thirteen, when she went to work as a household servant. She married my immigrant grandfather, himself a widower and father of
one small son, at the age of nineteen. She had little formal education to bring into her marriage, and very little knowledge of
healthy family relationships. What she did bring, however, was
a merry laugh, tried-and-true homemaking skills, the ability to
prepare delicious and beautiful meals, canning skills, and a gift
for baking that is still spoke of by anyone who knew Margaret
Sayad.

When my grandfather died, my grandmother moved to my
home, bringing all of her worldly possessions with her—and
one of these was passed to me. It is a plain, sturdy wooden rolling pin, lacking any particular natural beauty. Yet the worn
handles and carved middle are beautiful to me as I remember my
grandmother, her kitchen, and all the endless hours she poured
into preparing food for those she loved. Every pie I bake brings
a brimful of tears to my eyes remembering my dear grandmother
and her love for God and others. When this timeless treasure is
passed to my daughter, it will be four generations old.

> Likewise, teach the older women to be reverent in the way
> they live . . . Then they can train the younger women to
> love their husbands and children, . . . and . . . to be busy at
> home . . .
>
> —TITUS 2:3–5

Thought . . . Do you consider housework drudgery? Re-
evaluate. Every meal baked, floor washed, and bed
made, creates a *home* in which those you love are nurtured. Add a generous dose of God's love and it becomes a Heavenly haven.

The Lamb Box

BY SYLVIA A. LEFORT MASI

To work is to pray.

—SAINT BENEDICT OF NURSIA

One of the things I love best isn't much to look at. It's a round wooden box, about half the depth of a large Quaker Oat Meal box. The wood and dark metal band at the bottom are darkened by age because the box hasn't been used for its original purpose since the early 1900s. My mom, born in 1906, used the box for performing "her job" in her grandmother's busy household. It was her responsibility to feed the lambs. Of course, now that humble wooden box is an antique, which would fetch a good price at auction.

But that's not the value it holds for me. It sets in a place of honor atop a cabinet in our dining room. I treasure it because it is the only thing that has remained from Mom's childhood so long ago. It means so much to me because it brought her such pleasure to hold it and tell me again, "This is what I used to feed the lambs." Although it reminded her of her "chore," she had actually delighted in the work for which she used it.

Not only do I value the lamb box because Mom did, but because I, too, now "feed the lambs" twice each Sunday as I lead worship as a minister. Mom used grain to feed her lambs, and I use hymns, prayers, and God's Holy Word. Some might find it a chore, but I treasure "kingdom work" that makes my heart sing— work that leads little lambs to their Shepherd.

> . . . Jesus said to Simon Peter, "Simon son of John, do you truly love me more than these?" "Yes, Lord," he said, "you know that I love you." Jesus said, "Feed my lambs."
>
> —JOHN 21:15

Thought . . . Do you love your work? Any job "done unto the Lord" becomes a joy because it has purpose for all eternity.

The Empty Perfume Bottle

BY PATRICIA PERRY

Riches are a good handmaid, but the worst mistress.

—FRANCIS BACON

She turned the perfume bottle slowly in her hands, feeling the fine cut glass, running a finger along its smoky edges. My mother-in-law had just given up her home and moved into a studio apartment in a retirement community. After she was settled, we were left with the task of sorting and packing the rest of her possessions, giving away useful items she no longer needed, setting aside potential heirlooms and keepsakes.

"Wouldn't you like to take it with you?" I asked gently when she came to visit and saw the bottle among so many of her treasures setting on our dining room table.

"No," she replied, "I don't need it. I thought I would miss everything so much, but I didn't realize that I had most of it! I can't even remember from where this bottle came." She fingered the edges once more. "All these years I maintained a home—storing, dusting, paying for its upkeep. I feel so free and content now having only what I *need*—just enjoying life's simple pleasures." She set down the perfume bottle with a smile.

A wise woman, my mother-in-law. I resolved that when we finished with her things, I would start with ours—with closets, cupboards, shelves—all filled with "stuff" we no longer needed, which only complicated our lives. The excess would go to charitable organizations and to those in need. Just the thought brought me a lift and a sense of pleasure in simplicity.

". . . The man with two tunics should share with him who has none, and the one who has food should do the same."

—LUKE 3:11

Thought . . . Do you own things that you *need* or that you *want*? Determining the difference between the two can be a great life-simplifier.

In This Very Room

BY GRACIE MALONE

The steps of the good man are ordered by the Lord—and the stops, too.

—GEORGE MUELLER

I sat slumped in my recliner, exhausted, though I'd slept well the night before. For several days while their parents were out of town, I'd been trying to keep up with our two grandchildren, Luke, an inquisitive three-year-old, and, Connor, a bouncing toddler.

Having neglected my quiet time, I was also in a spiritual slump. As I refilled my coffee cup and reached for my Bible, I heard sleepy little voices coming down the hall. Luke stumbled into the living room in his pajamas, and Connor followed closely behind rubbing his eyes. As I gathered the little boys into my lap and held them tightly, I realized I'd missed my opportunity for spiritual refreshment again.

As we rocked, early morning rays of sunshine peeped over our fence, filtered through the curtains, and bounced off the prism hanging in my kitchen window. Luke spotted rainbows of brilliant color reflected on the walls. He wiggled out of my lap and stood transfixed for a moment, then with a flash of spiritual insight and reverential awe announced, "Grandma, God is here!" Connor climbed down and both boys jumped up and down in the sparkling light, making a myriad of colors dance on their faces.

The joy and wonder of that special moment reminded me of an important truth. God doesn't bless us with His presence be-cause we've been faithful to Him. He comes to us in His time and in His own way. Where there are children, and color, and sunshine, there is God.

Where can I go from your Spirit? Where can I flee from your presence? If I go up to the heavens, you are there; if I make my bed in the depths, you are there.

—PSALM 139:7–8

Thought . . . Have you ever gone on a "God-hunt"? "Look" for God. He will come to you in the most unexpected, delightful ways. He will transform the secular in your life into the sacred.

Grandma's "Love-Thing"

BY DORIS SMALLING

Children are the most wholesome part of the race, the sweetest, for
they are freshest from the hand of God.

—HERBERT HOOVER

As we waited in the doctor's office, I noticed a four-year-old boy
climb down from a seat between two women. He faced one, his
voice troubled. "Mommy," he questioned, "can Grandma love
me?"

His mother pulled him close. "Of course, Jamie. Whatever
made you ask that?"

"Cause she can't do other things, Mommy. I thought maybe
her 'love-thing' didn't work, either."

His grandmother reached for him. "Sweetheart," she stroked
his cheek with her finger, "when people get older, our body parts
get old, too. There's one part of us, though, that never, never
stops working. It just keeps working harder."

"What's that, Grandma?"

"Our heart's 'love-machine,' Jamie. It makes us want to give
each other love—like *this*." She hugged him tightly. He squealed
with delight.

"The more we share the love in our heart, Jamie, the more
love it makes. For example, doesn't it make you laugh and feel
happy when Daddy tries to hug you when he bathes you?"

The little boy laughed, wiggling in the joy of remembrance.
"He tries to hug me when I'm slippery." Suddenly, he looked
thoughtful. "Am I old enough to love, too, Grandma?"

"Of course you are, dear. God prepares our love even before
we're born." The boy climbed back up on his chair, hugging
each of his favorite "love-making machine" ladies. I wiped a tear
and praised God for these treasures—our grandchildren—and
for the gift of loving.

Do everything in love.

—I CORINTHIANS 16:14

Thought . . . How do you show love to your children?
Offer lots of hugs and kisses, but also thoughtfully an-
swer their questions, pointing them to God. It is with
God that love begins.

Big Mama's Cornbread

BY SUZANNE DALE EZELL

To live fully, we must learn to use things and love people, and not love things and use people.

—JOHN POWELL

The best treasures we have in life are the ones we don't even realize until it is too late—the rich family stories that every extended family has.

My grandparents, Big Mama and Big Daddy Dale, lived into their late nineties. They didn't worry a bit about how to live. They just lived each day to the fullest.

On a regular basis we went to Big Mama's house for lunch. Fried chicken, squash, okra, black-eyed peas, and green beans cooked in bacon drippings. And the cornbread! She insisted what gave her cornbread its extraordinary taste was the little metal bowl she mixed it in and the broken wooden spoon she stirred it with. No one has ever made cornbread exactly like that. We would eat until we had to have help getting up from the table.

George and Frances Jane Dale were a west Texas institution. Big Dad led more revivals, conducted more weddings, and preached more funerals than any ten preachers added together. When they retired, Big Dad and Big Mama "held court" in their tiny white frame house. People came to ask advice, get counseling, get married, or discuss church problems. They always had time to give a word from the Lord to every pilgrim who passed their way.

On their seventy-fifth anniversary, the White House called with congratulations. Their house was full of well-wishers. Big Mama answered the phone and when the operator said, "This is the White House calling," she answered without hesitating, "Well, could you call back later? I have all my friends here right now."

He who regards one day as special, does so to the Lord.

—ROMANS 14:6A

Thought . . . How can you live life to the fullest? When you fully treasure your family and friends by spending as much time with them as possible, you are well on your way!

The Treasure of Her Smile

BY KRISTEN JOHNSON INGRAM

Keep your face to the sunshine and you cannot see the shadow.

—HELEN KELLER

During my grandmother Elizabeth's girlhood, Victorian society had revived the ancient practice of catching a loved one's last tears in a little crystal vial, and sealing it to treasure for years afterward. But when Elizabeth was eight and both her parents lay dying of yellow fever, her mother refused to let her capture her tears in the little lachrymatory that her daughter had brought to the bedside.

"Remember my smile instead," my great-grandmother told her children. "Remember your father's devotion as a pastor. And always remember what we taught you about Jesus."

For Elizabeth and her four younger brothers and sisters left suddenly without parents, these instructions must have felt like small comfort; yet my grandmother's lifelong faith in Christ inspired my own, and when she was in her seventies, she said that she could remember almost nothing about her mother except the angelic splendor of her smile.

"I know that I'll see my mother's smile as soon as I get to Heaven," my grandmother told me, and she didn't have long to wait. She died shortly after we talked, and I pray that her mother's beautiful smile greeted her as she crossed the threshold to the Throne Room.

I doubt if God prefers to hold my tears in a bottle; I think He prefers to remember the times that I smiled at someone who needed His love.

Thou tellest my wanderings: put thou my tears into thy bottle: are they not in thy book?

—PSALM 56:8 (KJV)

Thought . . . Are you crying? Weeping may last the night, but joy comes in the morning (Psalm 30:5). Jesus said that those who mourn are blessed and will be comforted (Matthew 5:4). Therefore, you can smile through your tears, knowing that His joy also comes in the *mourning*.

Generations

BY FRAN CAFFEY SANDIN

Baby: Unwritten history! Unfathomed mystery!

—JOSIAH GILBERT HOLLAND

With my heart beating wildly, I turned the wrong way on a one-way ramp in the hospital parking garage. Luckily I managed to wheel around before facing a car head-on. My car needed a warning sign: "Watch Out! Here Comes a New Grandma!"

Beau, my son-in-law, had called that morning to say, "Angie is in labor at the hospital." Since the baby was coming three weeks earlier than expected, I needed a little extra time to make arrangements. Within the hour, Beau called again, "Emily Grace arrived safely and Angie is fine." Although relieved, I had hoped to accompany my daughter for the birth of our first grandchild.

Now I'm a grandmother! I thought repeatedly, while driving toward the Dallas-Fort Worth metroplex. As I anxiously slipped into my long-awaited role, I gained courage from my own grandmothers and their contributions to me, and I found myself locking arms with their remembrance.

Upon entering Angie's hospital room, I felt the divine presence of new life—a miracle— fashioned by His hands—made in His image. With beaming faces, Angie and Beau greeted me with their own sense of awe, and handed over their precious little bundle.

As I sat in the rocking chair, cuddling baby Emily and looking into her angelic face, I felt my heart would explode with love. That special moment has since been enhanced by the joy of watching my daughter become a beautiful, nurturing mother. Truly these are treasures of God that money cannot buy.

For the Lord is good; his lovingkindness is everlasting, and his faithfulness to all generations.

—PSALM 100:5 (NASB)

Thought . . . As a grandmother, do you pursue your own interests or see to those of your grandchildren? Invest in them the treasures of your time and faith, and your family will reap dividends for generations to come.

Family Ties

BY JO HUDDLESTON

The family is more sacred than the state.

—POPE PIUS XI

Every May, our family members travel to their place of origin like swallows flying back to San Juan Capistrano. On Sunday morning, we crowd into the small church located a few miles from the home place. This is "Decoration Day," and the church's cemetery is an ocean of flowers billowing across graves of remembered relatives.

After church we hurry to the family's traditional gathering. The white frame house has changed inside since Grandmother lived there, but its wide porch still stretches across the front, complete with roomy porch swing. A ten-foot-long wooden table stands underneath the black oak shade tree in the backyard and barely holds the food brought for Sunday dinner. Each year Grandmother's oldest son asks God's blessing on the food.

Afterwards, overstuffed and comfortable in unmatched lawn chairs we've brought in our car trunks, we commence a year's worth of catching up and reminiscing. Family members have served in our country's military from the rolling waters of the Pacific Ocean in World War II, to the frozen ridges of Korea, and to the steaming jungles of Vietnam. Some of us, at one time or another, have been "rich man, poor man . . ." Our family members have settled from Phoenix to Charlotte, from Miami to Detroit.

Whatever our financial status or residence, we're forever rich in the treasure of family ties. It's worth all our continued efforts to reach back and touch our roots, to connect with the magic of family.

Now about brotherly love we do not need to write to you, for you yourselves have been taught by God to love each other.

—I THESSALONIANS 4:9

Thought . . . You can choose your friends, but not your relatives. God creates families for His own purposes. Appreciate those family members He has given you as precious treasures. Don't take them for granted.

Nelephant

BY PAQUITA RAWLEIGH

A trusting child will love you forever. Do not disappoint him.

—PAQUITA RAWLEIGH

"Tita come, come!" my grandbaby called, his face full of anxiety. "See what happened to my poor 'nelephant'! He is diswasting and needs a 'doco,'" he insisted. "He needs to be 'fiker.'"

I couldn't understand his nonsense words. Not wanting to reveal my ignorance, as my grandson thought I was such a "neat" grandma, I tried to get enlightened about his predicament. Taking me by the hand, he led me to the garage. Then I understood. His stuffed elephant lay helplessly on the floor, its tummy torn, with beans flowing everywhere.

Suddenly, his explanation became clear as a bell. My grandson's "diswasting" comment (translation: "disgusting") resulted from seeing his pal torn apart. A "doctor" was needed to "fix" him. I immediately sewed the elephant back together. When I was finished, I called my grandson and showed him his "nelephant." He smiled and said enthusiastically, "I knew you could 'fiker' it, Grandma! Thanks a lot!" Happy as a lark, he went back to play. I will treasure his beautiful smile forever.

I think about how much I'm like my grandbaby. When I'm distressed, worn-out, and unhappy, I talk to my Heavenly Father, asking Him to "fix" things. Sometimes my words just spill out and don't seem to make much sense. Yet when God listens, He also understands my heart, even when I can't. Gently, He supplies just what I need, and mends my torn places. And when God's hand touches my heart, He "fixes" it as good as new.

Before a word is on my tongue you know it completely, O Lord. You hem me in—behind and before; you have laid your hand upon me.

—PSALM 139:4–5

Thought . . . Are you heartbroken? "Pour out your soul" to God Who understands (Psalm 62:8). Unburdening to One Whom you trust provides cathartic release. God will become your refuge.

Little Brown Bag Treasure

BY FERN AYERS MORRISSEY

The only lasting treasure is spiritual.

—MALCOLM MUGGERIDGE

Frayed and crumpled, the small brown paper bag is a treasure chest to me. Countless times I've emptied its contents, and reminisced. Even when my grandmother, MaMa, first gave it to me, the bag had a *worn* look. Undoubtedly, she had handled it many times through the years. Because, at ninety-seven, MaMa was anticipating God's final handling of her own worn-out life, she tenderly gave me the fragile bag, bequeathing to me little treasures she had cherished since young womanhood.

I pour out its contents: faded photos; little darkened tintypes; a decorated tintype resembling a plate; World War I postcards; scraps of old letters with handwritten script; an antiquated toy steel bell; a pair of tattered baby shoes. Most of these keepsakes pertain to my father, Ivan. In 1895, my dad, the baby in the plate-sized, faded green tintype, looked so permanently shy in a ruffled white dress, his thin fair hair gathered together with a few pale pink roses atop his head. This wisp of a babe became the serious rifle-bearing World War I soldier in the sepia postcard photo.

There are no jewelry, fancy lace, or money among these meager mementos. Yet, they are of priceless value to me because they represent the transcending gift of my grandmother, herself, and the godly gems of her character—humility, kindness, patience, and goodness.

And like the Holy Spirit's invisible fruit, these intangible treasures are permanently stored in my heart, where they blossom now and will through eternity.

But the fruit of the Spirit is love, joy, peace, patience, kindness, goodness, faithfulness.

—GALATIANS 5:22

Thought . . . Have you received a godly inheritance from your loved ones? Even if they did not know Christ, you can receive Him as your Savior now, and pass on His eternal treasures to your own progeny.

A Tea Party of Love

BY JANETTE OKE

For anything worth having one must pay the price; and the price is
always work, sacrifice, patience, love, self-sacrifice . . .

—JOHN BURROUGHS

"Say me, Mrs. Jones."

My granddaughter sat across the small table from me, with a
tiny teacup. At two, her words had not come out quite right, but
I knew what she meant. She wished me to call her Mrs. Jones—
not Ashley—when we tea-partied together.

"So, how are you, Mrs. Jones?" I asked, and her eyes sparkled.

"Fine." Another smile. She loved our little game. Ashley
stopped to refill her cup from the small teapot of weak-tea-
mostly-milk. Ashley poured in more milk from the dainty cream
pitcher and stirred in a bit of sugar. She loved to stir, the little
spoon going around in the small cup. With small hands, she
lifted the cup and sipped. "You like more?" she asked.

"Oh, yes. I'd love more, please." I loved the tea parties with
my granddaughter as much as she did. She beamed as I lifted my
cup and sipped.

Sharing. It makes life so much more fun. Motherhood takes
lots of sharing. But it is the sharing of good times, special secrets
and even down times, that make mothering—and grandmother-
ing—so special.

Motherhood. How wonderful of God to design such a delightful relationship. What if each new creation entered the world
fully grown? There would be no cuddling, no nurturing—no
mothering. The world would soon become a harsher place. For
in the sacrifice of mothering there is so much softening. I have
learned about God in the process of mothering—and grand-
mothering—and I understand just a bit concerning His heart of
love.

. . . so I will be with you; I will never leave you nor forsake
you.

—JOSHUA 1:5

Thought . . . Why can mothers show such tenderness?
Because God promises to tend His flock like a Shepherd and gently lead those who have young ones (Isaiah
40:11). Follow Him.

The Dropping Game

BY KATHLEEN HAGBERG

The steps of faith fall on the seeming void, yet fall on the rock beneath.

—JAMES WHITCOMB RILEY

Forty years later I can still hear my grandmother's laughter, more characteristic of a schoolgirl than a middle-aged grandmother. Laughter, the hallmark of her home, ruled when we played the "dropping game."

Lucille would line up my four younger brothers and myself next to each other in a row to face her. Stepping behind us and beginning with the youngest, she challenged us to stand "stiff and straight like a statue" so that we could fall backward full-weight into her outstretched arms. Our eyes filled with panic as we teetered midway between standing and falling. Predictably, panic melted into giggles as, one by one, we landed safely in Lucille's waiting arms.

My childhood memory gives way to an old refrain, "He's got the whole world in His hands." Moreover, the image summons up a word picture mirroring the total surrender to which God calls me if I am to grow in trusting Him. How often I teeter between "holding on" and "letting go." How easily I forget His promise that "Underneath are the everlasting arms (Deuteronomy 33:27)." A safe landing in His strong arms requires that I "let go." Each time I do, my trust deepens. The Lord has never failed to catch me.

The Lord upholds all those who fall . . .

—PSALM 145:14

Thought . . . To what treasure are you clinging which God wants you to surrender? Until you let go, and take a leap of faith, you will never know His abiding faithfulness, His abundant provision.

The "G" Word

BY LUCINDA J. ROLLINGS

Some of our modern grandmothers are so young and spry they help the Boy Scouts across the street.

—ANONYMOUS

The "G" word . . . it made me cringe to say it. I didn't want to be called *Grandma*. I preferred something cutesy like "GramMom" or "Grammy." Besides being common, *Grandma* sounded old. And fifty was definitely NOT old! Admittedly, I had a few gray hairs and unwanted bulges, and my energy level wasn't what it used to be, but . . .

Our three-year-old granddaughter, Amanda, was just beginning to talk and didn't say many words plainly. Sometimes she called me "Mom Mom," which I didn't mind. And sometimes, unfortunately, it came out "Mommy," which I would correct. "GramMom," I'd say, but it never caught on. Often she didn't call me anything. I began to think I would never have a name.

Then on my birthday, Amanda and her mother came to visit. Amanda rang the doorbell incessantly, which was my cue to say, in my best "big bad wolf" voice, "Who's that ringing my doorbell?" Amanda would giggle and shout, "ME!!!" Then, after the giggling had subsided, she burst out with "Happy Birthday, Grandma!" as plain as you please. What a precious gift! Nothing wrapped in ribbons could have made me happier. Suddenly, the word "Grandma" took on a whole new meaning!

Being Grandma means that God has granted me special blessings—my grandchildren. Our second granddaughter, Jessica, also calls me Grandma now. That former "old"-designating label, lovingly uttered from my granddaughters' lips, now takes on treasured significance. It's priceless.

Children's children are a crown to the aged . . .

—PROVERBS 17:6

Thought . . . Do you feel you're not old enough to be a grandmother? Trust God's timing, and be grateful that you have precious years of "living" and wisdom to share. Your grandchildren will "rise up and call you blessed."

Nettie Jones, Thank You

BY PATRICIA A. J. ALLEN

Music is well said to be the speech of angels; in fact, nothing among the utterances allowed to man is felt to be so divine. It brings us near to the Infinite.

—THOMAS CARLYLE

I heard its rhythmic breathing long before I could see it—the old pump organ singing in the corner of the antique store. A young lady sat on a modern bench as she played the ornately carved, red velvet–accented organ. Her legs moved in a dearly familiar rhythm. As I steadied myself on the display case of an estate jewelry collection, breathing in time with her "pumping," a long-forgotten memory newly resurrected itself.

How old had I been when Grandma first lifted me onto her lap in front of the organ? I wondered. I couldn't recall. I do remember that when I had insisted I could play by myself, I had to stretch to press on a key while Grandma pumped. I was too short to do both. Each time Mom and I visited Grandma Jones, I begged to hear the organ. Its bellows breathed energy into hymns about a "hill called Calvary" and "the Blood that flowed for me." How precious are the memories now that I'm a Granny, myself!

I still wonder . . . *Was it tedious for Grandma to play so often? Was it difficult for Mom somehow? Would they have rather talked than listen to a child enthusiastically play the ivories and sing off-key?* Maybe. Yet, they planted seeds of praise in my heart. I've learned that praise is the way to victory in life, bringing joy into saddened hearts. Thank you, Grandma, for the treasures of your patience and your time.

Whatever you have learned or received or heard from me, or seen in me—put it into practice. And the God of peace will be with you.

—PHILIPPIANS 4:9

Thought . . . Is music an integral part of your family's life? Psalm 100:1 (KJV) commands us to "make a joyful noise unto the Lord." Encourage family "hymn sings." Whether your singing is ethereal or noisy, it generates joy in the Lord and fun with each other!

No Shortcuts to Love

BY JOAN CLAYTON

Love is, above all, the gift of oneself.

—JEAN ANOUILH

We all looked forward to Sunday dinner at Mother's house. The aroma of freshly baking bread soothed my family as nothing else could. Yet three lively boys still sometimes tried my patience. "Trust them to the Lord," Mother reminded as she passed that plate of scrumptious rolls. Somehow we could weather the storm with trust in God in our hearts, and Mother's hot piping rolls in our stomachs!

"How come your rolls always turn out flatly?" my husband asked. I tried again and again, with no success. One day, determined, I watched Mother make her rolls, and traced every step.

"But Mother," I protested, "that makes such a mess! All of that flour and rolling all that dough. Isn't there a less messy way to do it?"

"You don't think about the mess or trouble it takes when you're doing it for those you love."

I learned a profound lesson from Mother that day, in breadmaking and in life. It changed my whole perspective. Although Mother has made her heavenly flight, her love and influence will always be with me. There are no shortcuts to love—it requires time and unselfishness. When I am pressured for time and tempted to take "shortcuts" (like buying rolls at the bakery), I remember Mother's words: "It's no trouble when you're doing it for those you love!"

Now I love to hear my own grandchildren coming through the door exclaiming, with a hug, "Mawmaw, I love to smell and eat your big fat rolls!"

And now these three remain: faith, hope and love. But the greatest of these is love.

I CORINTHIANS 13:13

Thought . . . Have you thought of love as an investment? The more care you deposit now into the lives of your family, the greater the reward later—their sincere appreciation and desire to extend love to the next generation.

The Spotted Gumball

BY GAYLE DeSALLES

> Good habits are not made on birthdays, nor Christian character at the New Year. The workshop of character is everyday life. The uneventful and commonplace hour is where the battle is won or lost.
>
> —MALTBIE D. BABCOCK

Thanking Grandma for the dime, I bolted for the corner market to buy a sack of my favorite "penny candy." Although I detested gumballs, a piece of paper taped to the dispenser outside caught my eye: "TRADE IN SPOTTED GUMBALL FOR FIVE-CENT CANDY BAR." Judging by the spotted gumballs that I could see, I surmised that my chances of winning were good.

I exchanged my dime for ten pennies and stuffed them in my front pocket as I walked out into the foggy San Francisco air. Dropping my penny into the slot, I turned the handle slowly. Immediately, out rolled a spotted gumball into the metal tray. I had won! Delighted, I presented my spotted gumball to the cashier. "Congratulations!" he said, handing my candy bar to me.

Although I realized that I might not be so lucky again, I still wanted to try to win. This time a plain blue gumball rolled into the tray . . . then a plain yellow one . . . and then another. *I'll try once more*, I thought. But as I reached into my pocket for another penny, I realized that I had spent them all. Disgusted, I stared for the longest time at the nine plain gumballs in my hand. Finally, I tossed them in the garbage can.

I solemnly walked back to Grandma's house, pockets empty of pennies or candy. But at eight years old on that dismal, gray afternoon, I had learned a valuable lesson: the risk of gambling could not be calculated after all.

> Do not wear yourself out to get rich; have the wisdom to show restraint. Cast but a glance at riches, and they are gone, for they will surely sprout wings and fly off to the sky like an eagle.
>
> —PROVERBS 23:4, 5

Thought . . . With casinos and lotteries abounding, do you gamble? Don't take a chance on getting "hooked." Scripture condemns greed. Workers are to *work* for their wages, trusting in God's provision.

Our Dwelling Place

BY LOIS WALFRID JOHNSON

Every experience God gives us, every person He puts in our lives, is the perfect preparation for the future that only He can see.

—CORRIE TEN BOOM

When we were children, our father took us home each August to the family farm. There, a few miles outside Walnut Grove, Minnesota, Dad helped Grandpa and the neighboring farmers bring in the harvest. For the men who worked and the women who served them food, the days were long and hot, but productive.

To us, as children, the days were filled with excitement, the nights with the harvest moon. Often our cousins joined us in the large white farmhouse. On hot summer afternoons we waded in Plum Creek. From where we played our make-believe games, the water flowed under a bridge into the land made famous by Laura Ingalls Wilder. But we had no knowledge of that then. We simply knew that we were home. We watched the grownups and remembered—the heads bowed, the times of prayer, the reading of the treasured Word.

When we needed to leave again, Grandpa and Grandma stood at the door, waving good-bye. Even as children, we knew we had tired them, but farewell tears welled up in their eyes.

Time passed, and it became my dad and mother who stood at the door for a final wave. More than once, I felt sure that they, too, brushed away tears.

Now my husband and I stand at the door, giving welcoming or good-bye hugs to children and grandchildren. We know the importance of that first or last moment and all the memories in between. We want to be sure that they are good.

Lord, you have been our dwelling place throughout all generations.

—PSALM 90:1

Thought . . . After your final farewell to your grandchildren, what will they remember? Have you shared the Good News of salvation through Christ so that you can welcome them again in Heaven?

Overcoming

Bear in Mind

BY NORMA HOWARD KIRKPATRICK

I have held many things in my hands, and I have lost them all; but whatever I have placed in God's hands, that I still possess.

—MARTIN LUTHER

Shiny brown eyes stared at me from a fuzzy face, almost real, like a puppy I once had. The teddy bear sat among a Christmas display of gift items in the store. It was almost Christmas and my husband, Bob, had been hooked up to tubes in the hospital for over a month. I needed something to hug, so I bought the soft, cuddly bear.

Frustrated, I went home to an empty house again after visiting Bob. I held "Bobby Bear" to my chest, burying my cheek into his soft shoulder. Pacing back and forth, I finally let the pent-up tears spill out. "Oh, Lord, how long must Bob suffer? Please, please, heal him or take him home to You."

Months later, after Bob's death, I attended a hospice bereavement support group meeting, accompanied by Bobby Bear. The dozen of us there shared the loss of a loved one, mostly spouses. Overcoming the temptation to withdraw into my own cave of sorrow, I told how the Lord had been my strength and how helpful it had been to hug my bear as I poured out my heart to the Lord. I offered to lend Bobby Bear for a month to whoever needed him.

A new widow took him home, returning in a month to say that Bobby had sat with her at her table for meals. We passed him along to other ladies who were similarly comforted. I treasure the memory of how God used a simple teddy bear to help me share Jesus' love.

Bear one another's burdens, and so fulfill the law of Christ.

—GALATIANS 6:2 (NKJV)

Thought . . . How do you live after you've lost your spouse? Receive Jesus' comfort through those who have suffered a similar loss. When you're stronger, comfort the newly bereaved.

A Spring of Hope

BY SUSAN M. WARREN

Our Lord has written the promises of the resurrection, not in books alone, but in every leaf in springtime.

—MARTIN LUTHER

Silent tears coursed down my friend's cheeks as she grieved the loss of her baby. I took her hand and held it, understanding her pain all too well. Five years earlier I had stumbled from the doctor's office in agonized disbelief. Our second child in three months had died in my womb. Pain . . . emptiness . . . how quickly a miscarriage turns joy to sorrow. At home, I held my two children, sobbing on their tiny shoulders. They patted me, confused, until their father came home and took over.

I was inconsolable. How could this happen twice? Would I ever have children again? Fear paralyzed me, and I was unable to cry out to God for help. Past midnight, I sat in the darkened living room, despair building a wall between me and my Lord. But He was there, a whisper of strength lingering in the silence. I knew that I had to confront the One Who held my life and my baby's in His hands. "Why?" I questioned, sobbing. I opened my Bible and read Psalm 107:35: "He turned the desert into pools of water and the parched ground into flowing springs." *What does that mean, Lord?* I agonized.

But I already knew. I wandered in a desert of grief, but ahead of me, and my baby, waited a spring of life. God then embraced me. Although my womb was empty, my soul was full, realizing the joy of eternity. Hope is the treasure of those who trust in Him. I knew that, in reality, my baby lived.

Why are you downcast, O my soul? Why so disturbed within me? Put your hope in God, for I will yet praise Him . . .

—PSALM 42:5

Thought . . . Have you lost a child? Your grief knows no bounds—except to God, Who sacrificed His Son so that you and your baby could spend eternity in Heaven with Him.

Living Stones

BY LUCI SHAW

A gem is not polished without rubbing, nor a man made perfect without trials.

—CHINESE PROVERB

"What is a Petoskey stone?" It's a fragment left over from a colony coral that grew across what is now Upper Michigan, when the land was covered by a tropical sea. Chunks of the fossil stone, rounded into pebbles by the action of lake waves, show the faint hexagonal structure that characterized this coral when it was alive. This Petoskey coral, named for the Michigan town where it was first identified, is a soft stone, easily polished with emery powder. When burnished, it is semitransparent—you can see deep into it, as if to its soul.

I gave my friend David two Petoskey stones—one "before" and one "after" polishing, with this inscription: "Can you see the difference between the rough pebble I found last week in a clutter of others at lake edge and the one I just finished polishing for you? You are a Petoskey stone, David, precious, imprinted by God with His own seeing image. First He formed you, then He chose you, when you were rough and dull, your secret beauty hidden, unsuspected. But you have gained gloss as the emery powder of criticism and conflict in God's hands has burnished you."

"Hold this polished stone in your hand and be reminded of how intricately planned you were and how splendid you are becoming. Expect the polishing to go on so that God's lovely image in you will show even more clearly."

And David said, "Now I have a new idea about what it means to be a 'living stone!'"

As you come to him, the living Stone—rejected by men but chosen by God and precious to him—you also, like living stones, are being built into a spiritual house to be a holy priesthood . . .

—I PETER 2:4–5

Thought . . . Are you holy like Jesus? Welcome the sandpaper of conflict to smooth your rough edges, making you a perfect surface to reflect His image.

In the Deepest Valley

BY RUTH E. McDANIEL

Faith is to believe what you do not yet see; the reward for this faith
is to see what you believe.

—SAINT AUGUSTINE

I was shaken to the core. If God were watching over me, how
could He have let this happen? My fifteen-year-old son, under
the influence of drugs, had stolen my credit cards and my car,
and now he was in an Illinois jail!

As my husband and I drove to the police department, we were
lost in thought. The entire family had been in counseling for
months. A troubled child normally comes from a dysfunctional
family, but we were Christians and our church had prayed for
us. We followed the therapist's advice and worked with school
authorities, but nothing seemed to help. I was filled with despair.

Suddenly, a favorite Psalm came to mind: "I will lift up my
eyes to the hills—from where does my help come? My help
comes from the Lord, the Maker of Heaven and earth (Psalm
121:1–2)." Then, Scriptures began flooding through me as if
some biblical dike had broken. Years of praying and reading and
studying the Bible had given me a firm foundation. The weaker
areas of my life might fall, but my faith foundation would not be
moved! I wasn't alone! God had not abandoned me! Now, in this
deep valley, I lifted up my eyes and looked to God for help!
Cleansing tears finally came, and my faith was renewed.

Our son was transferred to a drug rehabilitation program, and
the charges were dropped. The years that followed weren't easy,
but God lovingly molded him into a drug-free, law-abiding man
who has become one of my greatest treasures and a source of
unending joy. I have never doubted God again.

. . . Where does my help come from? My help comes from
the Lord. . . .

—PSALM 121:1–2

Thought . . . Do you have a teen who is troubled? Entrust
him to the only One Who can help. God will abandon
neither you nor him.

I Was in Prison, but He Was with Me

BY CORRIE TEN BOOM

Jesus Christ came into my prison cell last night, and every stone flashed like a ruby.

—SAMUEL RUTHERFORD

Years ago I was alone in a cell for four months. I cried to the Lord, and He answered: "Have I not said: 'Lo, I am with you alway, even unto the end of the world' (Matthew 28:20)? I am your peace. I can give you joy now."

I started to sing, first softly, later more loudly: *What a friend we have in Jesus, All our sins and griefs to bear.*

I waited a moment, and then I heard from another cell: *O what peace we often forfeit O what needless pain we bear . . .* It was an answer from a woman who also was in solitary confinement. Her husband had been shot before her eyes, then she had been put in prison. But she, too, knew Jesus as her Friend and Savior.

A guard banged on the door and shouted: "If you do not stop singing, I will take you to the dark cell."

I stopped singing and threw myself onto my dirty bed. There was peace in my heart. The guard did not know when I sang so softly that only my Savior could hear.

Not only in solitary confinement can one feel alone. In the company of others with whom you have no real fellowship you can be lonely. But Jesus is with you also. Have you asked Him to come into your heart? Then you can talk to Him without saying one word aloud. He hears and He loves you. You are very precious in His eyes. Hallelujah, what a Savior!

If anyone acknowledges that Jesus is the Son of God, God lives in him and he in God.

—I JOHN 4:15

Thought . . . Have you received Jesus as your personal Savior? When you belong to the Lord, you are never alone. He promises that His Holy Spirit will live in you forever!

Sean's Homecoming

BY JAN CLARK BUCKMAN

Our griefs cannot mar the melody of our praise; they are simply the bass notes of our life song: "To God be the glory."

—CHARLES SPURGEON

One summer evening, I opened the door to every parent's nightmare. Sean, our sixteen-year-old son, had been killed in an automobile accident. As unthinkable tragedy threatened to plummet me into the pit of depression, the God Who had saved me proved faithful to walk me through this devastation. Just the mention of His name—*Jesus*—brought the comfort of His presence. In days, months, even years to follow, I would continuously experience the sufficiency of that name.

The night before the funeral, sleep came grudgingly as I struggled with Sean's loss. I could not let go. The next morning I was totally unprepared for the joy that greeted me. God's "all is well," along with His gentle admonition, "Trust," moved powerfully into the depths of my heart. Suddenly, I knew with certainty that Sean's death was no senseless accident. My God intended to use it for good!

"Glimpses of good" became manifest. As friends witnessed our joy despite incomprehensible pain, broken hearts became hungry hearts, seeking relationships with the living Lord. Many made decisions for Christ or renewed their commitments. After joining our neighbors in prayer one evening, my mother tearfully affirmed, "Now, I *know* there is a God." We sat in silent awe. Before traveling to Mayo Clinic for Dad's open-heart surgery, my parents gave their lives to Christ. Dad died shortly after, and months later, Mother never woke from brain surgery. They were now with the Lord! Sean's homecoming had taught us to walk confidently, trusting in the sufficiency of God's unfailing promises.

He who dwells in the shelter of the Most High will rest in the shadow of the Almighty.

—PSALM 91:1

Thought . . . Do you trust God in the face of death? Because He is sovereign, your loved one didn't die without His knowledge or purpose. Ask Him to reveal treasures in tragedy.

Doves of Peace

BY BETTY HUFF

Jesus did not come to do away with suffering or to remove it. He came to fill it with His presence.

—Paul Claudell

At three o'clock one afternoon, I was transported by ambulance to our local hospital with severe abdominal pain. Three hours later, the same ambulance drivers brought my husband there with a fatal coronary.

Before my pastor and my daughter came to break the heart-rending news, I was heavily sedated. My pastor's words, "He's at *rest*. He's at *rest*," barely registered. When my daughter said, "Mom, it happened so quickly that he didn't feel any *pain*," I numbly agreed.

The next morning, however, I awoke to harsh reality and needed the comfort only the Lord could give. I reached in the bedside table for the Gideon Bible, that had never been opened. When I picked it up, it opened automatically to Psalm 55:4–6: "My heart is sore *pained* within me and the terrors of death are fallen upon me. Fearfulness and trembling are come upon me and horror has overwhelmed me. And I said, 'Oh that I had wings like a dove, for then I would fly away and be at *rest.*'"

Closing my eyes as they filled with tears, I wasn't aware of my visitor until she placed a gift box in my hand. Inside were two white porcelain doves, and the male's wings were open in full flight. Immediately the phone rang. It was my daughter calling from the mortuary. She needed my approval on a memorial card that she had found. It had a blue sky background dominated by a white dove in full flight! At that moment, my overwhelming pain took flight, and I felt peace.

. . . my peace I give to you. . . . Do not let your hearts be troubled and do not be afraid.

—John 14:27

Thought . . . Are you in deep pain because your husband has died? Remember that God, Himself, promises to be your Husband (Isaiah 54:5).

Just Believe

BY PHYLLIS WALLACE

Lord, Thy will be done in father, mother, child, in everything and everywhere; without a reserve, without a but, and if, or a limit.

—SAINT FRANCIS DE SALES

While I scurried around preparing for my annual Christmas tea, the background noises of four children blended with my hummed excerpts from Handel's *Messiah*. Little Hannah was so quiet, I thought she was just staying out of the way. Hours later my eyes "saw"a sick child whose skin literally stood up when pinched. The doctor confirmed severe dehydration, sending us to the emergency room. She lay in a tiny bed, IVs dripping, next to other babies attacked with the sometimes fatal virus. My heart was as heavy as the thirteen-inch snowfall outside. *Why hadn't I noticed sooner?* I wondered. *Would she make it through the night? How could I nurse her infant sister at home?*

My familiar rocking chair songs seemed to soothe her. Singing *Jesus Loves Me* through my tears, I saw a listless eighteen-month-old who wasn't responding to medicine. My Christmas wish list suddenly narrowed down to one thing. "God, please make Hannah well," I prayed.

In that instant, I realized that she was on loan to me for as long as our Creator decreed. He certainly knew about babies at Christmas. I "gave" Him mine, no strings attached. I thanked Him for the loan as I changed the prayer. Reflecting on the Virgin Mary's faith, I prayed, "Please, God, I believe. Help my unbelief. Help me trust You for whatever I'm facing."

Within ten hours, God restored the loan. The next day, the tea became a celebration of life. Hannah stayed in bed. I was up, but God laid down my fear.

". . . With us is the Lord our God to help us and to fight our battles." . . .

—II CHRONICLES 32:8

Thought . . . Can you pray, "*Thy* will be done" regarding your children? It's easier to do when you realize you are praying to a *Father* Who loves them more and cares for them better than you.

Treasure at the Beach

BY DONELLA DAVIS

God doesn't promise there won't be storms; He does promise to be present in them.

—ANONYMOUS

"What do you boys think the beach is like?" my mother asked my sons, Colten, six, and Kyle, four.

"It is a place where you find lots of treasure," they answered.

Realizing that they expected to find beach treasure, I planned to purchase cheap jewelry and plastic coins to bury on the beach for them to find. However, a week before vacation, the doctor found an unexplained lump on Colten's neck. The week turned into a blur of tests and specialist consultations. An MRI was scheduled for the day we returned from vacation.

The "treasure" was never bought. So, on the way to the beach, I explained to the boys that they would find no treasure in the sand. Upon arrival, we were greeted by a beautiful ocean view. We walked for miles on "our" secluded beach, played in clean white sand, watched dolphins play and crabs scurry, and fed the seagulls from our hands. On our last afternoon, a storm arose. In the storm, the crashing waves seemed to explode in praise of the majesty and power of their Creator.

As I stood in awe of God's creation, He confirmed to me that He was *still* in control. If He could bring forth the oceans and orchestrate all that is in them, if His thoughts of His children outnumbered the grains of sand, then surely He would display His majesty and power in our "storm." "Boys, mom was wrong. Someday I will tell you about the 'treasure' that I found at the beach."

Before the mountains were born or you brought forth the earth and the world, from everlasting to everlasting you are God.

—PSALM 90:2

Thought . . . Are you experiencing some "stormy" situation? Jesus is familiar with storms; He created them! Be sure to ask Him into your boat. Then you can face anything!

Autographed by the Author

BY RUTH BELL GRAHAM

As a Christian, you are primarily the product of the work of Christ on the Cross.

—NEIL T. ANDERSON

The heavy, flat package was from Canada. Quickly tearing off the wrappings, I discovered with delight a portfolio by the famous photographer, Yousuf Karsh. Wondering who had sent the book, I turned to the front and to my amazement discovered an inscription to Bill from the author, Yousuf Karsh. As I gathered the torn wrappings, I noted the customs sticker. "Autographed by the author" is what was written to describe the value of the contents.

I recently reread an essay I had written at the age of fourteen when I was a sophomore at the Pyengyang Foreign School in what is now Pyong Yang, North Korea. It is titled "The Name of Jesus," and it closes by quoting Revelation 3:12 ". . . and I will write upon him My new name." The essay concluded: "If His present name is so wonderful, what will His new name be which He has promised to write upon us if we overcome in this world?"

Some of us, however, feel more overcome than that we are overcomers. And we find comfort in Dr. Way's translation of Philippians 2:13: "Ye . . . have not to do it in your own unaided strength; it is God Who is all the while supplying the impulse, giving you the power to resolve, the strength to perform the execution of His good pleasure."

Our ultimate value will be that we were not only created, compiled and, as it were, written by the author. Our true value will rest in the fact that we have been autographed by the Author.

They will see his face, and his name will be on their foreheads.

—REVELATION 22:4

Thought . . . How do you bear Jesus' autograph? His "name" equals His character. He has inscribed His power, holiness, and love on your heart.

Alive

BY ANNETTE M. ECKART

Everything here but the soul of man is a passing shadow. The only enduring substance is within. When shall we awake to the sublime greatness, the perils, the accountableness, and the glorious destinies of the immortal soul?

—WILLIAM ELLERY CHANNING

After a car collision, I became bedridden. My career ended. All activities in which my husband and I were involved came to an immediate halt. My recovery became our world. Weeks in bed drew me closer to God. The biblical Word came alive for me as never before. His voice resounded with the sunrise and brought assurance at day's end.

My situation deteriorated. My weakened body had no reserves. Doctor appointments and therapies drained me. Months passed before we noticed any positive change. Every day I leaned on the Lord for answers. My husband and I began to pray together nightly. We took every decision to God.

When I began to drive again, I asked God if I might navigate the five miles to church. I sensed God's approval and made the journey. Moving stiffly, I managed to shuffle into a pew. Carefully sitting down, I sighed and closed my eyes. In my mind I said to the Lord, *Present.* I prayed to come into the present moment with God and to make a gift of my presence. God answered back, "And accounted for." I smiled. He knew my every move. Then I realized anew that the Blood of Jesus accounted for me. At that moment, I was grateful that I had survived the car crash. I treasured the guarantee of eternal life through Jesus Who ransomed me, because I knew if I had not survived, I still would have lived.

For even the Son of Man did not come to be served, but to serve, and to give his life as a ransom for many. . . ."

—MARK 10:45

Thought . . . To whom are you accountable? If you have received salvation through Jesus Christ, Who died on the Cross for you, you are accountable to Him as your Lord and Savior. He treasures you and paid a costly price to redeem you.

Full of Joy

BY JEANNE-MARIE GUYON

EDITOR'S NOTE: Madame Guyon, a French aristocrat and devout Christian who lived in the late seventeenth and early eighteenth centuries, was imprisoned by the corrupt King Louis XIV of France because of her faith in Christ.

The most visible joy can only reveal itself to us when we've transformed it, within.

—RAINER MARIA RILKE

During the time I was at Vincennes and Monsieur de La Reinie interrogated me, I continued in great peace, very content to pass my life there, if such were the will of God. I used to compose hymns, which the maid who served me learned by heart as fast as I composed them; and we used to sing your praise, O my God! I regarded myself as a little bird You were keeping in a cage for Your pleasure, and who ought to sing to fulfill her condition of life. The stones of my tower seemed to me rubies: that is to say, I esteemed them more than all worldly magnificence. My joy was based on Your love, O my God, and on the pleasure of being Your captive; although I made these reflections only when composing hymns. The central depth of my heart was full of that joy which You give to those who love You, in the midst of the greatest crosses.

I let others think what they please; for me, I find security only in abandoning myself to the Lord.

". . . for the joy of the Lord is your strength."

—NEHEMIAH 8:10

Thought . . . Are you imprisoned by circumstances? God has sovereignly allowed them. Because He loves you, you can sing, knowing that He permits trials for your good to make you more like Jesus (Romans 8:28–29)— knowing that this "momentary light affliction" is achieving for you an eternal treasure of glory, far outweighing the trial itself (II Corinthians 4:17).

The Treasure of Timing

BY ANN FOX CHODAKOWSKI AND
SUSAN FOX WOOD, THE TIGHTWAD TWINS

He knows not his own strength that has not met adversity.

—BEN JONSON

Our father was an animal lover, and we recall the many animal stories with which he regaled us when we were children. A favorite pertained to one of God's most beautiful creations, the butterfly. Daddy told us that one time he had watched a struggling butterfly for days as it tried to release itself from its cocoon. Finally, he couldn't stand watching it struggle any longer, so he opened the side of the cocoon, making it easier for the butterfly to emerge. To his disappointment, the beautiful wings that had formed could not even lift the small creature off the ground.

Later in the day he read about the butterfly, discovering that God had made the cocoon very tight so that natural oils could form on the butterfly's wings every time it struggled to free itself. At just the right time, the butterfly would break free and fly. Daddy had rushed the process. There was a purpose for the butterfly's adversity!

As children, we often wondered why God would not bless our family with more money and an easier life. Later, as single parents who struggled with a tight budget just as the butterfly had with a tiny cocoon, we became strong from the lessons we learned from our poor childhood. God had prepared us for skills we would later need to use in life's many cocoon-like situations. And now we have a ministry that helps set people free from tough financial experiences. Though we had tried to rush God, thankfully, He didn't listen!

There is a time for everything . . ."

—ECCLESIASTES 3:1

Thought . . . From what struggle are you trying to break free? Patiently persevere, knowing that God is using this trial to strengthen the treasure of maturity (James 1:2–4). Don't rush His work in you.

Why the Hurt, Lord?

BY JOYCE LANDORF HEATHERLEY

Sorrow is Knowledge: they who know the most must mourn the deepest o'er the fatal truth, The Tree of Knowledge is not that of Life.

—GEORGE NOEL GORDON

It's been many years since David, my infant son, died. One day when I saw a blond, blue-eyed boy about eight years old, I remembered David and the hurt was fresh and painful. He was with me for only a brief flash in time. Yet I think any bereaved mother will always yearn and miss the little one that slipped away.

I've been wondering about the *whys* of our yesterdays' hurts. Maybe one of the reasons God allows us to remember grief from time to time has to do with His developing a new *awareness and sensitivity to other people.* Another reason God allows the hurt seems to be in connection with *empathy.* Having walked in death's valley has enabled me to reach out to friends in their grief. I don't need to worry about what I'll say for we are silently bonded together. A hug or a look shows our compassion.

One reason for the heartache concerns my *understanding* of the grieving process. Yesterday, when I saw the boy, I asked the *why* of David's going for the hundredth time and patiently, for the hundredth time, God answered. "My child, stop asking, 'Why, Lord?' and ask instead, 'What do You want me to learn?' I want to teach you many things. Death is a part of life. I've allowed you to experience sorrow to refine your living. You are my child. I am in control, even in David's death and I will continue to direct your path. So trust Me, dear child."

Even though I walk through the valley of the shadow of death, I will fear no evil, for you are with me . . .

—PSALM 23:4

Thought . . . Do you suffer your child's loss? Change "Why, Lord?" to "What can I do, Lord?" Help another grieving parent. God will strengthen you both as you help each other.

Of Dads and Root Beer

BY PENNY J. CLARK

If souls can suffer alongside, and I hardly know it, because the spirit of discernment is not in me, then I know nothing of Calvary love.

—AMY CARMICHAEL

As a child, I adored my father and relentlessly imitated him, learning from him important life lessons: Hammer nails straight. Don't let car salesmen intimidate you. Sing descant, even if you're off-key. And always drink root beer.

Drinking root beer was a particularly bonding activity for Dad and me. Our mutual fondness dictated that outings end with a cold drink of the sweet stuff. After Dad helped me lift a bottle from the grocery cooler and pop the cap, we'd sit under a tree, sharing small talk and sips of our icy prize. In my mind we were best friends.

As I grew older, however, our relationship deteriorated. Dad, himself a victim of childhood abuse, increasingly responded to life's pressures with rage. Sometimes I drew comfort from a mental treasury of happier days; more often, even after becoming an adult and a Christian, ironically after Dad's death, I stubbornly focused on the pain of his betrayal.

Determined, I visited Dad's grave one muggy July day, and knelt on cool grass shaded by a nearby tree, mourning our lost years. Jesus' words, "Forgive . . . for they know not," echoed in my heart. I imagined Dad's own bewilderment as a rejected child, and grieved his struggle to cope as an adult. As I repented for letting my pain blind me to his, my bitterness melted, and I relaxed in my Heavenly Father's love.

Then, reaching into my insulated backpack, I pulled out an icy cold root beer and took a long drink.

Above all, love each other deeply, because love covers over a multitude of sins.

—I PETER 4:8

Thought . . . Is it impossible for you to forgive someone, ever after his death? Perhaps his wrong behavior toward you resulted from some wrong he suffered. Stop sin's cycle now. Forgive!

Tending the Fire

BY GAIL MACDONALD

There is in every heart a spark of heavenly fire which lies dormant in the broad daylight of prosperity . . .

—WASHINGTON IRVING

Years ago, I found myself in an arena with thousands of people. A retired missionary nearing his eightieth year spoke.

The man caught my attention with a simple word picture as he challenged people to seek something greater. He said, "Untended fires soon die and become just a pile of ashes."

The fire presumably burns in the heart of the one who follows Christ. It is a flame that cannot go unmanaged, for if it is allowed to dwindle into ashes, the outer person is destined to a life of coldness.

He proposed that we give serious attention to the condition of the "fire within." "Is it burning with force, or dying? Is it being fed or starved?" he asked. "Until this matter is resolved, all attempts at finding one's way through the challenges of life will be relatively futile."

From that day to this one, the vitality of my inner fire has been my priority. Tending the fire within is another way of talking about being open to the presence of Christ. It is what makes me long for His likeness, offers direction and stability, establishes proper motives and responses.

When I become aware that my attitude and conduct are drifting toward an un-Christlike perspective, I've learned to ask, "Have you been with Jesus at the fire, Gail? Have you allowed the fire to die down? Are there more ashes than flames?" Usually the alarming realization arises: He has been there at the fire within, waiting, but I've been a no-show.

You, O Lord, keep my lamp burning; my God turns my darkness into light.

—PSALM 18:28

Thought . . . Has your love for Jesus grown cold? Fan the flame through repentance. Then Jesus will continue to allow your "lamp" to burn brightly (Revelation 2:4–5).

Delivered from Fears

BY SANDRA JENSEN

You need not cry very loud; He is nearer to us than we think.

—BROTHER LAWRENCE

Anxiety attack! My first harrowing experience was a heart-thumping episode in the middle of the night. But before long, my nighttime terrors spilled over into my waking hours as similar attacks struck while driving the freeway.

"You can't let this get control of you," a friend advised after she gave me the name of a therapist who specialized in helping clients overcome anxiety. But by now I couldn't even drive beyond my own town.

I made an appointment with the therapist and was thrilled to discover that he was a Christian. Over the next several weeks he taught me specific techniques, but one in particular worked the best.

"Memorize a verse from the Bible," he said.

The following week I summoned the courage to venture onto the freeway alone. The anticipation of my solo trip sent my heart soaring, but I was determined. Armed with prayer, a cellular phone, and a Bible verse, I set off. With my legs weak from fright and my heart galloping, I repeated these words aloud: "I sought the Lord, and He answered me, and He delivered me from all my fears." The soothing words reassured me as I drove, but even more amazing was the awe I experienced each time I repeated the verse. When I needed the Lord He answered me, and just as I had asked, He stripped away my fear. I suddenly realized, more than ever, that the Lord's words are a treasure chest of promises—promises He keeps for all of His children.

Do not be anxious about anything, but in everything by prayer and petition, with thanksgiving, present your requests to God. And the peace of God, which transcends all understanding, will guard your hearts and your minds in Christ Jesus.

—PHILIPPIANS 4:6–7

Thought . . . Are you anxious? Are you praying? Often, we let fear overcome us before even expressing our anxiety to God. Memorize Scripture. The Holy Spirit will bring to mind specific truths as you need them.

God Works in Conflict

BY KAY ARTHUR

> God works in affliction, and those times when we're afflicted are the times when we're open to see it. Suffering ceases to be suffering in some way at the moment it finds a meaning.
>
> —VICTOR FRANKL

Jack and I saw something negative in our youngest son's life, and we confronted him. I knew it would be hard. It brought conflict, and in that conflict I had to hold on to what I knew was my husband's stand and what I knew about the faithfulness of God.

I got peace by running into the arms of my Heavenly Father crying, "Father, You understand. There's nothing too hard for You. You know we're doing this for our son's good."

Then our son left to go back to college. As he walked out the door I thought, *What if he drives too fast and has an accident?* The remembrance of one of our dear friends who had just been killed in a car wreck was too much for me. I ran out to remind David about Beth, hoping this would calm him and make him drive carefully. But he had already driven away.

Later he called us from college and said, "You and Dad are right, and I was wrong. Will you forgive me?" I was so proud of him! I knew he would come through. But in those three days I prayed and talked to the Father a lot more than ever for David. I had to embrace all that I knew from God's Word.

Sometimes you think you won't survive, but eventually you see "it was good for me that I was afflicted, that I might learn His statutes."

> ". . . But he knows the way that I take; when he has tested me, I will come forth as gold. . . ."
>
> —JOB 23:10

Thought . . . Is it hard to confront your child? Don't condemn him. Simply present the truth of God's Word, and let the Holy Spirit convict him.

Treasures from Tragedy

BY SANDRA J. BUNCH

Every experience God gives us, every person He puts in our lives is the perfect preparation for the future that only He can see.

—CORRIE TEN BOOM

Being newlyweds, our minds had naturally turned to the treasured desire of having a baby. However, it wasn't long before we discovered that we would face the tragedy of infertility. I was angry with God. I could not understand why He had chosen us to fight such a hopeless battle.

One day I was watching our two-week-old foster child sleep. He was the youngest we had nurtured thus far and had stayed with us for the shortest time, yet God had used him in a mighty way to touch our lives. As I lay there, I marveled over his little hands and face. It amazed me that this tiny miracle could even be breathing. I prayed, "Lord, why can't you create something as precious as this inside me?" Suddenly, clearly, I heard Him say, "Because if I had, you would not be doing what you are doing. Someone has to take care of My children."

What a revelation! It made sense of all the struggles and tears. At that moment, I uttered a prayer that I had thought I never would. I prayed, "Thank you, God, for my infertility. Without it, I would have missed out on so many blessings."

It should not be *our* plans that we follow, but *His*. Jeremiah 29:11 states, "For I know the plans I have for you," declares the Lord, "plans to prosper you and not to harm you, plans to give you hope and a future." I am glad that God planned my infertility. Through it, He has given me treasures out of tragedy.

"For my thoughts are not your thoughts, neither are your ways my ways," declares the Lord.

—ISAIAH 55:8

Thought . . . Do you anguish over infertility? Surrender to God's will and allow Him to "birth" in you His perfect plan. Ask Him to show you abused, unwanted children who need all the love you can give.

Love & Romance

Wedding Preparations

BY ANNE GRAHAM LOTZ

Heaven is a place prepared for those who are prepared for it.

—ANONYMOUS

The morning of my wedding day, I stayed in my bedclothes resting, so I would be fresh for the marriage ceremony and the reception that would follow. Several hours before I was to leave to go to the church, I began to get ready. I started with my makeup, carefully applying it to enhance any physical beauty I might have and hide the many flaws I did! I worked on my hair, sweeping it up so it would stay under the veil. My mother came to my room and helped me get into my wedding gown, fastening the dozens of small buttons up the back and adjusting the veil. When I had done everything I knew to do to get myself ready, I stood in front of the full-length mirror and gazed at the young woman enveloped in ivory silk and lace. I was tense and eager as I wondered, after months of preparation if I would be beautiful and desirable to my husband.

As elaborate as my preparations were as a bride seeking to be beautiful for my husband, they were feeble in comparison with God's preparations for His bride. The preparations I made for my wedding are nothing compared with the preparations being made for our heavenly home! Jesus promised, "I am going there to prepare a place for you." What God begins, He always completes. Our heavenly home will be ready. With loving eagerness and anticipation of joy, God will present the new Jerusalem—Heaven—to His children only.

> . . . "No eye has seen, no ear has heard, no mind has conceived what God has prepared for those who love him"—but God has revealed it to us by his Spirit. . . .
> —I CORINTHIANS 2:9–10

Thought . . . God has prepared Heaven for you, but are you prepared to enter His home? Only those who have received Jesus Christ as Lord and Savior can cross the threshold of Heaven.

The Day He Prayed for Me

BY JOYCE E. TOMANEK

You pray in your distress and in your need; would that you might pray also in fullness of your joy and in our days of abundance.

—KAHLIL GIBRAN

Frank and I have been married thirty-two years. Before we married, he attended church with me and my children. He was a believer, but quiet about his faith. I was grateful for a husband who would attend church faithfully with me.

Through the years, my faith became stronger and more vital as the Lord brought me through many trials and tribulations, sustaining me during times when I lost those dear to me, when loved ones had long and fatal illnesses. I wished that Frank's faith would grow stronger, too. I longed for him to become the spiritual leader of our home, but that did not happen.

Six years ago, cancer struck me. The morning of my surgery, a friend who is a priest came and kept us company. He prayed for me, a long and profoundly beautiful prayer, and anointed me with oil for healing. When the attendants came to wheel me to the operating room, Frank stopped them. "Just a minute," he said. He was afraid to let me go, for fear he'd never see me again. Then he prayed this prayer: "Lord, please don't let anything happen to my baby girl." No flowery phrases, just this plea from his heart.

There was so much love wrapped up in that one-sentence prayer. I treasure that prayer even more now than I did that day. Frank is now eighty-two and I'm sixty-three, and to him, I'll always be his baby girl.

And the prayer offered in faith will make the sick person well; the Lord will raise him up. If he has sinned, he will be forgiven.

—JAMES 5:15

Thought . . . Do you long for your husband to be more verbal about his faith? Actions speak louder than words. Treasure your husband's trust in God and love for you. They speak volumes.

He Is the Bridegroom

BY LIZ CURTIS HIGGS

Hallelujah! I have found Him Whom my soul so long has craved!

—CLARA TEAL WILLIAMS

Flying home, I sat next to a young woman who was impeccably groomed, except for the streaks on her cheeks where tears had removed some of her blush. My heart went out to her.

"What brings you to Louisville?" I asked softly.

A fresh flow of tears began as she moaned, "I don't know! I'm g-g-getting married," she stammered.

"How wonderful!" I exclaimed.

"I'm not so sure," she said, her voice still shaking. "My family and friends live in Florida, plus I have a great job there. I'm leaving my whole life behind."

"I moved to Louisville from far away, too," I said, trying to encourage. "It's a great place to live."

"I guess so," she said, unconvinced.

Despite my efforts, I was not helping. Then, the perfect question presented itself: "Do you love him?" Her expression changed instantly. "Oh, yes!" she said, then blushed at her enthusiasm. "He's very kind and considerate, really intelligent, and handsome, too." I smiled, knowing no further questions would be needed.

When we landed, I picked him out of the crowd instantly. He was obviously a fine young man. Tall, strong, yet with a warm and gentle smile and armed with a dozen red roses that matched her red suit perfectly. When she ran into his arms with a teary smile, I made myself look away rather than invade their privacy, but found a few happy tears had sneaked into my own eyes. The truth is, when you find the right One, it's easy to forsake all others and follow him.

> . . . as a bridegroom rejoices over his bride, so will your God rejoice over you.
>
> —ISAIAH 62:5

Thought . . . Has God led you to marry? Then abandon yourself to the mate He has chosen. Don't second-guess your decision. It's a big step, but with God's leading, you won't slip.

My Tweety Bird

BY NISEL PARDO-MCDONALD

Lovers should see things in the ones they love that others do not see.

—DR. ED YOUNG

"Over there," I said excitedly, pointing to a parking space near the mall. It wasn't often that my husband volunteered to go shopping with me, but when he did, he enjoyed it.

Strolling through the mall, we spotted a giant Tweety Bird balloon. He wasted no time in buying it for me. Our eyes locked and emotions deepened, as he handed me the balloon. Words were unnecessary. We both knew what the other was thinking. Two years before, I had endured six months of chemotherapy and had lost all my hair. It was during this time that William had shaved his own head, and had bought me a Tweety Bird knit cap to keep my bald head warm. He picked Tweety because it was bald, too. Every night before going to bed, I would don the cap and every morning upon my waking, William would ask, "How is my Tweety Bird doing this morning?"

After weeks of enjoyment, I trashed the deflated balloon, but somehow the wind blew it in front of my husband's home office window. For an entire day it bobbed up and down, grabbing his attention.

Finally, walking into the kitchen with balloon in hand, he said emotionally, "Tweety just doesn't want to die and leave us!" Tears welling up in both our eyes, we embraced tightly, grateful that my life had been spared and thankful to God for the intimacy and love that we share.

Many waters cannot quench love; rivers cannot wash it away.

—SONG OF SONGS 8:7A

Thought . . . Are you and your husband enduring some terrible trial? Cling very closely to each other and to God. As you lean on Him, you will grow even stronger as a couple, discovering "treasures in darkness," impossible to mine in the light (Isaiah 45:3).

God's Ways Are Always Best

BY MARITA LITTAUER

Obedience is not servitude of man to man, but submission to the will of God Who governs through the medium of men.

—POPE LEO XIII

The nature of crisis is that when it's yours, it's huge! For months I wrestled in my spirit over my crisis. Because of upheaval in his industry, my husband, Chuck, was forced to seek employment out-of-state. I didn't want to move and was beating both of us up over this decision.

My biggest concern was my business. I had always enjoyed moving, but my business was well established. I loved it and had great employees. I couldn't just "pick up and move." Once I faced my fear, I could stop and ask God His will. It didn't take a theologian to know His priority. Put my business first, or my marriage? Because I believe that the Bible is God's Word, I knew I had to put my marriage first and accept the move.

Amazingly, the moment I surrendered to God and was willing to submit to Chuck's needs, my sense of crisis lifted. I was totally at peace. Chuck and I talked at length, and prayed. Because my business had been supporting us during this difficult transition, and because it would take awhile for him to establish his, we have agreed to live separately in two states and commute back and forth to be together on weekends. We will re-evaluate in six months, with the possibility of my relocating in the future. I don't know how long we will have this "commuter marriage," but I do know that God's ways are always best. And I know that God is in control!

Wives, submit to your husbands, as is fitting in the Lord.

—COLOSSIANS 3:18

Thought . . . As a wife, do you find submission to your husband difficult? You are actually submitting to the Lord. It is easy to put your husband's needs first, when you put God first.

Still the One

BY LYNN WORLEY KUNTZ

Love is more easily demonstrated than defined.

—ANONYMOUS

When we met, my husband, Darryl, was building a tree house in the woods. I liked that. His dog accompanied us on our first date, a hike. She ate the cherries that we picked from a sunlit orchard, and spit out the pits! I was impressed! We first prayed together in the front seat of Darryl's Land Cruiser. We held hands, and thanked God for what we were coming to mean to each other.

We married five months after we met. We'd never seen each other without a suntan, or with a cold. We had two cars, but no bed. For Valentine's Day, Darryl bought me red knee socks and a kitchen sink trap. I baked him crunchy granola. We thanked God for how we were growing together.

We scraped, painted, and papered our first tiny house. We camped in the mountains, fished at the beach, planted gardens, raised two geese, and bottle-fed an orphaned raccoon. We made love and four beautiful babies, enjoyed ice cream cones and some great laughs in three dozen states and five countries, started two businesses, won a jitterbug contest, bought land and built a cabin in a remote valley. We held hands at funerals for his mom and my dad, and prayed for our children in waiting rooms of four hospitals.

We've been a team for twenty-five years. Darryl's still my sunshine. I'm his old flame. He's my best friend. I'm his one. He's my only. Thank you, God, for such a treasure chest of love and romance, past, present, and future.

For this reason a man will leave his father and mother and
be united to his wife, and they will become one flesh.

—GENESIS 2:24

Thought . . . Do you no longer love your husband? Write about all the experiences that you've shared over the years. The memories are irreplaceable, never to be repeated with another partner. Treasure what you have!

To Forgive Is Divine

BY PATRICIA PERRY

Common sense suits itself to the ways of the world. Wisdom tries to conform to the ways of heaven.

— JOSEPH JOUBERT

Even though my husband and I were on vacation, we awoke early and crept out quietly to the deserted pool deck. There we beheld a sight not often seen by Californians—we watched the sunrise over the ocean. We were on the Island of Catalina, facing east.

As the sky turned apricot to pink, I turned and looked at my treasured husband of thirty-one years and thought of how closely we had come to ending our marriage. Years ago, we faced a terrible financial and emotional crisis. We weren't in love anymore; we weren't even in "like." It was during this trial, when the world's wisdom insisted that the marriage was doomed, that God spoke to me. If He could forgive my sins, how could I not forgive my husband's? Could I demand a higher standard for my husband than God demanded of me? Humbled, I decided to forgive him, even though I didn't *feel* it.

Forgiveness, however, wasn't enough. God persisted in reminding me of our first love for each other. I realized that we both had started to focus on what was wrong with each other, not on what was right. I began to remember the qualities my husband had when we first met and how I loved those character traits in him. To my surprise, when I looked earnestly, they were still there. As I focused on the positive, a remarkable thing happened. I fell in love with him all over again—and he with me.

> Bear with each other and forgive whatever grievances you may have against one another. Forgive as the Lord forgave you. And over all these virtues put on love, which binds them all together in perfect unity.
>
> —COLOSSIANS 3:13–14

Thought . . . Do you struggle to keep love alive? À la Elizabeth Barrett Browning's poem, *How do I love thee? Let me count the ways* . . . write down every positive quality of your husband. You will realize why you loved him in the first place. Treasure your relationship!

Cookies for Breakfast

BY MARILYN MEBERG

EDITOR'S NOTE: Marilyn's husband was dying of cancer when he gave her this tea party three days before Christmas.

Love is a canvas furnished by nature and embroidered by imagination.

—VOLTAIRE

I am a light sleeper, so I was aware of Ken's restlessness. Aware of mine as well, Ken broke into the silence at 3:50 A.M. "Marilyn I've got a great plan for us."

"Really . . . I assume it doesn't include sleep."

"Right! I must get up and you are to stay in bed for ten minutes. Then you get up, come down to the living room, and the plan will unfold!"

"Okay, Babe."

At 4:00 A.M. I got up and went into the living room where Ken had a fire going, a pot of tea on the hearth, and an arrangement of cookies on a silver tray. He had drawn one of the love seats close to the fire, lit Christmas candles, and turned on the tree lights. Christmas music was playing softly. "Ken Meberg, you have the soul of an artist. What a gorgeous scene!" With happy enthusiasm, he poured each of us a cup of tea. He handed me the cookies and said, "Eat as many as you like, Madam."

"You mean I can eat cookies instead of breakfast?"

"Indeed you can, my dear. This is a special occasion."

We sat in front of the fire slurping tea, munching cookies, and giggling like naughty children. I don't know when I have enjoyed a tea party more, and have had better company. I was intensely aware of needing and wanting to savor those moments with my husband, and indeed I did. In fact, I still do.

My lover spoke and said to me, "Arise, my darling, my beautiful one, and come with me. . . ."

—SONG OF SONGS 2:10

Thought . . . Do you and your husband treasure "joy breaks"—imaginative moments you create for each other just for the fun of it? Life is short. It's important to have no regrets.

Rainbow Seeds

BY ANNETTE M. ECKART

Some of us will be seed-sowers in the hearts of people.

— JOYCE SACKETT

New marriages are full of "firsts"—first apartment, first house, first anniversary. Our marriage is twenty-seven years old, but we are still sharing "firsts."

We celebrated our latest anniversary with a "first" by going hunting together. We packed camping gear and went "rainbow hunting" in Hawaii. Ruthless in our pursuit of shimmering, colorful arcs, we drove through a mountainous region described in our guidebook as "the birthplace of rainbows." Around noon, we stopped at a roadside produce stand. My husband, Eddie, selected mangoes for lunch, and I quizzed the young woman manager, sportsman-style. "See any rainbows from here?" I queried. "Yup. All the time."

We continued our search in the direction of the beach. Blue-gray clouds draped the verdant mountains, hiding the sun's glare. The cloud canopy sharpened distinctions between shades and shapes of lush foliage. Intrigued with the vividness of the scene, we hadn't noticed that a shadow had fallen over the road. Unexpectedly, huge droplets of rain began a thundering rhythm on our windshield. Eddie noticed my cloudy expression as the downpour continued. I knew that on this part of the island it could rain all day. "Hey," he encouraged, "great rainbow seeds!"

Sunshine had broken out for me, even though rainbow seeds kept pouring down. My husband plants hope. He drops the right word into the bare soil of the soul, and new attitudes flourish. The rainbow I spotted that day was Christ's hope-filled light in my husband. My search had ended. I had married a treasure.

Whenever I bring clouds over the earth and the rainbow appears in the clouds, I will remember my covenant between me and you and all living creatures of every kind. . . .

—GENESIS 9:14–15

Thought . . . Are you planting "rainbow seeds," colorful glimmers of hope, in others' lives? Write a letter, place a phone call, arrange a personal visit. Plant treasures of kindness. The pot of gold at rainbow's end is God's "Well done, faithful servant!"

More Precious than Silver

BY KAREN O'CONNOR

Cast all your cares on God; that anchor holds.

—ALFRED LORD TENNYSON

One year while my husband was establishing a new career, I took advantage of an opportunity to earn some additional money to tide us over. But the strain of keeping everything afloat—our home, family, church work, and my usual writing and teaching—began to burden me. I was suddenly resentful of my self-appointed role as *super wife*.

"Dear Lord," I prayed one day as I flew home from an exhausting two-week consulting job out of state, "You know my needs and the needs of my home and family. I can't do it all. Please work it out. I'm too tired to even think of a solution. I need a 'helper angel'!" I said, smiling at my own whimsy.

I arrived home later that day to a sparkling-clean kitchen, freshly scrubbed bathroom, and a newly painted living room, dining room, and hallway. Every picture and painting on our walls (and we have a collection to rival any small museum!) and every dish and glass in the china cabinet had been cleaned and replaced. The silverware was tarnish-free. The furniture throughout the house was freshly oiled and the carpets had been perfectly vacuumed.

The "angel" behind this miracle? My husband, Charles. My treasure! "Just wanted to surprise you," he said, smiling from ear to ear. "If you can help with the earnings for awhile, it's the least I can do to help with the chores around here. Welcome home, honey!"

I glanced heavenward and whispered a humble, "Thanks!"

For he will command his angels concerning you to guard you in all your ways.

—PSALM 91:11

Thought . . . Do you value traditional roles in marriage? God does. Yet, He also tells everyone to submit to each other in love. There are times when both husband and wife can submit to each other out of reverence for Christ (Ephesians 5:21).

The Joy of Yielding

BY MARTICIA BURNS MCKINNEY

Independence is not strength, but unrealized weakness and is the very essence of sin. There was no independence in our Lord; the great characteristic of His life was submission to His Father.

—OSWALD CHAMBERS

Several years ago, I married my husband, Dale. Because we had both been single awhile and were set in our ways, adjusting to our marriage was a challenge. I especially had trouble yielding to a husband after many years as a single mom and "head of the household." Dale had a very conventional view of the roles in marriage and maintained that there were certain things that only a man could do. As a result, we had some lively discussions about wives submitting to their husbands.

Dale had taken down the bedroom door to replace the hinges, and I was impatiently waiting for him to finish the job. Though he had told me to let him handle it, one weekend when he was out of town I decided to remove the old painted-on hinge myself with a razor blade. Unfortunately, the razor slipped and I had to have six stitches on my thumb.

To my surprise when I got home from the hospital, Dale was there. When he couldn't reach me, he got worried and came home. I braced myself for a lecture, but instead when I told him what had happened, he didn't even say, "I told you so." Without a word, he put his arms around me. It was then I realized that submitting meant what he had said all along—letting him do the things he could do best, not just for his good, but for mine. Submitting to a loving husband wasn't so bad after all.

Submit to one another out of reverence for Christ.
—EPHESIANS 5:21

Thought . . . Do you stumble over submission? Jesus, Himself, submitted to God. He could do nothing by Himself (John 5:19). We, as "students," are not above our Master (Matthew 10:24).

The Treasure Box

BY PAT DEVINE

Life can only be understood backward, but it must be lived forward.

—NIELS BOHR

I try to recall the occasion—an anniversary, a dance, a birthday? My fingers fondle the crumpled pink ribbon on the parched sepia flower—a gardenia—my favorite gift from my favorite beau of fifty years and more.

A theater program still glows with deep, clear colors announcing: The American Theater presents *Porgy and Bess*, November 27, 1949. The house lights dim, the opera begins. In Row H, Seats 11 and 12, a young man, a girl, a ring—they pledge their troth.

My hands move deeper into the dusty old box. I open a folded paper, smoothing brittle creases, and find orders, dated August, 1951, summoning my young husband to ORD. The panic echoes across the years and causes my heart to race as it did then when he explained that ORD meant Overseas Replacement Duty in Korea. I was to be left behind, pregnant with our first child.

I smile as another snapshot reveals the rest of the story. A chubby baby girl, with a pink ribbon tied around a topknot of silky brown hair, kicks her fat little legs in the air. On the back I read, "Kathy, age three months—San Antonio." I sigh again at remembered relief when word arrived: "I'll be serving stateside—come to Texas."

I close the once-white cardboard box, return it to the shelf. Some day I will take it down again when my heart needs to be reminded where my treasures lie.

". . . For where your treasure is, there your heart will be also. . . ."

—MATTHEW 6:21

Thought . . . Where do your treasures lie? Be honest. Even if the box of inexpensive mementoes was destroyed, would you know that *real* treasure is wrapped up in the memories that it contained? Memories—those are treasures of the heart.

Missing Things

BY LUCI SHAW

Never look at what you have lost; look at what you have left.

—ROBERT HAROLD SCHULLER

My friend Martha was on the phone, her voice barely controlling her panic. "Please pray," she said, "I've lost my rings." She had been spring cleaning and had removed her wedding and engagement rings for safekeeping. She and her husband searched the now-glistening kitchen—shelves, cupboards, drawers, probing even the drain of the kitchen sink. Nothing. The precious twin symbols of their marriage had disappeared without a trace.

"But they couldn't have just vanished," I protested over the phone line. "Diamonds and gold don't simply evaporate. They're there, somewhere."

I began to ponder the persistence of material things, and beyond physical realities I thought of all the other precious gifts that we give, and are given, and of the words we speak into the air. Even though they are invisible, nothing will ever obliterate them. I thought of the lavishing of love on someone dear who may, at the time, appear to be indifferent to it, so that the love seems wasted.

Eight years later, Martha and her husband decided to renovate their kitchen. As they lowered one of the old metal cabinets from the wall, they could hear a muffled rattle. For the first time they realized that the shelf was hollow. They turned the shelf upside down and shook it. The rings fell, gleaming one by one, into Martha's hands—gifts twice-given.

When she called me, with elation and excitement in her voice, she reminded me of the New Testament woman who lost one of her betrothal coins and who, when she found it, celebrated with her friends and neighbors.

". . . 'Rejoice with me; I have found my lost coin.' In the same way, I tell you, there is rejoicing in the presence of the angels of God over one sinner who repents."

—LUKE 15:9–10

Thought . . . Have you wasted love on someone who is unappreciative? Love never fails—even when it's not returned. We love because God commands it. We strive to please Him, not man.

New Love, New Life

BY NORMA HOWARD KIRKPATRICK

People are lonely because they build walls instead of bridges.

— JOSEPH FORT NEWTON

His voice broke. Tears streamed down his face as he told of his wife's recent death after fifty-three years of marriage. Our bereavement support group painfully empathized with him. "And I'm totally lost in the kitchen," he continued.

"I know how you feel," I answered. "I had been married forty-seven years, and I'm totally lost with using tools, not knowing how to install hooks or hang pictures in my new home." All the women agreed. So I suggested that we pool our talents. Jack wiped his eyes and said, "Well, I guess I could help you." My voice breaking, I replied, "I'll make you homemade soup."

The discussion turned to different ways we had coped, and I said, "I couldn't have gotten through without the strength of the Lord." Another lady shared, "Well, I'm an agnostic, but friends helped me." Jack added, "I guess I'm an agnostic, too."

In the following weeks, Jack visited occasionally and did handiwork for me and I shared my homemade soup, *and* my faith. A few months later, he received Christ and was baptized. We suddenly felt alive again, like teenagers, in our interest in each other. We were married a year later. "Miraculous, isn't it," we often agreed, "how the Lord brought us together. Not only do we have new love, but new life in Christ!"

We had a wonderful three years before Jack succumbed to cancer. I often wonder, *What if I'd never spoken up at that first meeting?* Now I'm comforted that Jack and I will spend eternity together.

Therefore, if anyone is in Christ, he is a new creation; the old has gone, the new has come!

—II CORINTHIANS 5:17

Thought . . . Do you share the Gospel at every opportunity? Don't hesitate. You never know how close someone may be to death—to Heaven or to hell.

Hugs, Kisses, and Reese's Peanut Butter Cups

BY JULIE EVANS

> You're still the one I run to. The one that I belong to. You're still the
> one I want for life. You're still the one that I love. The only one I
> dream of. You're still the one I kiss good night.
>
> —SHANIA TWAIN

My husband, Dave, and I recently celebrated our eleventh anniversary. The amazing thing is that in this disposable world, we
actually still *like* being married to each other! We are both "still
the one" for each other—a very comfy-cozy thing. We just fit
together . . . like a Reese's Peanut Butter Cup. Even more than
peanut butter and jelly, peanut butter and chocolate simply belong together. Ask any woman on the planet and she will tell
you that this is a truly blessed union. Peanut butter and chocolate fit together perfectly.

Once, when my hubby and I were eating a Reese's Peanut
Butter Cup together (ever notice how there are two in a package—one for him, one for her—who said candy bars aren't romantic?), I said to Dave, "I wonder how they get the peanut
butter inside the chocolate?" It was a question that had baffled
me for years, but this was the first time I had dared voice it to
anyone. But in marriage, especially, one must risk vulnerability
in order to achieve intimacy.

Dave looked at me as if he had just fallen in love with me all
over again; then he burst out laughing and said, with equally
precious vulnerability, "I was just wondering how they ever got
the chocolate around the peanut butter!" A true story.

Now, could there be a more perfectly yummy match? Us, I
mean.

> How beautiful you are, my darling! Oh, how beautiful! . . .
> How handsome you are, my lover! Oh, how charming! . . .
> —SONG OF SONGS 1:15–16

Thought . . . Do you long for compatibility with your
husband? Appreciate that his strengths offset your
weaknesses. Look for interests to share. Above all, share
compatibility in Christ.

Repeated Sunrise

BY ANNE MORROW LINDBERGH

Love is not a state, it is a movement. Personal contact is not a state, but a fleeting movement that must be ceaselessly rediscovered. Marriage is not a state, but a movement—a boundless adventure.

—PAUL TOURNIER

Husband and wife can and should go off on vacations alone and also on vacations alone *together*. For if it is possible that woman can find herself by having a vacation alone, it is equally possible that the original relationship can sometimes be refound by having a vacation alone *together*. Most married couples have felt the unexpected joy of one of these vacations. How wonderful it was to leave the children, the house, the job, and all the obligations of daily life; to go out together, whether for a month or a weekend or even just a night in an inn by themselves. How surprising it was to find the miracle of the sunrise repeated. There was the sudden pleasure of having breakfast alone with the man one fell in love with. Here at the small table, are only two people facing each other. How the table at home has grown! And how distracting it is, with four or five children, a telephone ringing in the hall, two or three school buses to catch, not to speak of the commuter's train. How all this separates one from one's husband and clogs up the pure relationship. But sitting at a table alone opposite each other, what is there to separate one? Nothing but a coffee pot, corn muffins and marmalade. A simple enough pleasure, surely, to have breakfast alone with one's husband, but how seldom married people in the midst of life achieve it.

However, each one of you also must love his wife as he loves himself, and the wife must respect her husband.

—EPHESIANS 5:33

Thought . . . Can you repeat the sunrise of early marriage? This miracle is possible by rediscovering the purity of your love through simple pleasures and solitude *together*. Setting aside even a half hour daily to bask in the warmth of your love, brings fulfillment when the sun sets.

Spiritual Journey

It's All in the Hearing

BY SANDRA PALMER CARR

The minister lives behind a "stained glass curtain." The layman has opportunities for evangelism which a minister will never have.

—JAMES McCORD

Several churches in our city met together for a Thanksgiving Eve service, where each pastor participated in the program. One pastor particularly impressed me as he introduced himself. "I'm from the Sootentai people," he said. I turned to my husband, Chuck, wondering if he knew where the Sootentai lived. I fully expected to hear an exciting story with missionary flavor, set among a remote people, somewhere on a distant island. Their primitive existence would make us thankful for our many blessings.

As the pastor continued to speak, it gradually dawned on me that he hailed from a special group of well-dressed men, native to nearly every country in the world—the "Suit-and-Tie" people, and he was the only pastor present wearing a suit and tie. I laughed quietly.

But as I seriously began to think about it, I realized the need for missionaries to evangelize the "Suit-and-Tie" people—executives and businesspeople who are searching for Truth, and feel that they will never get off the career treadmill long enough to find it.

So now I remember to pray for the "Suit-and-Tie" people, because God brought them to mind in a unique way. He often uses humor to teach me about the value of souls. God especially treasures the "Suit-and-Tie" people, who often feel separated from Him on their remote islands of self-sufficiency and busy isolation. God can speak to them and to us in surprising ways, even when we're slow to hear or comprehend His words.

. . . Faith comes from hearing the message, and the message is heard through the Word of Christ.

—ROMANS 10:17

Thought . . . Do you think that the professional, well-educated, or wealthy don't need to hear the Gospel? Their self-sufficiency masks their need for Christ. They need God's salvation message. Be a missionary without leaving your workplace.

Why, Lord?

BY JANE PARRISH

Faith is now in the crucible, it is being tested by fire, and there is no fixed resting place for the heart and mind but in the Throne of God.

—ARTHUR W. PINK

It was dinnertime. Opening the refrigerator, I paused to read the Scripture I'd taped to the door: "Blessed are those whose strength is in You, Who have set their hearts on pilgrimage. They go from strength to strength, till each appears before God in Zion (Psalm 84:5, 7)." It was food for my soul—the answer to *Why?*— Why go on? Why won't this end? Why, Lord? Each question tempted me to greater discouragement in facing the strained relationship that threatened my peace, that grew worse each day with no end in sight. *I am so tired today, Lord,* I silently reasoned with God.

Yet, the truth of these Scriptures showed me reality, drawing my attention to God. "If I weren't sure of who You are, Lord, I might not continue," I confessed. As I refocused, God reminded me that neither the length nor depth of the trial was mine to define. Although I wanted to set limits to control the pain, I was but a pilgrim on a journey that God had ordained. As I leaned on Him, I would go and *grow* from "strength to strength."

As I finished dinner, I whispered, "Oh Father, I would not choose this cross, but I submit to it. Thank You for turning life's pressures into treasures of intimacy with You, knowing that You, alone, are my strength and that You are in control. And thank You that I do have a destination. One day I will appear before You, home with You in Heaven."

The Lord has established his throne in heaven, and his kingdom rules over all.

—PSALM 103:19

Thought . . . Have you given up on life? No trial lasts forever. And God will strengthen you every moment of your earthly journey, bringing you safely to your Heavenly home.

Never Alone

BY LYDIA E. HARRIS

One man with courage makes a majority.

—ANDREW JACKSON

For twenty-six years I saw my husband, Milt, as quiet and unassuming, so it surprised me when he announced his plan. "I'm going to organize a prayer gathering at work for the National Day of Prayer." I was proud of his courage, his bold allegiance to God, and the example it set for our children. He chose the time, noon, and the place, the flagpole outside his six-story building. He advertised the event, tacking computer-made flyers on bulletin boards throughout the building. Together, we prayed that others would notice the posters and join him to pray.

Who are the Christians at work? we wondered. With hundreds of employees, surely there were others who would want to participate. *Would this lead to a regular prayer time or Bible study?* Our anticipation mounted as the National Day of Prayer arrived. Throughout the morning I prayed, "Lord, please send others to pray with my husband."

As Milt walked through the front door that evening, I greeted him with eager questions. "What happened? How many came?"

"There were three besides me," he replied with a grin.

"That's great! Who were they?"

"The Father, Son, and Holy Spirit!"

I was proud of my husband's courage that day and still am. Other *National Days of Prayer* have come and gone since then, but the first Thursday in May, 1993, stands out as a treasured day. It was the day that I learned a valuable lesson: with God's triune presence, we are never alone.

". . . Have I not commanded you? Be strong and courageous . . . for the Lord your God will be with you wherever you go."

—JOSHUA 1:9

Thought . . . Are you courageous to share your faith in the workplace? Respect restrictions your employer makes upon religious displays. Be bold in sharing your faith on "personal time," like lunch, and by the godly, honest example you set.

A Sign of Hope

BY JERI CHRYSONG

I am as my Creator made me, and since He is satisfied, so am I.

—MINNIE SMITH

Feeling used, abused, and tossed aside after my divorce, I went to the beach to walk off some stress. On one particular day, however, I did not want to be consoled. I wanted to pout. As I began to think, *Nobody loves me . . . nobody will ever love me,* I sank deeper into a pathetic funk. I refused to focus on the positives and chose to rehearse my negatives: the wrinkles, sporadic gray hairs, surgical scars, and stretch marks from childbirth.

And then I stumbled upon a shell—a black murex, I think, like the type sold in gift stores. With its barnacle holes, it had seen better days. "Kind of like I am," I griped. However, upon closer examination, my artist's eye noticed its delicate ruffles and ridges. I no longer saw the barnacle holes, chips, or flattened color, but imagined what the shell once had been. I was delighted with my find. "What a treasure!" I exclaimed.

"Like you, Jeri," I felt the Lord say, as I cradled the shell, "Someday, someone will come along and look past the physical flaws on which you so love to dwell, to see the treasure you are and exclaim, 'What a treasure I've found in Jeri!'"

In spite of the mushy sand beneath my feet, my steps had a little more spring to them as hope accompanied me home on a new journey.

> . . . We also rejoice in our sufferings, because we know that suffering produces perseverance; perseverance; character; and character, hope. And hope does not disappoint us . . .
> —ROMANS 5:3–5

Thought . . . Are you suffering over rejection after divorce? God will be your Husband (Isaiah 54:5) and Jesus won't forsake you (Hebrews 13:5b). Treasure their faithfulness.

God's Jewels

BY HELEN STEINER RICE

God has a bottle and a book for His people's tears. What was sown as a tear will come up as a pearl.

—MATTHEW HENRY

We watch the rich and famous
Bedecked in precious jewels,
Enjoying earthly pleasures,
Defying moral rules—
And in our mood of discontent
We sink into despair
And long for earthly riches
And feel cheated of our share—
But stop these idle musings,
God has stored up for you
Treasures that are far beyond
Earth's jewels and riches, too—
For never, never discount
What God has promised man
If he will walk in meekness
And accept God's flawless plan—
For if we heed His teachings
As we journey through the years,
We'll find the richest jewels of all
Are *crystallized* from *tears*.

Better the little that the righteous have than the wealth of many wicked; for the power of the wicked will be broken, but the Lord upholds the righteous.

—PSALM 37:16–17

Thought . . . Do you envy arrogant people who flaunt their prosperity? Like David, enter God's sanctuary; see the destructive end of those who make riches their god (Psalm 73). Don't envy them; pray for them! Your journey will be easier without riches to weigh you down.

Where to Turn?

BY DORIS SCHUCHARD

One alone is true to us; One alone can be all things to us; One alone can supply our need.

—CARDINAL JOHN HENRY NEWMAN

Cradling the grocery sack against my hip, I reached into my pocket for the car keys. Empty. Purse, empty. School ended in ten minutes and I was on car pool duty today. Where were those keys? *Stay calm,* I told myself. *Just retrace your steps.* Down the bread aisle, past the dairy case—nothing shiny glinted up at me from the floor. *I'll call my husband. Maybe he can pick up the kids.* But he had just left the office. Even the school's phone was busy; I couldn't call to say I'd be late.

I glanced at my watch—five minutes left. My last idea was to try the store's customer service department. Embarrassed by my mistake, I explained my dilemma to the clerk. She smiled and held up a set of keys attached to a familiar pink plastic key chain. "A gentleman just found them on the floor."

I had never been so happy to see three tiny metal objects. But as I drove off—*quickly*—I laughed. A little key had opened a hidden treasure of understanding. I often try to solve life's problems through my own abilities, but whenever I do, I usually find that my wisdom is limited. Only as a last resort do I go to where the answer has been all along—to the One Who knows my future and cares enough to want the best for me. If only I would always start at the top and ask God, Who is the answer to all my questions!

. . . Turn to the Lord your God with all your heart and with all your soul.

—DEUTERONOMY 30:10

Thought . . . When you need answers for life's journey, where do you turn? Go first to God, Who promises to give generously the treasure of wisdom to all who ask (James 1:5).

The Flock: the Treasure of Safety

BY KRISTEN JOHNSON INGRAM

The soul can split the sky in two, and let the face of God shine through.

—EDNA ST. VINCENT MILLAY

The spring's goldfinches had just arrived when I heard the television broadcaster announce, "CNN breaking news . . . shooting at Thurston High, Springfield, Oregon . . ." Tragedy had occurred just four blocks from my house!

That afternoon, as my teenage grandson told me how frightened he had been at school, I was transported back to Cuban Crisis days. My son, then in the first grade, came home late, covered with dirt. I accused him of fighting, something he sometimes did on the way home. "I wasn't fighting," he explained. "I passed the high school on the way home and a bell rang. I thought it was an air raid and jumped in the gutter to duck and cover." *As if ducking and covering would protect you from nuclear attack*, I thought, as I wrapped him in my arms.

My grandson wasn't afraid of The Bomb. He feared the school cafeteria!

"Look," he said suddenly, and pointed out the window. Goldfinches were surging through the air, lighting on branches, kiting from tree to tree, swooping down onto the bird feeder. "It's a celebration," he said. "A bird party!" Then he said, "I guess God will take care of me."

Goldfinches usually move on after a week; but this year, they stayed all summer. I'm not one who looks for signs, but the fluttering yellow of their graceful flights has given me hope that angels will descend to protect our children, that movies will quit glorifying violence, that one day we will beat our weapons into plowshares and teach our children to love God and each other.

> In God, whose word I praise, in the Lord, whose word I praise—in God I trust; I will not be afraid. What can man do to me?
>
> —PSALM 56:10–11

Thought . . . In these unsettling times, do you fear the future? Jesus is the same yesterday, today, and *tomorrow* (Hebrews 13:8). He will never fail you.

A Fork in the Road

BY SUSAN TITUS OSBORN

Obstacles are those frightful things you see when you take your eyes off your goal.

—HENRY FORD

I gripped my son's hand tightly as we hiked along the path through the towering redwoods. The massive trees obscured most of the sunlight. A light fog made the trail difficult to see, but I treasured this special time together.

Suddenly, we came to a fork in the road. My son asked, "Which way do we go, Mom?" His eyes conveyed trust. He assumed I knew the direction out of the woods, but I was caught up in listening to him and hadn't paid attention to where we had walked.

I paused for a moment and thought of how often forks in the road of life confront us. Frequently, when met by a fork, I have made split-second decisions that have affected my entire life. How different my experience might have been had I chosen other paths.

Yet, our decisions need not be made alone. God wants us to consult Him concerning even the smallest decisions in life. Through prayer and reading the Scriptures, we can stay in tune with God's direction for our lives.

I looked down one fork of the trail, which divided the world's tallest living trees. Then I gazed down the other. In the distance I saw a faint amber light, which I recognized as the sign on top of the mountain cabin resort where we were staying. With confidence I said, "This is the right path. Let's go."

Show me your ways, O Lord, teach me your paths; guide me in your truth and teach me, for you are God my Savior . . .
—PSALM 25:4–5

Thought . . . Are you at a crossroads in your spiritual journey? Stop. Look. Ask God to show you the good choice—the "ancient paths" of Scripture. Walk according to His will and find rest (Jeremiah 6:16).

You Can't Get There from Here

BY LESLIE WHITWORTH

What seems to be the end may really be a new beginning.

—ANONYMOUS

Just as dew sparkles at dawn then vanishes like a mirage, so there is a fragile, crystal silence in our house just before daybreak. Night noises fade and nature seems quietly suspended between darkness and morning's golden orb. On one such morning, as I watched the sunrise, a hummingbird beat against the inside of the screen door, desperate for freedom. I tried to shoo her out, to no avail. I eased toward her, my heart pounding in my ears. Her prickly claws clung to my extended finger. Whenever I moved, she took off in frenzied flight. Startled, I said, "I know what you want, but you can't get there from here." Again she perched on my finger. Cupping my hand over her buzzing wings and pushing the door with my hip, I released her into the glistening morning.

Still feeling the tickle of tiny talons on my finger, I wondered how many times I had beaten my head vainly against an obstacle. Recently divorced, I longed for the comfort of knowing the minute details of my children's lives. Did my son sleep all night at his dad's? Did my daughter eat breakfast? Did they have enough covers? Questions incessantly caromed around in my mind.

Yet, in that morning's experience, I felt the gentle guidance of God. I could not break down the barriers divorce had created in our lives. But if I could be still, perch in peace, and let myself be carried by His grace, God would bless us.

I can do everything through him who gives me strength.

—PHILIPPIANS 4:13

Thought . . . Are you suffering after divorce? God is the God of treasured fresh starts. His faithfulness is new every morning. Give this "new day" of your journey to Him. He promises to work *all* things out for your good (Romans 8:28).

A Record of Footprints

BY CAROL KUYKENDALL

Lives of great men all remind us we can make our lives sublime, and, departing, leave behind us footprints on the sands of time.

—HENRY WADSWORTH LONGFELLOW

Moms are the Keepers-of-Memories. For many of us, that instinct is knit deeply within our souls. That's one reason I started keeping track of my Footprints of Faith. I wanted a record of God's faithfulness in my life to remind me of His constant presence.

I started by writing down the defining moments or major milestones—places where life seemed to stop or change direction: some childhood memories; my marriage; the birth of our first child; the death of my father . . . Amazingly, I could see that God met me in each place, and I began to believe at least one of His promises in each experience. At each milestone, I took a step of growth in faith.

How about recording some of your own Footprints of Faith? Below are questions to get you thinking. Ask what you learned about God in each situation. If you answer, you have discovered your Footprints of Faith.

1) What is one of the most difficult experiences you've ever faced? What did you learn? 2) What is a time in which you really felt your mother's love? Your father's? 3) What experience has helped you recognize what matters most in your life? 4) What are your greatest temptations? 5) If you are married, what was your greatest adjustment? 6) If you are single, what is your greatest struggle? 7) If you have children, what was the most difficult challenge in adjusting to motherhood? 8) Describe a personal experience in which God seemed real to you.

A man's steps are directed by the Lord. How then can anyone understand his own way?

—PROVERBS 20:24

Thought . . . Do you have difficulty seeing God's interaction in your life's journey? Answer the above questions, and you will be amazed at how intricately He is involved in every "footstep" you take.

The Key to Joy

BY SUSAN M. WARREN

God's way may be harder for you, but it will be easier on you.

—H. HANSON

Oh, how it hurt. Although he tried to be gentle, my husband's words ripped open my heart. "I'm sorry, I just cannot allow you to do this job any longer." *Cannot allow?* My pride, my rebellious spirit bristled. "You are tired and crabby, and our family is suffering." I knew that he was right; my job as an accountant was taking its toll on our ministry and family life. From cold noodle dinners to canceled Bible studies, I had become a walking nerve. And now, expecting our fourth child, I knew that something had to give. "Please quit," he said, as I slammed the bathroom door in his face and collapsed, crying.

Surrender. It never came easily to me. I was the child who pushed curfew, the Christian who danced on the fence of disobedience. I had been known to shake my fist at God while He waited, patiently. But *this* submission would mean sacrificing a part of my identity, slicing off some self-esteem. My past journey with God reminded me that when I surrendered, He gave me the key to a closet of unimagined treasures . . . peace, untried spiritual gifts, blessings, joy. So why was I hanging onto this job like some sort of tenacious bulldog?

I slowly peeked through the door, and then abandoned myself into my husband's waiting arms, and into God's.

Six months later, I rocked my cooing baby, lingering in the precious treasure of "quantity time." Again, surrender had unlocked the door to true joy . . . just another step upon my spiritual journey.

". . . For I know the plans I have for you," declares the Lord, "plans to prosper you and not to harm you, plans to give you hope and a future. . . ."

—JEREMIAH 29:11

Thought . . . Do you refuse surrender to God? Because He loves you unconditionally, knows your future, and wants the best for you, surrender is the only thing that makes sense.

The Attitude of Christ

BY PAT PALAU

Whenever we sacrifice something—a circumstance, situation, notion—God always gives us something back that's far greater than we could dare ask or imagine!

—JONI EARECKSON TADA

Not long ago, during a time of personal turmoil, a childhood memory verse returned to my mind: "Thou God seest me." What a wonderful promise! God not only sees me, but He knows me.

In today's culture, we want to know ourselves. We desire to look inside, understand what we see, and verbalize it to others. Then we go a step further and ask the rest of the world to understand us, too.

People often say to me, "It must be so exciting to travel, to minister, and to see so much of the world." Such comments, however, reveal that the speaker doesn't fully comprehend all that is involved in the type of ministry that my husband and I have. I'm constantly tempted to offer a long explanation of the "flip side" of worldwide evangelism: that everyone does not love you, exotic food is not great as a steady fare, hotel pillows are often hard, and on and on.

Yet I can rest in that promise—"Thou God seest me." I can release the desire to receive the credit I feel I deserve, the bitterness of feeling misjudged in my motives, and the feeling that no one understands.

"Oh Lord, You have searched me and You know me (Psalm 139:1)." He has known me and has not turned away from me. He is the One Who truly understands me. And He dwells within me wherever I journey! Jesus Christ is my Maker. He will be faithful to develop a strategy to make me more like Himself.

Each of you should look not only to your own interests, but also to the interests of others. Your attitude should be the same as that of Christ Jesus.

—PHILIPPIANS 2:4–5

Thought . . . Are you lonely because no one understands you? Tell Jesus. He knows you, *and* He understands your feelings. He, too, was misunderstood. Receive His treasure of comfort.

Bible Sights Are Worth the Trip

BY ANN M. VELIA

God's Book is packed full of overwhelming riches; they are unsearchable—the more we have, the more there is to have.

—OSWALD CHAMBERS

Carlsbad Caverns is one of New Mexico's most beautiful treasures, and I love to take out-of-state friends to see it. We make the three-mile descent by foot along dank, dimly lit trails that wind steeply between fantastic formations.

We take our time—time to reflect about how the unobtrusive entrance belies the majesty hiding below—time to marvel at Jim White's bravery in exploring its virgin depths and the work it took to pave trails, set handrails, string electric lights, and construct the elevator that will eventually lift us back to the top—time to reflect on how God fills even the underside of our world with wonder like stone icicles and draperies, and glassy pools. The deeper we go, the more beautiful the sights we discover.

Reading God's Word is similar to a Caverns' visit. At first, my Bible seemed as murky as White's first look into the Caverns must have been. A friend suggested that I begin reading John's Gospel and his three epistles. In I John 4:8–10, I found the message of salvation that God offers through faith in the Living Word, Jesus Christ. Then the lights came on!

I've made many trips through the Bible now, alone, and in the company of skilled teachers. There's still much to discover in that eternal treasure. The deeper I go, the more beautiful the sights.

Oh, the depth of the riches of the wisdom and knowledge of God! How unsearchable his judgments, and his paths beyond tracing out!

—ROMANS 11:33

Thought . . . Like David, do you rejoice in following God's statutes as one who rejoices in great riches (Psalm 119:14)? You can't put a price tag on mining truth for yourself.

Grace for the Journey

BY KATHRYN THOMPSON PRESLEY

There is nothing but God's grace. We walk upon it; we breathe it; we live and die by it; it makes the nails and axles of the universe.

—ROBERT LOUIS STEVENSON

Iris testified to a thousand spellbound women at a retreat. She had been a prostitute and a drug dealer before the Lord drew her to Himself. Finally, she told of how she had knelt at the altar one night, a hooker, and "got up from my knees a lady!"

There were few dry eyes in the auditorium. I thanked God for Iris, but was uneasy that I had to follow her on the program. What could I possibly say—saved as a child, grown up in the Church, lived a squeaky-clean life? How blessed, yet how boring in comparison to Iris!

The words formed on my tongue on the way to the podium. "You've just heard a wonderful testimony from the Prodigal Daughter. Well, I'm the Elder Sister, but I want you to know, it took no more of God's grace to save Iris, nor any less than it did to save me."

It's a lesson I've had to relearn again and again. Earlier, as a teenager, I was concerned that so few had responded when I witnessed to classmates. When I talked to my pastor, he was kind, but straightforward: "Kathryn, do you think it's possible that you feel superior to your lost classmates? Perhaps they resent that. Remember that 'while we were yet sinners' our Lord loved us and died for us. Witnessing is only one beggar telling another where to find bread."

I've remembered that over the years; my pastor (and Iris) made a tremendous difference in my ministry and in my gratitude for God's grace.

But we have this treasure in jars of clay to show that this all-surpassing power is from God and not from us.
                                        —II CORINTHIANS 4:7

Thought . . . What keeps you from pride in sharing your testimony? What gives you the courage to share it? It's in knowing that you are a sinner, saved by God's grace, and that you still need His grace to live every day.

Letter from a Friend

BY MARGARET FISHBACK POWERS

We get no deeper into Christ than we allow Him to get into us.

—JOHN HENRY JOWETT

I am writing to say how much I care for you and how much I want you to know Me better. When you awoke this morning, I exploded a brilliant sunrise through your window trying to get your attention. You rushed off. Later, I spotted you walking and talking with some friends. I bathed you in warm sunshine. I perfumed the air with nature's sweet scent. You rushed off. You didn't notice Me. Then I shouted to you in a tornado. I painted you a beautiful rainbow in the sky. Then you gave Me a glance. Still you rushed off. That evening I spilled moonbeams in your face. I sent a cool breeze to rest you and take away your fear. I watched over you as you slept. I shared your thoughts. You were faintly aware I was so near. I've chosen you. I have a special task for you. I hope you will talk to Me soon. Only I brought you through the storm. Others saw no morn. I remain near.

I am your Friend. I love you very much.

Your Friend,
Jesus

We must pay more careful attention, therefore, to what we have heard, so that we do not drift away.

—HEBREWS 2:1

Thought . . . Has Jesus been trying to get your attention? Do you realize that the Lord of the Universe *longs* for "the treasure of your company" as you journey through life? Don't put Him off. Write a letter of apology, then of praise!

The Announcement

BY LaSARAH MONTGOMERY

In jealousy there is more of self-love, than of love to another.

—ROCHEFOUCAULD

I guessed the news by my husband's reaction: my sister-in-law, a bride of three months, was pregnant. Stunned, I grabbed the phone and called her, squealing my congratulations, but after hanging up, I felt that the wind had been knocked out of me. I had never thought of myself as being jealous, but it took that surprise announcement to reveal the twisted spirit of my heart.

I had initially liked Trina, but began to feel threatened by her after she married my brother-in-law and suddenly became the perfect daughter-in-law to my husband's family—the daughter-in-law that I felt I was not. I became cold toward her, convinced that she was unkind and hypocritical; but in my heart, I knew that the real problem was my jealousy.

I tossed and turned all night. I had always dreamed of having the first grandchild for my husband's family, offering something to them that would make them completely accept me. Now, I felt as though Trina had won hands down in the pageant of family devotion.

There was so much sludge in my heart that I didn't know where to begin to remove it. Jealousy was squelching what should have been a grateful heart, submitted to God's perfect plan. Somehow I had to grasp that this was *God's* best for my life's journey, even though I felt it was His worst. Slowly but surely, as He changed my attitude, He gave me the priceless treasure of a pure heart.

I could finally embrace the woman I had envied, and praise God for what I had originally found undesirable.

Therefore, rid yourselves of all malice and all deceit, hypocrisy, envy, and slander of every kind.

—I PETER 2:1

Thought . . . Is jealousy eating you alive? As you accept God's sovereignty, realizing that He only chooses His best for your life, you will learn to trust His plan and not envy others.

Lifeline

BY ANNETTE M. ECKART

Let nothing disturb you, nothing frighten you; all things are passing;
God never changes . . .

—SAINT TERESA OF AVILA

From the window of a Boston bagel shop, I watched thirteen awed preschoolers totter along a steamy street. Each clung with one hand to the bright red rope that passed between them. A parade of little legs, some chunky and sure, others slender and faltering, marched in a crooked line. Haphazardly they tripped along, oblivious to briskly passing adults. The tots' brightly colored clothes created a brilliant summer garden against a drab business suit landscape.

The children's heads turned in every direction, as if loosely affixed to their necks. The tinkling sound of ice-cream truck music, the sight of swan boats gliding over a lake, and the smell of grilled pretzels caused their heads to swivel. Startled by the roar of a passing bus, their eyes grew wide. Little fists clenching the cord indicated that the new tourists viewed the city as a scary place. Despite numerous distractions, they never let go of the safety of the rope.

Suddenly, I saw myself as one of them, tottering through a world filled with overwhelming sights and sounds. Obeying God's call to walk in a childlike way, I cling to the red rope of Jesus' Blood, the priceless treasure that keeps me safe. Jesus is my lifeline, my constancy in a frightening, constantly changing world. I need not fear becoming lost as I hold onto the lifeline of salvation. The children knew protection by holding the rope; they let nothing separate them from it. Jesus is the treasure Whom I grasp, journeying securely in His safekeeping.

For I am convinced that neither death nor life, neither angels nor demons, neither the present nor the future, nor any powers, neither height nor depth, nor anything else in all creation, will be able to separate us from the love of God that is in Christ Jesus our Lord.

—ROMANS 8:38–39

Thought . . . Do you have the treasure of eternal life?
Jesus' atoning blood is your only lifeline to salvation.
No one comes to God, except through Him (John 14:6).

It's Your Life, Lord

BY CYNTHIA HEALD

All to Jesus I surrender, Lord I give myself to Thee.
—JENNIE EVELYN HUSSEY

When my husband, Jack, and I moved to a new town some years ago, we had three small children all under three years old. Jack was beginning his veterinary practice. Because he treated large and small animals, he was usually gone twelve to fourteen hours a day. Besides having three small children, an absent husband and father, we lived in a very old house that had mice! I had no close friends—only One, Who heard my cry, "Lord! I can't go on anymore. I'm tired, I'm lonely, I want to give up." Unmistakably, I heard God's voice in my heart saying, "Good, I don't want you to go on in your own strength. I want to live your life for you." That was my initial surrendering. From that time on I began to understand that the Christian life is not imitation, but habitation. It's an exchanged life—His life for my life. Really, it's not an even exchange, as Elisabeth Elliot says. "What is ours belongs to Christ, but also what is His belongs to us!" Since I'm still in the process of becoming, I am continually challenged to surrender circumstances to Him daily. When I'm irritable and frustrated over situations I cannot control, God will gently ask, "Cynthia, whose life is it?" I have to answer, 'It's yours, Lord, it's yours."

> I have been crucified with Christ and I no longer live, but Christ lives in me. The life I live in the body, I live by faith in the Son of God, who loved me and gave himself for me.
> —GALATIANS 2:20

Thought . . . Have you surrendered your life to the Lord—not just when you received salvation, but by asking Him to take control of your daily living? When you do, the Lord is free to live His life *through* you. What have you got to lose, except your weakness?

Tennis Ball Blessings

BY JULIE EVANS

He does not bless us begrudgingly. There is a kind of eagerness about the beneficence of God. He does not wait for us to come to Him. He seeks us out, because it is His pleasure to do us good.

—JOHN PIPER

It was to be one of those bedtime chats for which my four-year-old daughter, Amanda, was famous. This time I was stumped. "Does God love Barbie?" she asked, with an earnestness that made me wish for her sake that He did. Not wanting to burst her bubble and not wanting to lie, I punted. "What do *you* think, sweetie?" She reasoned that He probably didn't, since dolls didn't have spirits. We were both satisfied. Sometimes a punt goes through the goal.

Four years later, I still ponder that conversation as I watch Amanda, and her questions, grow up. She is a deep little thinker as she lays herself down to sleep. During those times, I treasure her heart, listen to what's on it, and pray about those things. But God is even more intimately involved with the matters of Amanda's heart. He is building faith in her, allowing her to blossom as a believer in Him.

Last summer, Amanda wanted to learn how to play tennis. Elated at the thought, I bought her a racquet and we hit the courts. After a fun-filled first lesson, over a Mountain Dew, we talked about how "cool" it would be to find a big box of tennis balls at a garage sale. The very next week, we found exactly that.

I am reluctant to say that God cares about tennis balls. But He does care intimately about little girls who care about tennis balls and Barbie dolls. And He lets them know it!

For the eyes of the Lord range throughout the earth to strengthen those whose hearts are fully committed to him.

—II CHRONICLES 16:9A

Thought . . . How do you help your children grow in their journey with the Lord? Teach them to pray *specifically* for things that affect their little worlds. When God answers, they'll receive the treasure of a living faith.

Virtues

Wash Your Hands

BY KAREN BURTON MAINS

Christ is full and sufficient for all His people; . . . A Treasure to enrich; A Sun to enlighten; and a Fountain to cleanse.

—JOHN SPENCER

Although a child might protest having his head washed, he could spend endless moments with the plastic wind-up water toys—whales that spouted water, boats that chugged through bathtub lakes.

Getting a child into the tub could be a chore, but getting a child out of the tub could be a chore, as well.

I remember teaching a child how to wash his hands. I remember the chubby fingers and little palms. I remember rubbing the bar of soap and then rinsing them under the running water.

I remember the clean hands and face, the still dirt-streaked neck, and the bathroom towels stained with residue from too-hasty washings. I remember dirty denims in a pile on the floor, and grubby knees and matted hair and baby shampoo. I remember the miracle of that beautiful cherubic body all clean and soft and new; and the great terry towel smelling fresh from the laundry; and wrapping a child—hair and limbs washed, sweet and compliant now—in the folds.

"Tra-la! Tra-la!" I'd cry to my child in his terry cloth royal robe, "Here comes the little King!"

I remember the magic feel of a washed child in clean pajamas.

Our Heavenly Father takes intense pleasure in the washing of His children, too. He's a parent Who continually leads His children, soiled with the world, to the laver. He plunges our hands into the basin of water; we protest, "But I was playing!" Like any good parent, He teaches us how to become clean.

Come near to God and he will come near to you. Wash your hands, you sinners, and purify your hearts, you double-minded.

—JAMES 4:8

Thought . . . Do you need to "come to the laver"? Only Jesus' blood can cleanse you fully. Receive His salvation. Then ask God to cleanse sin's daily dirt from your feet (John 13:6–11).

Poetically Speaking

BY LYNN D. MORRISSEY

Do you wish people to speak well of you? Don't speak well of yourself.

—BLAISE PASCAL

One thing I treasure most is God's use of humor to correct my character flaws. As a beginning writer, I was convinced I was another Elizabeth Barrett Browning. Yet, despite my pride, I still enrolled in a university poetry workshop. Led by a free-spirit-starving-graduate student in ballooning blouses and long skirts, would-be poets dissected poems and the poets who wrote them. Having my wonderful work picked apart like a leftover turkey carcass, feeling my bare bones scraping the page, was no fun, but began God's humbling process.

The capstone was the "Poetry Potluck " at our teacher's apartment. I joined the circle of promising poets, ready to recite what I considered to be my latest *masterpiece*.

Before we began, our teacher left to go find Sophocles. While I failed to understand how philosophy pertained to poetry, nothing my eccentric mentor did surprised me! She flowed out of the room and in again, and we commenced.

She began talking to her sleeve in saccharine, high-pitched squeals. Suddenly, it became apparent that Sophocles was her pet gerbil, until he had crawled completely out of her sleeve, revealing his long *rat's* tail! Emitting countertenor squeals in harmony with his mistress, he scampered gleefully from poet's lap to poet's lap.

Rising in a flamboyant Shakespearean gesture, I recited my poem on my feet, *pacing!* I had been upstaged by a rat! Completely humbled, I offered to do the dishes, and made a sweeping exit, stage left, to the kitchen. I did not wait to hear applause.

Pride goes before destruction, a haughty spirit before a fall.

—PROVERBS 16:18

Thought . . . Are you proud about your talents and achievements? Humble yourself before the Lord before He humbles you. Any talent you have is a generous gift of grace from God.

Choosing Life

BY GAIL MACDONALD

You can't do anything about the length of your life, but you can do something about its width and depth.

—EVAN ESAR

A friend of mine had sought to define purpose for herself. "Choose life," she wrote as she put an entire life's purpose into two words. That simple affirmation springing from the Book of Deuteronomy meant that whenever she had a choice to make, the life-giving solution was the one that would help her make up her mind. "We can eat a candy bar or an apple," she said. "But which leads to a greater quality of health? We can watch TV or read a book. But which leads to a greater quality of growth? We can say the loving word or critical word. But which conveys the quality of personal nourishment?" And so she chose to drive her purpose—the choice of vital, healthy, growth-oriented life. Her dream is to help others choose life as well. Will they embrace life as Christ offers it or resist and break themselves over His truth?

As I pursued the formulation of a formal statement of purpose, . . . it was important to me that my purpose sprang from the Scriptures, so I began to scan them for someone whose life rang true to what I believed God was asking me to become, someone whose devotion to Christ would stretch me beyond where I was or ever dreamed I could be. And I found her! Mary of Bethany—sister to Martha, sister to Lazarus, and friend to Jesus—a fascinating woman who understood perfectly how to make a difference whenever she was with Jesus and His friends.

> . . . Mary . . . sat at the Lord's feet listening to what he said. . . . the Lord answered ". . . only one thing is needed. Mary has chosen what is better, and it will not be taken away from her."
>
> —LUKE 10:39–42

Thought . . . What is your mission? Write a "motto" based on how you will use your spiritual gifts and life-experiences to glorify God. Live with purpose!

Time for a Change

BY PATTY STUMP

A smile is the light in the window of your face that tells people you're at home.

—ANONYMOUS

It was time for a change! Without any reservations, I informed the hairdresser to chop my locks in order to give me a "new look"! Carefully, she snipped and clipped, styled and smiled, leaving me with a snappy "new do" that I was sure my family would appreciate. When I returned home, my eight-year-old daughter exclaimed that I looked *different*. "It's my new haircut!" I responded. Thoughtfully, she studied me before commenting that it wasn't the haircut that made me look different. Hesitantly she added, "You look different with a big smile on your face!" *What? A smile?* "Don't I usually smile?" I inquired. "Nope," she said.

I suddenly realized that amid the hustle and bustle of life I had become preoccupied with tasks to be done and piles to overcome. As I struggled to juggle it all, I had lost perspective on what was most important and, in turn, failed to reflect a joyful countenance to my family. Proverbs 15:13 states, "A joyful heart makes a cheerful face." What I project to others will be a reflection of what I treasure deeply within my heart.

My daughter was right; I hadn't smiled in awhile. As I prioritized my relationship with God, my countenance began to reflect a joy that came from time spent with Him. In essence, as I adjusted my heart towards Him, I began to experience a "facelift" that others were bound to notice! The next time I consider redoing my *external*, I will first review what's *internal* and, in response, make certain I'm prioritizing what's *eternal*!

A cheerful heart is good medicine, but a crushed spirit dries up the bones.

—PROVERBS 17:22

Thought . . . Are you smiling? Even though a smile usually indicates a joyous mood, try smiling or singing even when you're unhappy. Often when you "set the stage" for joy, the real treasure soon follows.

Taking the Road Test

BY CHARLOTTE ADELSPERGER

Stewardship is not a classroom exercise in fractions. It is a homework assignment in total living.

—KENNETH L. WILSON

One spring many years ago, near the end of my first year of teaching, I proudly purchased my first new car. It was a shiny light blue compact, paid for in full from my careful savings. Before I took my new prize out on its first drive, I stood beside it and prayed something like this: "Oh God, thank You for this beautiful car! All that I have is from You, so I dedicate this car to You right now."

Within a week, a test of my stewardship came as I was driving home from school in a downpour. I saw a drenched elderly woman dragging along, lugging a shopping bag. I offered her a ride. When she climbed in, the whole front seat of the car sunk down. Her feet were covered with soggy mud that squished all over the floor of my new car.

She directed me to her home up a gravel muddy road, climbed out, and mumbled, "Thanks." As I drove home I saw slush hardening on the floor, and I heard mud chunks flying off the wheels. I cringed. Then it hit me: that woman was one of the "least of these" who happened to come queen-sized—with mud. God had allowed me to take *my* treasure out for a road test, where I encountered one whom *He* treasured, a woman in need.

> "The King will reply, 'I tell you the truth, whatever you did for one of the least of these brothers of mine, you did for me.'"
>
> —MATTHEW 25:40

Thought . . . When you meet the needy, do you help like the "good" Samaritan, or cross the road like the Levite? People treasure your smile, touch, words, and material aid. Jesus treasures your obedience.

A Little Night Work

BY ELIZABETH GEORGE

As every thread of gold is valuable, so is every minute of time.

—JOHN MASON

When I began working at night rather than plopping down in front of TV, I struggled! Making the commitment to use evenings to help my ministry, I learned to use my evenings in useful and creative ways. Now I value evenings that were a hidden treasure.

Finding this gift of time for a little night work opened up a new life. Christian Development Ministries was birthed by Jim and me ten years ago. A wiser use of evenings has given me the time to develop and use my spiritual gifts to enrich lives of Christian women. I shudder to think what I would be doing if I had continued to throw away God's gift of evenings!

Make evenings count! Hopefully these steps that revolutionized my life—and my evenings—will encourage you.

1. *Evaluate your evenings*—I heard the highest paid sports agent in the world speaking on the importance of time [state] that he plans his day in twenty-minute increments. Do you know how you spend every twenty minutes of your evenings? This can be quite an eye-opening exercise!

2. *Plan your evenings*—One Sunday at church I walked past a friend. Thankfully she grabbed my arm so I could share in a wonderful thing that had happened—she had lost forty pounds! When I asked her how she had done it, she told me that she had decided to exercise every night after work. Her goal for the new year had been to incorporate that one activity into her evenings. In other words, she planned her evenings—and she's definitely enjoying the payoff!

For there is a proper time and procedure for every matter . . .

—ECCLESIASTES 8:6

Thought . . . Before you say good night, do you have a *good* night—a productive one? If you've run out of time, discover evening's gold mine of minutes. For most, they're hidden treasure. Use them wisely.

Monkey Love

BY RACHEL ST. JOHN-GILBERT

To know even one life has breathed easier because you lived . . . this is to have succeeded.

—RALPH WALDO EMERSON

"That guy's got a lot of guts," I mumbled under my breath. "It's not just anyone who can walk around with a gorilla wrapped around his neck."

Yet there he was, Dr. Sandy Outlar, with a stuffed gorilla dangling down his torso. The newly hired, highly touted superintendent of Norfolk Christian Schools was busy captivating the imaginations of the knee-high brethren. He was introducing the concept of spiritual "gorilla warfare"—punctuating each point with an ear-piercing *SCREECH!*

Dr. Outlar captured my heart, as well, during that September morning safari. I had recently begun to theorize that people who have been broken in some way—emotionally, relationally, financially—tend to take more initiative and risks in reaching out to others.

This theory proved to be true of the esteemed Dr. Outlar, as I later learned that his childhood had been marred by living with an alcoholic father. Small wonder that he would risk his pride and reputation in the eyes of some in order to brighten the day of even one child.

It's so tempting to want to hide behind the facade of appearances, falsely believing that each golden brick of accomplishment will somehow validate our existence. Maybe what God is looking for instead are a few good primates—believers willing to make monkeys of themselves for the sake of love.

Therefore, as God's chosen people, holy and dearly loved, clothe yourselves with compassion, kindness, humility, gentleness and patience.

—COLOSSIANS 3:12

Thought . . . Do you have the courage to touch someone's heart with the truth of your past—whether revealing your own sin or those perpetrated against you? When you do, you validate God's presence in an often cold, uncaring world.

Do What?

BY CAROLE MAYHALL

Anger is quieted by a gentle word just as fire is quenched by water.

—JEAN PIERRE CAMUS

Joyce was a small explosive brunette with a temper the size of an atomic cloud. She was not one to cross! Our teacher left the room and put me in charge as monitor. Joyce immediately began acting up. I asked her as nicely as I could to please stop disrupting. I was forced to report her conduct to the teacher who gave Joyce a stern lecture. Joyce hissed, "Just you wait until recess!" In my imagination, I saw a banshee-from-hell pulling out my hair.

At noon I fled home, scared and miserable. Mom asked, "Honey, what's the matter?" I poured out my tale of woe. Mom listened calmly, then said, "Carole, take her an apple." I wailed, "What good will that do?" "The Bible says to 'do good to those who are spiteful to you.'"

I wrestled with her suggestion, but after lunch, stepped up to Joyce's desk and put the apple before her, and mumbled, "I'm sorry you are so angry." Joyce's mouth dropped open. She finally stammered lamely, "I guess I deserved it." Situation diffused, Joyce and I eventually grew to be friends.

The concept of doing something nice for someone who doesn't like you has stayed with me as I saw Mom live out that concept. When a jealous lady at church began spreading ugly rumors about Mom, Mother sent her a red rose every day for a week with an encouraging Scripture verse. That woman became one of Mom's most staunch defenders.

Mom taught the command of Jesus, ". . . Do good to those who hate you . . ."

A hot-tempered man stirs up dissension, but a patient man calms a quarrel.

—PROVERBS 15:18

Thought . . . Can you let go of your pride and love your "enemies" when they have treated you unjustly? You'll obey Jesus' command, and possibly gain a new friend.

He's My Friend

BY DORIS SMALLING

Wisdom comes alone through suffering.

—AESCHYLUS

"No, Roger," I interrupted my fourteen-year-old son, "I don't want you testifying for Tom."

"Mom, I can prove that Tom didn't take anything from the equipment room."

"The janitor saw Tom, not you, so don't get involved."

"Tom and I saw the door open, and he shut it."

"Tom's family is moving soon, but you'll still be here. The kids will pick on you. In a new school, Tom will soon forget."

Roger mumbled, "I won't."

"I said no. That's it."

With my hectic work schedule, I nearly forgot Roger's problem. He reminded me the following week. "Tom won't speak to me even to say good-bye. I don't blame him." Tears sprinkled his "starting-to-fuzz" face. "I wonder if Tom would have deserted me."

Later, the guilty confessed. Tom moved. Roger and his hurt were still at home. My son valued friendship above all. In attempting to fend off his hurt, I unwittingly had inflicted more. Gratefully, I learned early not to try insulating my children from life—not to become a lifetime buffer for them. I could instill a moral foundation, using God's Word, but I couldn't step in front of life's challenges. God doesn't say, "Shield a child . . . " He says, "Train a child in the way he should go . . . (Proverbs 22:6)." Time heals, and the boys restored their treasured friendship. Repentant, I placed this experience deep within a small box that I've labeled, "Lessons Learned the Hard Way."

Coral and jasper are not worthy of mention; the price of wisdom is beyond rubies.

—JOB 28:18

Thought . . . When you make a judgment error in either disciplining or protecting your child, do you apologize? Children treasure a parent's humility, and it becomes a great teaching tool.

Virtue's Résumé

BY ARMENÉ HUMBER

Gratitude is an offering precious in the sight of God, and it is one that the poorest of us can make and be not poorer, but richer for having made it.

—A. W. TOZER

"The skill I'm most proud of is . . ." She glanced nervously at her classmates, then finished the sentence, " . . . communicating." The woman next to her began the sentence again, continuing this final exercise of the day.

To identify a skill, then publicly announce it, was a challenge for most of the women struggling in this Job Seeker's class to forge a career from shattered confidence and outdated skills. Each faced unique obstacles—long résumé gaps, computer illiteracy, age discrimination, and more. Each needed to find the treasure within her that would give her the confidence to face the career search process. As a new instructor, I was fascinated by how effectively this simple exercise built confidence.

I glanced ahead to Carmen, wondering how she would handle it. Carmen concerned me most. A new believer, she had recently escaped a long, abusive marriage and had come to us from a shelter in donated clothes. To add to her difficulty, English wasn't her first language, and she struggled simply to express herself. Several times, she had run from class in panic. *Where would she find confidence for an interview? What skill would she treasure?* I wondered.

Suddenly it was her turn. "The skill I'm most proud of is . . . gratitude." Gratitude? A *skill?* It wasn't on our skill list. But that didn't matter. Carmen had found her treasure. In spite of all she had overcome and all that she faced, she had learned that gratitude is a skill highly treasured by God, the giver of lasting confidence. It's there for the taking. We need only use it.

And whatever you do, whether in word or deed, do it all in the name of the Lord Jesus, giving thanks to God the Father through him.

—COLOSSIANS 3:17

Thought . . . Do you feel impoverished, lacking talents, skills, and possessions? Count your blessings. When you are grateful for what you already have, you'll be amazed at how rich you actually are.

Potato Chip Moments

BY GAIL MACDONALD

If we are ever in doubt about what to do, it is a good rule to ask ourselves what we shall wish on the morrow that we had done.

—SIR JOHN LUBBOCK

A friend returned to the United States after spending four years in a developing country. "What has been your biggest shock in reentering our culture?" I asked. "Walking down the potato chip aisle in the supermarket," she answered. I laughed because on the surface her comment did not seem profound. She went on.

"The potato chip aisle is symbolic of everything our family seems to be facing on this visit home. Four years ago when I went shopping, there were only a few varieties of chips. Now I find I am faced with more choices than I have time for. I'm almost paralyzed by indecision. Why should I spend important minutes deciding what kind of a chip I'm going to buy?

"My friends aren't aware of the energy it's taking, they've gotten so used to the subtle enslavement. When the truly important issues need our attention, our energies have already been squandered on trivia."

What a difference my friend's insight has made in my life. "Potato chip moments," I have begun calling them—times when one gets inundated by insignificant choices. If we lack a perceived purpose, we are slowed to a crawl because we aren't sure what is truly important.

Unless there is a strong sense of purpose lurking somewhere within us, we can expect our lives either to bang about like the ball in a pinball machine or to come under the control of those who are more than glad to create purposes for us.

Be very careful, then, how you live—not as unwise but as wise, making the most of every opportunity, because the days are evil.

—EPHESIANS 5:15–16

Thought . . . Are you traumatized by trivia, accomplishing little? Eliminate life's potato chips and concentrate on the meat and potatoes of God's Word. It shows you what's truly important.

A Little Child Shall Lead Them

BY PENNY J. CLARK

Well done is better than well said.

—BENJAMIN FRANKLIN

Attending a Christian preschool, my daughter Emily learned the alphabet by memorizing Scriptures beginning with each of the letters. On weekends, she proudly brought home her growing collection of alphabet cards, asking her father and me to help her practice.

On weekend five, the preschool recitation became a memorable lesson in practical theology.

"All have sinned and fall short of the glory of God; Believe in the Lord Jesus and you will be saved; Children, obey your parents in the Lord, for this is right; Do to others what you would have them do to you; Even a child is known by his Deweys."

Startled, I asked Emily to repeat the *new* verse.

"Even a child is known by his Deweys. You know, Mom, like Mr. Dewey at church."

Her obvious sincerity made me stifle the chuckle in my throat. Bob and Carolyn Dewey, a lovely young couple active in our church, were recognized role models throughout the congregation.

Now, assuming the preschool teacher hadn't clarified week five's verse, my husband pointed out the correct word "doings (KJV)." We discussed what a child's doings might include, and how they should reflect Jesus to others.

"Like Mr. Dewey at church," Emily repeated firmly.

It was one of those moments that parents dread: we quoted the verse correctly, but our preschooler understood it better. We, too, are known by our doings. Will those who meet the Clarks recognize Jesus? Will He be known accurately by our "Clarks"?

". . . let your light shine before men, that they may see your good deeds and praise your Father in heaven."

—MATTHEW 5:16

Thought . . . Are you setting a godly example for your children? Remember that your "doings" speak louder than your "tellings" . . . your actions, louder than your words.

Full of Beans

BY JOHN-EVA B. ORSA

If your desires be endless, your cares and fears will be so, too.

—THOMAS FULLER

I was a hunter. There it is! I've said it . . . and I'm still somewhat embarrassed to admit it.

I had quite a trophy case filled with "treasures" I had trapped, bagged, and dragged home. It had started innocently enough when I acquired two of the furry little things. And then a friend invited me to go hunting with her!

We had rushed off hastily, just before dawn and, as we rounded the corner to our intended hunting ground, we were dismayed to find that sixty hunters had arrived before us. Camped out in front of the toy store, they obviously desired the coveted Beanie Babies, even above sleep! I wish I could say that that was my first and last expedition, but I went on several other safaris to track down what had become my heart's desire.

However, hunting season came to an abrupt end one day when I was standing in line with a few dozen adults and several bewildered children. Suddenly, it hit me like a lightning bolt when I thought about why we were there. We were all waiting for the two Beanies from the *Hercules* movie, appropriately named Pain and Panic. God's wonderful still, small voice appealed directly to my heart: "Who in his right mind would want to acquire Pain and Panic?!" It was just the treasured wisdom that this hunter needed to hear to recapture my wayward heart . . . and to empty out a trophy case!

". . . But store up for yourselves treasures in heaven, where moth and rust do not destroy, and where thieves do not break in and steal. . . ."

—MATTHEW 6:20

Thought . . . Are you collecting "treasure," in reality "stuff," that clutters your house and that will one day be destroyed? Dig for gold in God's Word like one who finds great spoil (Psalm 119:162). His Word is eternal (Psalm 119:89).

Consecration

BY HANNAH WHITALL SMITH

EDITOR'S NOTE: Mrs. Smith was a Quaker and well-known nineteenth century Christian writer.

Consecration is handing God a blank sheet to fill in with your name signed at the bottom.

—M. H. MILLER

I was once trying to explain to a physician who had charge of a large hospital the necessity and meaning of consecration, but he seemed unable to understand. At last I said to him, "Suppose, in going your rounds among your patients, you should meet with one man who entreated you earnestly to take his case under your especial care in order to cure him, but who should at the same time refuse to tell you his symptoms or to take all your prescribed remedies, and should say to you, 'I am quite willing to follow your directions as to certain things, because they commend themselves to my mind as good, but in other matters I prefer judging for myself, and following my own directions.' What would you do in such a case?" I asked. "Do!" he replied with indignation, "Do! I would soon leave such a man as that to his own care. For, of course," he added, "I could do nothing for him unless he would put his whole case into my hands without any reserves, and would obey my directions implicitly." "It is necessary, then," I said, "for doctors to be obeyed if they are to have any chance to cure their patient?" *"Implicitly obeyed!"* was his emphatic reply. "And that is consecration," I continued. "God must have the whole case put into His hands without any reserves, and His directions must be implicitly followed." "I see it," he exclaimed, "I see it! And I will do it. God shall have His own way with me from henceforth."

Commit your way to the Lord . . .

—PSALM 37:5

Thought . . . Have you put every aspect of your life into God's hands—no holds barred? When you do, He promises to give you the desires of your heart, and to make your righteousness shine like dawn (Psalm 37:4–6). For what are you waiting?

Eighty-Six That Broad?

BY BETTY HUFF

The quality of mercy is not strained, it droppeth like the gentle rain
from Heaven.

—WILLIAM SHAKESPEARE

It was 2:00 A.M. and I was working the graveyard shift at a busy
restaurant. The bars had just closed and their boisterous, inebri-
ated patrons were filling our booths and counter stools, loudly
demanding coffee and food.

One was so quiet, though, that except for her clothes, I hardly
noticed her. She was wearing a paint-spattered tee shirt over
torn pedal pushers and furry pink bedroom slippers. Her hair
was wrapped around oversized rollers, and makeup smeared her
puffy face.

She ordered a chef's salad and, after I served it, I forgot all
about her until the cook yelled, "Eighty-six that broad!"—a restaurant term meaning "kick her out." Her head had dropped into
the salad, and her face was covered with ham, cheese, and
Roquefort dressing. She looked so pitiful that I couldn't put her
out in that condition, so I helped her to the ladies' room and
gently cleaned her face.

Months later, an attractive woman sat at my counter. "You
don't recognize me, do you?" she asked. "You waited on me one
night when I was in such bad shape that the cook wanted to
'eighty-six' me. I had been painting the living room that evening
when a policeman knocked on my door. He told me that my
only child had just been killed in an accident. Driving home
from the morgue, I planned to commit suicide, but turned into
your restaurant instead. You were so compassionate, it gave me
the strength to go on."

"Do to others as you would have them do to you. . . ."

—LUKE 6:31

Thought . . . Are you quick to judge others by their
appearances or actions before understanding what's
behind them? Reach out with the treasure of Christ's
tenderness and you might find a hurting heart in need
of His touch.

A Heart Attitude

BY EDWINA PATTERSON

Those who can see God's hand in everything can best leave everything in God's hand.

—ROBERT C. SAVAGE

When our son was in high school, he and his dad built a car from scratch. The hours they spent under the car together were wonderful teaching experiences, and my husband, R. J., took advantage of this opportunity to teach spiritual truths, as well.

When they couldn't get the motor to run, they prayed together for God's guidance and wisdom. They discussed perseverance—the importance of not quitting just because life gets difficult. When they were wiring the windshield wipers and air conditioning, they discussed the wonders and intricacies of the working mechanisms of the car. R. J. wove into the conversation the intricacies and wonders of our human bodies that God has created. They learned to depend upon our omniscient God to direct every single item they assembled.

It took them a year and a half to complete the car. When it passed inspection, we all celebrated—not so much because of the resulting vehicle, but because of the rewards of perseverance and patience. Most importantly, a young teenage boy learned the necessity of taking everything to the Lord in prayer, completely depending upon Him to guide every decision.

I learned that family devotional times do not have to be every Tuesday night at 7:00 P.M. They can be anytime. True worship can occur in your backyard, in the kitchen, or under the hood. True worship is an attitude of the heart!

> These commandments that I give you today are to be upon your hearts. Impress them on your children. Talk about them when you sit at home and when you walk along the road, when you lie down and when you get up.
> —DEUTERONOMY 6:6–7

Thought . . . Do your children only learn about God in church? Teaching them God's truth is your responsibility. Opportunities to apply truth abound, if you use daily experiences as the training ground.

Simple Acts of Love

BY STORMIE OMARTIAN

The Christian home is the Master's workshop where the process of character-molding is silently, lovingly, faithfully, and successfully carried on.

—RICHARD MONCKTON MILNES

When our children were small, my husband and I worked at home. We had a treasured saying we found necessary to keep repeating to each other: *Remember, love is letting someone help you even when you can do it better by yourself.*

Countless times one of us would call across the house to the other, "Please remind me what love is again!"

This was a signal that one of us was trying to get some work done, but it was taking far longer than expected because one of the children was "helping." The person responding would either come to the rescue and divert the "helper" into performing another important task, or simply quote the treasured saying with an understanding smile.

We learned that acts of humble and sacrificial love happen when we include someone else in our lives, even when it would be far more convenient not to do so.

Love is patient, love is kind. It does not envy, it does not boast, it is not proud.

—I CORINTHIANS 13:4

Thought . . . What's one definition for love? Learning to Overlook a child's Voluntary Endeavors to help, even when they're not helpful. Children love to be involved in your life. Welcome them!

Gifts

The Angel

BY ANNETTE SMITH

Only the heart knows how to find what is precious.

—FYODOR DOSTOYEVSKY

Newly employed, I looked forward to attending my first hospital Christmas celebration. Weeks before, the party committee had chosen a menu, set a date, and supervised the drawing of names for the gift exchange. Adding to my anticipation was the fact that I'd drawn the name of my new friend, Yvonne. Choosing her present would be easy. She loved angels.

I crafted her gift using scraps of inexpensive muslin and snippets of old lace. I gleaned from my daughter's hair ribbons a length of narrow, rose-colored satin. Tied in a soft bow, the ribbon shaped the angel's waist. From a frayed and faded antique quilt, I cut a pair of heart-shaped wings. A circle of tiny crystal beads formed a stitched-on halo. I thought the finished angel lovely. I was sure that Yvonne would be pleased.

However, at the party, when people began opening their packages, I realized others had brought elegant, expensive items. I began to feel embarrassed about my homemade angel, and wished I had brought something nicer. I watched Yvonne open my gift. "She's beautiful!" she gushed.

"I didn't know what to get you," I spoke apologetically. "So unique!" Yvonne exclaimed. "Just old bits and pieces," I mumbled.

"Perhaps so," Yvonne interrupted, "but put together like this, those bits and pieces make something wonderful. This angel reminds me of how God takes the scraps of our lives and, through His love, transforms us into something beautiful. Thank you. I will treasure her forever!" And I, Yvonne, will always treasure you.

How can we thank God enough for you in return for all the joy we have in the presence of our God because of you?

—I THESSALONIANS 3:9

Thought . . . What would your friend most treasure? Give what's most important—your time and heartfelt sharing. Consider her tastes *and* your budget. Make gift selections to accommodate both.

God's Greatest Gift

BY MOTHER TERESA

A world without children is a world without newness, regeneration, color, and vigor.

—JAMES C. DOBSON

Some parents feel great love and tenderness for their children.

I remember the instance of an Indian mother who had twelve children; the youngest of all was in terrible shape. I would have a hard time describing what the child looked like, emotionally or physically.

When I suggested taking the child to one of our homes, where we had many more in similar conditions, the mother started to sob. "Please, Mother Teresa, don't say that! This child is the greatest gift God has given my family. All our love is showered on her. If you take her away from us, our lives would have no more meaning."

> Blessed is the man whose quiver is full of [children]. They will not be put to shame when they contend with their enemies in the gate.
>
> —PSALM 127:5

Thought . . . Do you become easily exasperated with your children's antics or misbehavior? Think about what life would be like without them. You wouldn't trade them for the world!

Giving My Two Cents Worth

BY SANDI GORDON

Nobody is so poor that he or she has nothing to give, and nobody is so rich that he or she has nothing to receive.

—POPE JOHN PAUL II

I was waiting in the checkout line at a shoe store when I over-heard the cashier tell the man who was at the front of the line that his purchase totaled $48.02. Moments later, the cashier asked the man if he happened to have the two cents. The tall thin man, dressed in a plaid shirt and blue jeans, dug deeply into his pants pocket before shaking his head and replying, "No."

Surely I have two pennies, I thought. But simultaneously, another thought came to me. *Do I really want to get involved? Do I really want to bother getting out my wallet to check?*

Deciding that my walk with Christ would not allow me to ignore this opportunity to reach out, I pulled out my wallet and recovered two shiny copper-colored coins. As I set the pennies on the counter, the man was filled with gratitude. From his re-sponse, you would have thought that I had offered to pay his entire bill! The man thanked me numerous times, and a final time as he was leaving the store.

Why had such a small gift meant so much to this stranger? I am doubtful that it was the two cents. After pondering this ques-tion, I have decided that it was the tiny witness he had received that love is still present in this world—love that is willing to bother getting involved. For a mere two cents, I had given this stranger a gift for which there is no price tag.

And do not forget to do good and to share with others, for with such sacrifices God is pleased.

—HEBREWS 13:16

Thought . . . Like the Good Samaritan (Luke 10:29–37), do you become involved in the lives of those in need? Even the tiniest gesture (your two cents worth), is more than most people receive in a lifetime. Offer Christ's treasure of kindness.

Broken Pot

BY JANE TOD JIMENEZ

What is a friend? A single soul dwelling in two bodies.

—ARISTOTLE

The pot sits on the window ledge above my desk where I work every day. It links me to a treasured friend. Though forty years my senior, Marion seems like my sister. We've shared our faith, our writing, and books. Most importantly, we've shared the past three years of pain following the deaths of her husband and my mother. In the same month, Marion and I were united in the loneliness and grief that fills your soul where a loved one once lived.

We've cried, shared, traveled, and laughed. So I wasn't surprised when I found her gift on my doorstep. I opened the tiny box to find a delicate ceramic bowl made of overlapping leaves reaching up from the bottom in golds and greens, finishing at the top in a fluted edge of leaf points.

To my surprise, there was a web of yellowed cracks where someone had glued the broken pot back together. Puzzled, I wondered at Marion's gift. I knew that she had purposely chosen it for me. I chuckled, and wondered if I should ask her about the cracks. Had she even noticed them? Her handwritten card explained.

"How wonderful to find friends in life! And this little 'whatcha-macallit' is to remind you of the fact that God takes our lives, mends them, making them beautiful when we let Him . . . and to remind you of me—one fragmented life that God, in His mercy, has put back together." Amen, my friend.

. . . O Lord, you are our Father. We are the clay, you are the potter; we are all the work of your hand.

—ISAIAH 64:8

Thought . . . Have you let your friends see your "cracks"? As you reveal your vulnerability, it allows others to share their own hurts. Your pursuit of perfection may prevent them from releasing their pain.

Heaven-Sent

BY MARILYN WILLETT HEAVILIN

I have a song that Jesus gave me; it was sent from Heaven above.

—ELTON M. ROTH

When Nate died, I asked for a special gift from the Lord—[that] I would be able to remember the sound of his voice.

I started to play a cassette tape of myself when I was speaking at a luncheon [and] inadvertently placed the tape into the recorder on the wrong side. I listened to the woman speaking and thought, *Who is that? That isn't my voice.* I realized I had discovered a tape of one of Nathan's voice lessons! I prayed, "Oh God, please let me hear him clearly; don't tease me." As he began to sing, the teacher suggested he move closer to her, which was also closer to the tape recorder. I could hear him perfectly. God answered my prayer! I sat sobbing as I heard Nate sing one song and discuss it with his teacher.

She asked, "Nate do you have any more songs?"

He answered, "I've got one more. It isn't my favorite, but it's my mom's favorite and I want to learn it for her!"

I hungrily devoured each precious note as Nate sang the beautiful melody, "Pierce My Ear, O Lord."

The teacher said, "Nate, that was beautiful. I understand why your mom likes that song."

Nate said, "Yeah, not much melody, but kind of mellow."

Can you possibly imagine the joy I felt as I listened to my Nate sing? It was like a special delivery letter from heaven. More than two years after Nate's death, God answered my request that I would never forget the sound of his voice.

. . . watch yourselves closely so that you do not forget the things your eyes have seen or let them slip from your heart . . .

—DEUTERONOMY 4:9

Thought . . . Will you bequeath your children money only? Make a recording of your speaking or singing. When they miss you most, the sound of your voice will be Heaven-sent.

Appearances Can Be Deceiving

BY SUZY RYAN

Let me worship You in the cathedral of my heart, not just store spiritual information in the concordance of my mind.

—ANONYMOUS

What a perfect present! My son loved the baseball glove I had bought him. Unfortunately, it would not mold to his hand. We stretched it, oiled it, and rubber banded it, but the harder we tried, the stiffer it appeared. Then we looked carefully at the writing and saw the disclaimer: leather laces only. This rigor mortis glove was a fraud!

Later that day, a friend came over to bake Easter cookies with my children. She asked for a Bible, so I handed her mine thinking, *She will think that I'm so spiritual with my highlighted Bible!* Immediately, God convicted me of my pride. I realized how much I resembled that plastic glove. Embarrassed I prayed, "Forgive me, Lord, for always wanting people's applause. Help me quit bringing attention to myself, and not to You."

After my friend left, I thought about the flashy glove and its poor quality. Although the dazzle had deceived my untrained eye, God is never deluded by some cheap imitation. He knows our spiritual condition, our unspoken thoughts, and how worn our Bibles are. More importantly, He knows if His words have penetrated our softened, teachable hearts, or have boomeranged off our hard, synthetic faith.

Thankfully, God is teaching me to worship Him in the cathedral of my heart, and not just in the concordance of my mind. I am learning that quality, like real faith, often is understated and inconspicuous. Since He is not a phony god, but the one true living God, thankfully, His patience never wears out. Now, that's something to treasure!

The pride of your heart has deceived you . . .

—OBADIAH 1:3

Thought . . . Are you proud of your humility? The best way to overcome the deceptiveness of your heart, is to daily ask God to "search" it (Psalm 139:23–24) and confess the sin He reveals.

Priceless Gifts

BY ANNIE CHAPMAN

In the same way that "God's wondrous gift" came to Bethlehem, silently, so Christ comes into our lives today.

—KENNETH OSBECK

During years of giving and receiving Christmas gifts, I received four that have immeasurable worth.

My first Christmas with my husband, though money was scarce, Steve gave me three roses. Those roses represented so much that was true and lovely.

The second unforgettable gift was given by our son. Nathan gave me a basket with dried flowers. Inside was a card inscribed, "Thank you, Mom, for teaching me to read." Years later, when I see Nathan's Bible, where he reads it each night, I remember that note of thanks.

The third special gift came from mother. Mom had been diagnosed with cancer. Mom's gift changed a Christmas I didn't want to remember into one that I will never forget. Mom made an audio tape about her childhood. During that time of pain, disease, grief and dying, Mother shared her life. That tape, a treasure beyond all measure, is safely protected.

Our daughter, Heidi, gave the fourth special gift. When she was four years old, Heidi jumped with excitement as I opened a tiny package. Inside was a tiny nativity scene. "Mommy, Jesus glows in the dark," Heidi kept saying. She was right. Her glow-in-the-dark nativity scene did shine through the darkness; it has continued to be a reminder of God's greatest Gift. The Savior is with me even when times are dark. He is the Light of my path. Heidi's gift reminds me of that truth.

Priceless gifts have nothing to do with monetary value. Jesus, born in a musty stable, proved that long ago.

Thanks be to God for His indescribable gift!
                              —II CORINTHIANS 9:15

Thought . . . Are you always disappointed with your Christmas gifts? Let Jesus give Himself to you, illumining disappointment's darkness. No "present" can replace His *presence.*

Lessons Learned

BY PATTY STUMP

You aren't an accident. You weren't mass-produced. You aren't an assembly-line product. You were deliberately planned, specifically gifted, and lovingly positioned on this earth by the Master Craftsman.

—MAX LUCADO

As a mom, I often wonder what my children will remember. Time alone will tell if they'll grow up recalling my laundry list of "do's and don'ts," or perspectives that I've sought to instill, such as delighting in how God fashioned them.

One morning as I sat with my six-year-old son, I caught a glimpse into his perspective on this issue. Three months prior, he had received from his grandmother a doll that tremendously resembled him! My son treasured "Charles," his new companion, and took him wherever he went. This particular morning I marveled at how similar the two looked: same soft brown hair, olive skin, and big brown eyes. Yet, as I looked closely at Charles, something seemed odd. That's it! His left eye was missing eyelashes! Being an expensive doll, I was disappointed in the oversight and quietly phoned the company. I could either send the doll in for repairs or request a replacement. I knew that my son would never part with Charles temporarily or accept a replacement. Would he be disappointed when he noticed the flaw?

That night, as we ended our day in prayer, my son thanked God for Charles and "for making him just the way he was, even with the scratch on his head and no eye lashes on one eye!!" What?! He had known all along!! My son finished his prayer by also thanking God for making him just the way he was! What treasured moments these were as we both thanked the Lord!

For we are God's workmanship . . .

—EPHESIANS 2:10

Thought . . . Do you accept your children just as God created them? While you must discipline and mold them, don't remake them. Appreciate them as the unique treasure they are.

Looking Higher

BY LAURIE BETH JONES

... He came to lift us up to "the Heavenly places" where He is Himself ...

—OSWALD CHAMBERS

I was in an ice-cream store getting a chocolate yogurt snack. I noticed a three-year-old child oohing and ahhing over a birthday cake he saw in the display case. His mother stopped behind him and lifted him up. He began to howl at the prospect of being separated from the cake before him. She said, "No, Travis, that isn't the cake we're going to have for your birthday—THIS ONE IS!" She lifted him to the highest display shelf, and there, before his eyes, was a cake even lovelier than the one he had seen before. "DINOSAURS!" he shouted in glee. "Yes, we're getting you the cake with dinosaurs on it." His mother laughed as Travis clapped his hands in delight.

I thought later: God is like that mother to us—sometimes having to lift us away from what we see and want on the *lowest* shelf to show us what He really has in mind for us—there, at the very top.

Humble yourselves before the Lord, and He will lift you up.

—JAMES 4:10

Thought . . . Has God disappointed you by withholding your request? Ask Him to change the desires of your heart to match His. He delights to give you His very best gifts. All else pales by comparison.

Mother's Melody

BY LYNN D. MORRISSEY

The child, in the decisive first years of his life, has the experience of
his mother as an all-enveloping, protective, nourishing power.
Mother is food; she is love; she is warmth; she is earth. To be loved
by her means to be alive, to be rooted, to be at home.

—ERICH FROMM

She sang life to me unconditionally
as I grew in her secret cocoon
and bloomed to completion.
She sang contentment.
Nesting me at her breast,
we rocked and rocked in quilted quiet.
My curls rose and fell with her breath.
She sang ivory lullabies,
rock-a-bye babies, hush-a-byes,
by yon bonnie banks and farmers' dells.
The tunes soared and swelled 'til I was compelled
to sing a ring around her rosy beauty.
She sang comfort on rain-throated days
and brought tea and toast.
I floated in her blue-quilt sea,
gently bedded.
She sang love to me sacrificially.
I was in her.
Now she's in me.
I am my mother's melody.

But I have stilled and quieted my soul; like a weaned child
with its mother . . .

—PSALM 131:2

Thought . . . How can you repay your mother for her
gifts to you? Treasure her with your respect, love, and
time. Above all, live a godly life which brings her honor.

A Special Holiday Blessing

BY LEA C. TARTANIAN

Humanity is never so beautiful as when praying for forgiveness, or else forgiving another.

—JEAN PAUL RICHTER

"I hope that you will forgive me," I said to Michelle, a nurse at a branch office of the state institution where I worked. Two pages were missing from an important document she had sent me. I had torn my office apart looking for them, but to no avail.

In a snappish, condescending tone she said, "I'll have to make some telephone calls and locate the physicians who filled out the forms. It won't be easy, with Christmas only two days away!"

Outside my office window, gray clouds and chilling rain added to my discouragement. I felt terrible for the inconvenience I had caused Michelle.

Just before closing the office, Michelle telephoned. With an embarrassed giggle she stated, "You won't believe this. I found the documents. I never mailed them to you!"

Alone in the office on Christmas Eve, I was still furious with Michelle for making me feel guilty the day before, and then not apologizing. "God," I prayed, "I'm asking for a miracle. I'm disappointed with human beings who have no regard for others. I don't want to feel this way the day before Christmas!"

Around 11:00 A.M., our telephone operator handed me a special delivery package. It was a breathtaking centerpiece of red roses, white baby's breath, and pine needles. To this day I treasure the card pasted in my diary. It reads, "Merry Christmas. —Michelle."

God had answered my prayer.

". . . Forgive us our debts, as we also have forgiven our debtors. . . ."

—MATTHEW 6:12

Thought . . . Does someone doubt your forgiveness? Sometimes actions speak louder than words. Besides making an apology, reach out with some tangible gesture of reconciliation.

The Best Gift of All

BY ELISABETH ELLIOT

It is when you give of yourself that you truly give.

—KAHLIL GIBRAN

Frequently, the best gifts we receive come in small packages; and as mothers, we know that they often are bestowed by small hands, offered from big hearts, full of love.

When a tiny two-year-old greets us bearing a dilapidated dandelion in his sweaty fist, and proclaims, "A present for you, Mommy," it becomes our most precious treasure in the world. We know that the child offered all he had, out of great love.

I remember when I was a little girl and wanted to buy presents for Mother and Daddy. Mother had given me a dime, which I spent on an entire box of chocolates for her birthday. (In those days ten cents went a long way, and such an expenditure was actually possible!)

Although Mother had furnished the capital for her own gift, she dearly treasured it because she loved me, and knew that I loved her and had given all I had. It was the giving of myself and my *love* that had made the present special.

It's the same with our Heavenly Father. Any gift that we might "hand" the King—our time, talents, and material treasures—He has supplied. Yet, in comparison with His immeasurable spiritual wealth, this seems as insignificant as a child's crushed dandelion. Our offering is made from a heart of love and it is all we have. He greatly treasures it, because He knows that we have offered a part of our very selves.

Each man should give what he has decided in his heart to give, not reluctantly or under compulsion, for God loves a cheerful giver.

—II CORINTHIANS 9:7

Thought . . . What can you give God to express your love? He will treasure your cheerful obedience more than your sacrifice (I Samuel 15:22).

The Gift of Love

BY SUSAN M. WARREN

You need not cry very loudly; He is nearer to us than we think.

—BROTHER LAWRENCE

Only God can turn tragedy into treasure. I had just returned from overseas ministry to find that my mother-in-law had sold my belongings in a giant garage sale. Gone were a lifetime of treasures: clothing, knickknacks, souvenirs. The discount free-for-all stole my confidence in a God Who said He loved me. *How could He let this happen? Did He even care?* I felt like an unwanted refugee in the Kingdom of God—a stowaway, clutching my worldly belongings in a soft-sided Samsonite. From forty bulging boxes remained a lonely crate of John Denver records. I felt as if God were laughing.

I was barely treading the sea of sorrow when the storm arrived: sold were thirty years of heirloom Christmas ornaments. The decorations were memories from my mother, and my annual achievements—an angel skier, piano, roller skates, a crochet cross—silent symbols of her love, sold for a dollar. Grief crested over me.

I put up my Christmas tree, stared at the bare branches, and cried . . . forgotten, betrayed, unloved . . . by the One Whom I served.

Of all the glittering presents under the tree, *His* was the one that I least expected. Unmarked, save for my name, I opened it, and was blinded by the radiance of His love. Inside was a sea of delicate ornaments, hand-picked by my church. It was then that "Sonlight" broke through the clouds and shone upon my heart. He had given me new treasures for old—symbols of His intimate, unending love.

". . . The Lord your God is with you, he is mighty to save. He will take great delight in you, he will quiet you with his love, he will rejoice over you with singing."

—ZEPHANIAH 3:17

Thought . . . Have someone's thoughtless actions hurt you? Jesus understands mistreatment. Run to Him. The treasure of His comfort will compensate for any pain or loss.

The Gift of Wonder

BY JOYCE LANDORF HEATHERLEY

For all knowledge and wonder is an impression of pleasure in itself.

—FRANCIS BACON

One of the most precious things my mother ever developed in me was the sense of wonder. She left me this rich gift as a part of my inheritance. All children are born with a sense of wonder, but to reach adulthood with it intact is practically a miracle. I think my mother understood the wonder-factor about children and worked to develop mine.

I was in the second grade when I noticed a field of yellow dandelions on my way home from school. I waded into that glorious golden sea of sunshine, picked all the blossoms my hands could hold, and ran all the way home. Flinging open the front door I shouted, "Here, Mother, these are for you!"

My mother was teaching a Bible study and our living room was filled with ladies from Dad's church. My announcement left her two options: she could shush me up or develop my sense of wonder. With a look of what can be described as magnificent awe, she laid her Bible and notebook on the table, knelt beside me, and took my gift.

"Oh, they are beautiful, beautiful, beautiful," she said over and over again. "I love them because you gave them to me. I'm going to set them on our table for our centerpiece tonight."

Lord, our sense of wonder can open our eyes so that when we look at things we really see them. Please keep me constantly reminded of our heritage of wonder as I train my children to see everything there is to see.

The Lord has done great things for us, and we are filled with joy.

—PSALM 126:3

Thought . . . How can you develop your children's sense of wonder? Treat them as God's wonderful creations. Your sense of excitement in them will cause them to be excited about life.

Priceless Froggy

BY JOYCE E. TOMANEK

The manner of giving is worth more than the gift.

—PIERRE CORNEILLE

My fourteen-year-old son, Jim, normally Mr. Sunshine, came home from school in tears two days before Christmas break. "What's wrong?" I asked, offering him cookies still warm from the oven. He rejected them. This was serious.

"Oh Mom! I've been making a present in art class. It's ceramic. I had one finished, but someone knocked it off the table and broke it. The second one cracked when it was being fired. Today when I was cleaning the greenware, my tool slipped and poked a hole in it. It's hopeless. The teacher said the last batch has to be fired tomorrow morning. Now I don't have anything to give to that person for Christmas."

I asked, "Can you shape the hole? Maybe you can turn whatever it is into something else." His face lighted up. He snatched a handful of cookies and dashed off.

On Christmas, Jim insisted that I open his present first. I unwrapped a dark green ceramic frog with a silly grin on its face . . . and a coin slot in the top of its head. Our eyes met. He grinned as broadly as the frog. I choked down another frog—the one in my throat. We hugged.

Froggy has grinned at me from the shelf on my desk for twenty-five years. It is the last gift my son ever gave me, treasured because it came from his heart. Jim had a massive brain aneurysm two months later which suddenly ended his life. God transformed his life on earth into something else—eternal life in glory.

> For if the willingness is there, the gift is acceptable according to what one has, not according to what he does not have.
>
> —II CORINTHIANS 8:12

Thought . . . Do you insist upon perfection in your children? When you realize that God loves you just as you are, you can accept your children in the same way. Receive all that they give you, gladly, in love.

Just Like a Blanket

BY CAROL KENT

Everything has its beauty, but not everyone sees it.

—CHINESE PROVERB

When J. P. was born, we were showered with a remarkable endowment of heirloom-quality blankets: handmade quilts, pink and blue afghans knitted by the hands of praying grandmothers, christening blankets trimmed in exquisite lace, blankets with satin borders. J. P.'s nursery was well stocked with the most elegant baby blankets on which I had ever laid eyes.

I was chagrined when J. P. attached himself to the only truly ugly blanket in the pile. His favorite was an unattractive polyester "blue-light special" from K-Mart. After a short time, the graying white comforter developed unattractive balls of knotted material on the surface. The binding was shredding. The blanket embarrassed me. I hid the treasured rag and pulled out one of the exquisite blankets from the nursery closet. But all were rejected by my son.

On one occasion, I rationalized that he was old enough to be permanently severed from this unwholesome relationship with the tattered blanket. I replaced it with a bed covering of much finer quality. I carefully placed the polyester castoff in the wastebasket. A bit later, I looked up from my work and found my son clutching the discarded blanket to his face as tears streamed down his cheeks. He had just started praying with his own words instead of using the memorized prayers we had taught him earlier.

With his head bowed over the precious blanket so recently saved from destruction, I heard him pray aloud, "Dear Jesus, You're just like a blanket, and I won't ever stop loving You."

I love you, O Lord, my strength.

—PSALM 18:1

Thought . . . Is Jesus your "security blanket"? Many reject Him finding nothing attractive about Him (Isaiah 53:2–3). But when you realize all He sacrificed for you, you'll never stop loving Him!

Harvest Time

BY DORIS SMALLING

Love, like a spring rain, is pretty hard to be in the middle of without getting some on you.

—FRANK A. CLARK

"Hey," exclaimed sixteen-year-old Josh pointing to the painting on my wall, "that's a neat picture!" Two boys from our church youth group were visiting. Their interest in my picture surprised me. "Yes, Josh. The harvest is beautifully depicted. But I treasure that picture for other reasons. I remember the incredible teenagers who gave it to me."

"*Incredible?*" Caleb quizzed.

"Yes. Most of those teens had a choice between our school or juvenile detention. They started the year miserable and mean, but left happy, loving, and hopeful for a bright future."

"How?" Caleb's interest sparked.

"Mike is a perfect example. He was sarcastic and belligerent and sneered when I announced, 'We have only one rule, The Golden Rule. We'll discuss and pray about it every morning.' Also, his terrible temper caused trouble."

"What happened?" both questioned.

"He started a fight in class with a boy named Tom. Trying to stop him, I took the blow intended for Tom and was knocked out cold. Just as I gained consciousness, the principal walked in. 'What are you doing on the floor?' he asked."

"Mike's helping me." He never noticed that I didn't answer. Mike, shocked, almost numb, asked for my forgiveness. I had dialogued all year about various harvests—including souls. Mike and the class found this picture, symbolizing our personal harvest that year."

Josh grinned, "No wonder you treasure that picture so much."

"Yes, Josh, but not nearly as much as God treasures the 'soul harvest' He will reap for eternity!"

Then he said to his disciples, "The harvest is plentiful but the workers are few. . . ."

—MATTHEW 9:37

Thought . . . Are you planting seeds of God's Word in teenagers' hearts? Treasured souls will perish for eternity if they don't hear God's Word.

Buried Treasure

BY KAREN O'CONNOR

Nature is but a name for an effect whose cause is God.

—WILLIAM COWPER

I remember a time when my life felt like a giant landfill! Everywhere I looked were bags of trash: financial setbacks; career struggles; marriage challenges; family relationship difficulties. Nothing worked anymore! To get away from the pain and confusion—at least for a day—I ran off to the mountains with some hiking friends. A good workout was just what I needed to gain some perspective.

After the first hour on the trail, I could barely stand. The rough patch of road undulated up and down like a roller coaster, and we lost ground almost as quickly as we gained it. "Not sure I can go on," I called out breathlessly to my companions. Others echoed my viewpoint.

Hal, one of the stronger hikers, charged ahead and then turned and shouted, "Come on! The real treasure is up here. You've got to see this view!" His enthusiasm caught my attention. I plowed ahead. What a sight it was—treasures as far as the eye could see. Beautiful peaks poked above the clouds, tall trees and flowering shrubs dotted the hillsides, and small lakes and streams sparkled in the sun. Hal was right. And to think I had almost missed these gifts—all because I was so "weary and heavy-laden."

I came home that day a different person, ready to face my problems with a new and higher point of view. Could it be that what I saw as trash God saw as "buried treasure"? With His help, I couldn't wait to find out!

> . . . if you call out for insight and . . . understanding, and if you look for it as for silver and search for it as for hidden treasure, then you will understand the fear of the Lord and find the knowledge of God.
>
> —PROVERBS 2:3–5

Thought . . . Do you seek God's perspective on problems? From His vantage point, they're opportunities to take you to new heights in trusting Him, and in building your character muscles.

The White Elephant

BY KAREN L. RILEY

The perfect surrender and humiliation were undergone by Christ: perfect because He was God, surrender and humiliation because He was man.

—C. S. LEWIS

The invitation to the Christmas party came in the mail. My roommate and I were delighted at the prospect of attending a party. There was only one catch—we were to bring a "white elephant" gift to share with the group. Today, I have a house full of items I could designate as "white elephant" gifts, but at that time the request seemed impossible. We were fresh out of college and neither of us had landed that "career" job, so we were working at minimum wage.

For days we scoured our tiny apartment for something—something we could afford to give away. We came up empty. The evening of the party, as we were getting ready to leave, my roommate appeared from her room carrying a tiny hand-carved crêche. She had received this precious treasure as a gift, and I knew how much she cherished her manger scene. Horrified, I questioned her decision and she replied, "You've seen the other one I have. I really don't need two of them." But I saw in her face a telling wince.

That night my roommate had to endure the snickers of people who passed along her cherished gift, naming it a "dashboard derelict," and making other not-so-nice remarks. I looked at the small manger scene and was reminded of how God gave up His precious Treasure, despite the ridicule that He knew Jesus would endure. He gave his Son to bear the pain and abuse of the Cross. And for those who receive Christ, our salvation becomes priceless eternal treasure.

". . . For whoever wants to save his life will lose it, but whoever loses his life for me and for the gospel will save it. . . ."

—MARK 8:35

Thought . . . Do you suffer cruel ridicule? Knowing what Jesus suffered on the Cross, you can endure because you know that He understands, and because He endured far worse.

You Can't Take It with You

BY EMILIE BARNES

In the end, it's the treasures we give away that will be most surely ours.

—EMILIE BARNES

It has been nearly ten years since I lost fourteen of my favorite teacups. A glass shelf shifted, and those cups shattered on the floor. They were just teacups, but a little part of my heart shattered with them. Some were family heirlooms, others represented treasured memories.

I went away to speak at a seminar. My hostess welcomed me and showed me around her lovely house. I especially admired a beautiful set of dishes, a complete setting for twelve, with dainty pink roses.

"They are special," she agreed when I exclaimed over them. "I wish the pattern hadn't been discontinued."

We talked. We got to know each other. We became friends. With sadness, I shared my story about the shattered teacups.

The next morning at breakfast, I found a pink-sprigged teacup next to my plate. Tears filled my eyes.

"Thank you for sharing your teacup with me this morning," I said.

"It's your teacup now," she told me. "It's my gift to you."

Tears spring to my eyes when I think of that gift. Whenever I see it, I think of that beautiful woman and her now incomplete set of eleven teacups. She taught me how important it is to hold all my treasures with a light hand, caring for them with gratitude but being willing to hand them over joyfully when the time comes. When love commands. It's a lesson worth remembering whenever we are contemplating our beautiful treasures because, after all, we can't take them with us.

". . . Whoever finds his life will lose it, and whoever loses his life for my sake will find it. . . ."

—MATTHEW 10:39

Thought . . . Do you lament the loss of some possession? Let it go. Sometimes God will surprise you with greater treasure, but most of all with the blessing of His presence.

Ticket to Ride: an Unforgettable Wedding Gift

BY AMBERLY NEESE

Love is a verb.

—CLARE BOOTH LUCE

The doctors never expected my father to live long enough to see me married. The cancer had permeated my dad's body, and the chemotherapy had weakened his once strong will. Yet, despite the prognosis, my dad had walked me down the aisle at my wedding.

Of all the lovely items we received for wedding presents, the gift from my father was the most memorable. Although the cancer treatments had depleted his finances, he scrounged enough money together to purchase two roller coaster tickets. The enclosed card read: "For you and your new roller coaster partner. —Love, Dad." Through this special gesture, Dad was "passing the baton" to my new spouse, giving his blessing upon our union.

Years after my father's passing, my sister married. I was sad that Dad couldn't be there to see his youngest marry. Although my sister and dad had not shared a passion for roller coasters as we had, they were ardent movie fans. Saturdays were often spent at the local cinema.

On my sister's wedding day, I visited the local movie house and bought two tickets and a package of candy. Placing them in a card, I scribbled, "I'm so proud of you. This is for you and your new movie partner. —Love, Dad."

As my sister and I held each other and cried, I realized that Dad's love for us was an incredible treasure that had transcended his passing. He would always be with us.

Listen, my sons, to a father's instruction; pay attention and gain understanding.

—PROVERBS 4:1

Thought . . . What can you *do* now to show your children that you love them, which they will never forget after you die? Reading Scripture, praying, and attending church together are love investments that will reap eternal dividends.

Simple Pleasures

Simple Pleasures

BY MADELEINE L'ENGLE

Pleasure is seldom found where it is sought; our brightest blazes of gladness are kindled by unexpected sparks.

—SAMUEL JOHNSON

One of my happy memories from the days when our children were little is summer evenings when family and friends gathered for the sparkler parade. Even the toddlers could hold a sparkler with moderate safety, and the grownups would watch the children, led by the older ones, dance in and out of the fruit trees in the orchard.

This past July we had our picnic with another generation of children. I had been sent a large box of sparklers from Texas, and the children, four little boys, waited for dark and then ran around the field making great sweeping patterns with their sparklers, and it was beautiful.

There was a special poignancy for me in watching the faces of the parents who had, a couple of decades ago, been part of the sparkler parade, now looking with love at their own children making patterns of light.

Life is full of such small moments, simple pleasures. Each year I cultivate a greater appreciation of such simple feasts. In their own way, they are as satisfying as sumptuous banquets.

The true light that gives light to every man was coming into the world.

—JOHN 1:9

Thought . . . How can you keep the heart's torch lit as you pass it from generation to generation? One way is to make moments matter and keep the memories alive through family storytelling.

Moonlight Rendezvous

BY ALISON JOY HUTCHINS

How soon unaccountable I became tired and sick, / till rising and gliding out I wander'd off by myself, / in the mystical moist night-air, and from time to time, / look'd up in perfect silence at the stars.

—WALT WHITMAN

I hugged my sleeping bag tightly around me as the nighttime sounds of summer surrounded my tent. My sleepy eyes closed and I prayed, "Father, thank you for . . ." I left the thought unfinished, too tired to make the mental effort. I was too tired to make anything—including a trip to the bathhouse several campsites away. At the moment, all I could concentrate on was the cloud of sleep pleasantly numbing my brain. I yawned an apology to God and surrendered to exhaustion.

I woke hours later to an intolerable need to visit the ladies' room. My sleepiness dissipated as I scrambled from the tent, tripping and stubbing my toe in the process. Shuffling along the path to the bathhouse, I couldn't help but smile and say, "So, Lord, this is what I get for standing you up?"

I studied my shadow, which blanketed the ground as clearly as if the sun stood at my back. When I paused to look up at the night sky, it took my breath away. Millions of shimmering stars dusted the canvas of space. The moon, though a sliver, glistened with ethereal brilliance, hypnotizing me with its beauty. This very night I had asked the Creator of the galaxies for a rain check and, instead, He summoned me for a private exhibition of His masterpiece. My smile returned as I treasured the simplicity of such a marvelous blessing.

"Father, thank You for Your love," I whispered, and this time sleep was the last thing on my mind.

When I consider your heavens, the work of your fingers, the moon and the stars, which you have set in place, what is man that you are mindful of him, the son of man that you care for him?

—PSALM 8:3–4

Thought . . . What does it mean for the Lord of the universe to desire your company? He has made you a little lower than angels, crowned with glory and honor (Psalm 8:5). Spend time with Him!

No Prayer Too Small

BY DONNA MESLER NORMAN

Let us not be content to pray morning and evening . . . but let us live in prayer all day long.

—FÉNELON

Chicago! Our niece and nephew were ecstatic about visiting us in the Windy City. Traveling to a new and distant town, seeing a lake the size of an ocean, and riding a *train* just to go downtown fueled their appetites with a craving for adventure!

No planned activity, however, created greater zeal than the promise of "fishing with Uncle Phil." A tiny lagoon snaked lazily through our apartment grounds, its cascading fountains bubbling like a coffee pot. Now and then, a slippery bluegill squirmed just below the surface, but a fisherman's mecca it was not. No matter to the kid brigade! That first night Shannon and Scott barely paid homage to grilled burgers and fries before dashing from the table. Jauntily donning caps, and carrying poles and a "fish container," they scampered off to the high seas!

A wave of apprehension washed over me. "Lord, this is *so* important to them. *Please*. Couldn't they catch just one little fish?" I hardly had time to repeat the urgent request before shouts from water's edge propelled me to the window. Crammed into that little plastic bucket were seventeen bluegills! How in the world . . . and from *where* did they come? The triumphant pride gleaming on two cherub faces carved an indelible treasure deep in my soul.

God had heard my humble prayer, enfolding His answer around the dreams of children . . . around their quest for simple pleasures.

" . . . If you believe, you will receive whatever you ask for in prayer."

—MATTHEW 21:22

Thought . . . Do you honor your children by praying for their dreams? No prayer is too small, no dream too insignificant to the God Who loves them.

I Sat. I Sipped. I Savored.

BY JUNE L. VARNUM

Blissful are the simple, for they shall have much peace.

— THOMAS À KEMPIS

As I sat down in my old wooden rocker early one morning, I closed my eyes and slowly began to rock. How sweet these moments were—a far cry from my usual routine of gulping coffee, scribbling a to-do list, then hurriedly reading a Bible lesson, always conscious of passing time. Tick. Tick. Tick. The clock on the mantle seemed to call, "Hurry. Hurry. Hurry. The day is slipping away."

Usually I jumped up and obeyed that "hurry" warning. But this morning, an unexpected calmness surrounded me, and I knew it was okay just to sit for awhile. Sipping fragrant coffee from my china cup, I watched through the living room window as night faded to morning. The shadowy forms of two barn swallows flitted past, their day just beginning. A large bluebird momentarily preened before the rearview mirror on my car. *How funny he looks, Lord,* I thought. *You make such delightful creations, Father.*

Smiling now, I slowly sipped the last flavorful dregs from my cup. Because my day, the "doing" part, was about to begin, I deliberately savored these quiet moments, a gift from God. Not wrapped in tissue and tied with ribbons, not held in my hands, I held these treasures in my heart. I thanked my Lord for simple pleasures—early morning minutes in an old rocker, a cup of flavored coffee, and time to savor just *being*.

> "In . . . rest is your salvation, in quietness and trust is your strength . . ."
>
> —ISAIAH 30:15

Thought . . . Mary, Mary, anything but sedentary, how do your mornings go? If you are always on the run, take "time out" each morning to literally *sit* in God's presence. Pray, read Scripture, and meditate. You can easily afford this luxury (*really a necessity!*), if you organize the night before and retire early.

The Pleasures of Print

BY KAREN HAYSE

A man who does not read good books has no advantage over the man who cannot read them.

—MARK TWAIN

Shimmering waves tossed by a summer's wind . . . hot, glazed doughnuts melting on your tongue . . . the scent of rain as lightning sears a blackened sky . . . To billions of people who cannot read, these phrases carry as much meaning as an evening of watching television when the cable is down. Fortunately, I am not one of them.

Sometimes, I mistakenly assume that being able to read is my God-given right. But, as an elementary teacher who listens to children labor as they try to pronounce simple words, I am reminded that reading is a God-given treasure. If everyone in the world opened a book in his native language, only thirty percent of us would be able to comprehend it.

My favorite part of the day is the thirty minutes before bed when I delve into a gripping book or colorful magazine. It is then that the twenty-six little symbols that comprise our alphabet transport me to majestic places and distant times. What lessons and pleasures I would miss if I could not decode their messages!

I am thankful that when I pull envelopes from my mailbox, I can understand the loving words printed inside cards and letters. I see a library as a literary candy store. And my heart stirs even more as I pore over God's words on the onionskin pages of my Bible, bringing praise to my lips. I thank Him that, unlike seven out of ten people in this world, I can read.

How sweet are your words to my taste, sweeter than honey to my mouth!

—PSALM 119:103

Thought . . . Do you treasure books? You are reading this one, so likely you do. Why not tutor a child or illiterate adult in reading? You'll foster their ability to read and understand God's Word for themselves.

Hoarfrost and High Heaven

BY LUCI SHAW

Never once since the world began has the sun ever stopped His shining. . . . His face very often we could not see, . . . For His love is always shining.

—JOHN OXENHAM

It was one of my favorite places in our old house—the little landing halfway up the stairs. There through the evening window I could see the whole wide sky uninterrupted by streetlights or lights from other houses.

One severely cold winter all the windows in the house were decorated with flakes and scrolls of frost like a baroque patterned foil, all silver and white. That night I stood on the landing and looked out through the glass, between the stars of frost, to where, millions of light-years away, the stars twinkled through space. The infinitely far stars seemed as close to my eyes as the tiny touches of frost on the glass. And when I breathed on them, lightly and warmly, they melted and melded, swimming together, the very far joined to the very near.

Years later, after photography had become my passion, I loved to record on film this aspect of the cold. The images were clearest on early mornings, with the rising sun highlighting the window frost. The marvel was that once again the far and the near, the immense and the infinitesimal, the powerful and the fragile were collaborating to create a moment of beauty and revelation for me. The sun was in service to these small frost feathers—lighting them into radiance. Is it fanciful for me to think of the sun on the frost as a metaphor of God's face shining on me, small and insignificant as I am?

". . . the Lord make his face shine upon you . . ."

—NUMBERS 6:25

Thought . . . Are you far from God? God, Himself, came from Heaven to earth—from far away to very near—as a tiny baby. Jesus is the light of the world Who is as close as your heart, if you'll invite Him to enter.

Gales of Giggles

BY CRISTINE GRIMM

Laughter is the closest thing to the grace of God.

—KARL BARTH

One busy afternoon my nephew, a blue-eyed handful, began playing with my hair. He does it often, gazing deeply into my eyes and revealing an astounding sincerity and awareness beyond his two years. On this day I'm held in rapt attention while he carefully folds my hair over his tiny hands and across my face. Strand by strand, he repeats the routine that he perfected as a baby. His weightless body reminds me of his tender age as he smiles, awaiting my reaction. His breath catches, and I exhale fast and hard, blowing long, now-tangled strands everywhere. They tickle his face in their flight.

His usual "Again!" is forgotten. Instead, he immediately convulses backwards, giggling, completely trusting my ability to hold him, to protect him from a fall. I do so, barely, and his joy rises to greet my now-exposed face. His giggles multiply, coaxing me to join. Our laughter cascades over itself, bouncing off walls, echoing through hallways, and tickling spines. We "feed" off each other, becoming hysterical, completely mystifying our family by our joyful outburst.

We stop. I wipe away the tears. Ready for new adventure, he gets down and wanders over to his one-year-old brother, carefully explaining exactly which key starts Mommy's car, which pedal makes it go, and how he'll back it into the boat hitch because "brover's still too yiddle."

I return to my busy day feeling renewed and invigorated by life's simple pleasures—grateful to God for this gift of a child, and his natural enjoyment of each small moment.

Our mouths were filled with laughter, our tongues with songs of joy.

—PSALM 126:2A

Thought . . . Are life's pressures preventing your laughter? Spend time cavorting with a child. Not only will you receive the treasure of laughter, but joy, innocence, and freedom, as well.

208

That Dingblasted Farm!

BY EVELYN ANDERSON SHEETS

We put our love where we put our labor.

—RALPH WALDO EMERSON

What about this dingblasted farm—half woods, one-quarter swale, prone to flood and frost—this place called home? What about this hardscrabble maze of circumstances with no escape?

Our father had wrestled small fields from their surrounding woods. He had built a barn, a house, and a few small outbuildings. No lap of luxury, this. Plenty of firewood to cut at one's "leisure." No shortage of weeds; ample potato bugs; stones aplenty. Taxes, anyone? Forty-five dollars, you say. Just do without the necessities. Piece of cake.

But how do folks measure growth from a struggle? By how many millimeters is the sinew of the backbone increased by, say, a decade of such labor?

There were days when the skies *were* a glorious blue, and yellow butterflies flitted over the garden. The smokehouse *did* put out savory bacon. Papa said, "It'll taste good when the snow flies." When the snow did fly, we played card games under the hanging kerosene lamp suspended over the table. A steady fire burned in the heater. We slowly rotated around the table, cold side to warm side, as we played.

Then it was summer again. We could almost touch the sky from the swing in the basswood tree. When we patted the horse's nose, soft as velvet, and said, "Good boy," he'd bob his head as though to say, "My pleasure."

That dingblasted farm! I guess I did love it after all.

As you know, we consider blessed those who have persevered.

—JAMES 5:11A

Thought . . . Is your family struggling with hard times? Lean on the Lord and on each other. Look for "treasures of togetherness" that far outweigh the difficulties.

Prayers of Simplicity

BY LAURA SABIN RILEY

And there is no greatness where there is not simplicity, goodness, and truth.

—LEO NIKOLAEVICH TOLSTOI

I smiled as I listened to the simple, heartfelt prayers of my three-year-old at bedtime one night: "Thank you for Mommy, Daddy, cousin Jaimee, Grandma . . . and thank you for my Winnie the Pooh books. Amen." Smiling triumphantly, Seth said, "I pray, now Mommy pray." I smiled back at him and agreed, wondering how I could be as simple in approaching God as he. Suddenly, my prayers seemed long and complicated.

As I finished the dinner dishes, I thought about Seth's prayer. It was straight from the heart—*genuine*. I realized how full of rhetoric and fancy talk my prayers had become. Listening to Seth helped me to see that I just needed to say what was on my heart—no more, no less.

A few days after discovering the value of simple prayer, I was in the backyard playing with Seth when I noticed a beautiful sunset. I picked him up, pointing toward the sky and said, "Thank you, God, for the pretty sunset."

A few days later when he was eating lunch, from his chair he could see the skyline of the backyard out the bay window. As he was munching on his raisins I heard him say quietly, "Thank you, God, for the pretty sky." I smiled, and thanked God for a child who was learning that the true treasure of prayer is not found in mounds of glossy, golden words but in a few small, simple nuggets.

". . . And when you pray, do not keep on babbling like pagans, for they think they will be heard because of their many words. . . ."

—MATTHEW 6:7

Thought . . . Do you struggle with prayer? Employ what Richard Foster calls "simple prayer"—praying simply and unpretentiously anything that is on your heart in everyday language. You will never run out of things to say, nor struggle with how you say them.

No Hurry

BY DORIS HAYS NORTHSTROM

Don't hurry, don't worry. You're only here for a short visit. So be sure
to stop and smell the flowers.

—WALTER C. HAGEN

Mom and I cross the damp grass and brush by camellia petals,
christened with dew. We pause, caught in the ethereal spell cast
by soft wind and the Big Dipper's brilliance. She fumbles in her
purse and apologizes, "My keys are here somewhere. Sorry."

"No hurry, Mom," I assure, and squeeze her shoulder. Taking
her hand, I lead her past the rose garden along the walkway.
Today we had found the old spot on the lake, shared egg salad
sandwiches from our picnic basket, and fed the ducks. I remembered other picnics when she shared her peanut butter sandwiches and raisin-filled cookies with kids in the neighborhood
park.

Tonight, I hold my breath in the stillness as our faces catch
lances of moonlight. I tuck a sprig of honeysuckle into silver
curls behind her ear. We giggle like children on a scavenger
hunt. Mom's hand shakes as she scrambles deeper into her purse
for her key. "I found it!" she boasts. "Now we can go inside."

Someday I'll stand here alone as winter shadows lace the
unswept path. And I'll remember her eyes, our day at the lake,
her touch in the night, and our walk across the stars.

"No hurry, Mom. No hurry at all."

Honor your . . . mother . . . that it may go well with you . . .
—EPHESIANS 6:3

Thought . . . Are you hurrying through life? Spend time
and enjoy simple pleasures with the elderly, who have
lots of it to give, plus wonderful memories to share.

Enough Is Enough

BY LUCI SWINDOLL

Contentment is an inexhaustible treasure.

—ARABIAN PROVERB

A few years ago a friend was spending the weekend with me, and when we awakened on Saturday morning she asked, "What shall we do today? Where would it be fun to go? The mall? The movies? The museum?" I think she was pretty stunned when I suggested we stay home. "And do *what?*" she questioned. "Shouldn't we go someplace? It's Saturday!"

I said, "Why don't we do something here and enjoy what we already have?"

"Oh," she muttered. But she became intrigued with the idea as I explained how I feel that we sometimes go running around looking for and buying more things—things we might already have. Why don't we just stay home and enjoy them?

That's what my friend and I did that day . . . *and she loved it.* We worked a jigsaw puzzle, listened to our favorite music, read to each other, played a game, made little meals, all the while having wonderful conversation. We went to bed that night completely satisfied.

Since that day, my friend has said to me many times, "That helped me so much. I've learned to stay home and enjoy what I already have." Now when she comes here she never wants to leave.

What we learned that day is that enough is enough, even though there are times we're afraid to test it. We're kind of scared that what we have won't be enough to satisfy us.

> . . . I have learned the secret of being content in any and every situation, whether well fed or hungry, whether living in plenty or in want.
>
> —PHILIPPIANS 4:12

Thought . . . Do you often run away from home? Mall-mania (shopping 'til you drop) breeds discontent and is *expensive*. Don't flit around like a butterfly. *Land.* Stay home and "cocoon." Spend "free time" doing things for free. Your heart and wallet will be full!

Letting Go

BY LINDA ROSWIT

May the countryside and the gliding valley streams content me. Lost to fame, let me love river and woodland.

—VIRGIL

During a trip to the Arkansas Ozarks, my husband, Bill, and I were excited to discover a new river to float. Although not particularly challenging, it held many pleasant surprises. The water was remarkably clear, its turquoise hue shining in the sunlight.

Floating on a weekday, we had it all to ourselves and felt positively rich! Sometimes we quit paddling and let the current take us where it wanted, reminding me that I should quit controlling every aspect of my life and let God do the steering. As I relaxed, I felt my worries and cares melt away—no annoying phone calls interrupting my thoughts—no distressing world news upsetting my peace.

In silence we observed flocks of turkeys flaunting their feathers as they courted. Blue herons fluttered overhead while a woodchuck ambled up a hillside. Even two deer, their white tails flashing, joined us at river's edge to quench their thirst as we ate lunch.

I felt totally accepted by God and enjoyed a "kinship" with His creatures. I gave thanks for this river that had not been dammed and was allowed to run free the way God had intended it. "Lord," I prayed, "I desire to know more about Your world, because when I do, I'll know more about You." This was the most delightful surprise of all—a unique opportunity to worship God. I had a sacred awareness that in experiencing untamed nature, face to face, I was experiencing the very hand of God in all creation. I bowed my head in awe.

As the deer pants for streams of water, so my soul pants for you, O God.

—PSALM 42:1

Thought . . . Do you doubt God exists? Explore the treasures of nature. If you search with an honest heart, you cannot help but know that almighty God created the heavens and earth (Psalm 19:1–4).

Treasures at Twilight

BY SUSAN M. WARREN

We do not remember days, we remember moments.

—CESARE PAVESE

The hamper overflows, toys litter the floor, and leftovers harden in the supper dishes. From the bedroom, young voices crescendo into argument, and I feel my head throb. The sun is falling, a brilliant mandarin squeezing its juice onto the horizon, and I stop, a toy in my grip, and enjoy His magnificence, a symbol of His love.

A tug on my shirt tears me from worship. Annoyance flickers briefly, but is doused by a tender smile, a book gripped in chubby hands. "Read to me, Mommy." I sigh. I have no energy and my headache screams in protest. "Okay," I say and pull my toddler to my lap. "Good night, moon. Good night, room . . ." I begin quickly, then slow to the gentle rhythm of the story. Too quickly it is done. My boy's eyes twinkle. "Again?"

"Okay." Again we say good night to bears on chairs, mittens and kittens. We are done, and another son climbs aboard. "Read this one, Mommy." We read about a steam shovel named Maryann, a little Engine that could, and Horton the Elephant.

The sun is sleeping, and my children follow. They kiss me and slide from my lap, laughing, happy. My headache is gone. The shadows of dusk hide the scattered toys. I shut the laundry room door, tightly. Kisses, hugs, prayers, and suddenly the house is quiet. But my heart sings. In the magic of twilight God has reminded me of the simple treasure of creating for my children a memory of moments—a memory of love.

". . . A new command I give you: Love one another. As I have loved you, so you must love one another. . . ."

—JOHN 13:34

Thought . . . Is the complexity of your schedule precluding your pleasure of enjoying simple moments? Spend time with children. They enjoy life through simplicity. They enjoy what counts.

The Longer Way

BY SYLVIA DUNCAN

I travel not to go anywhere, but to go. I travel for travel's sake.

—ROBERT LOUIS STEVENSON

My usual way to a discount grocery store proceeds over major streets, with electric signals at each intersection. Cars and trucks impatiently maintain the speed limit. Fast food restaurants, gas stations, and office buildings line the way. On a hot afternoon, I huffed and puffed inwardly. There was a traffic jam and I was thirsty. I needed a shortcut.

I made a right turn onto a narrow, unfamiliar side street. I had to drive more slowly, stop completely, and look carefully at each of the four-way stop signs in the quiet residential section. I headed my car in what I thought would be a roundabout way home. I wended my way through quaint areas, delighted to see rose gardens, sleeping puppies on porches, and three small girls beside a lemonade stand. I grinned at the sight. I stopped the car, rolled down the window, and handed over my fifty cents.

"We make it fresh. It takes awhile," was the proud comment as one girl squeezed a lemon and another added iced sugared water from a thermos jug. It tasted delicious. Each sip of my cup of cold, sweet juice was treasured.

Though my journey took quite a few extra minutes, those lost minutes were regained in a different way. My head was clear, my patience untried, and I felt refreshed. I decided then to vary my routes each week, turn off at new corners, and allow time for full stops. The quieter way takes a bit more time, but is well worth the investment!

Make it your ambition to lead a quiet life . . .

—I THESSALONIANS 4:11

Thought . . . On life's journey, are you taking time to "drink the lemonade"? Sipping life slowly, savoring each simple pleasure, is more rewarding than swallowing life whole. It goes so quickly; don't help it along by hurrying.

Just Plain Folks

BY JUNE HUNT

True humility comes from being grateful for our good fortune and talents and aware of our flaws and shortcomings.

—MITZI CHANDLER

Dad may have been a world-renowned industrialist and financier, but when he and Mom were at home, it was hard to imagine him being anyplace else. On the front porch he loved to watch the "show" (his term for watching the moon and the stars). Some may find it difficult to imagine H. L. Hunt and his wife enjoying such simple pleasures, but frequently I found them sitting quietly on the porch holding hands. They had been together a long time and words were not always needed for conversation between them.

My father always delighted in singing for anyone with a listening ear. The one they called their song is "Just Plain Folks." In part it goes: "We are just plain folks, your mother and me, Just plain folks like our own folks used to be. . . . Yes, we're just—plain—folks."

This song never fails to affect me deeply. That's my favorite time to imagine my dad—holding Mom's hand and singing, "We're Just Plain Folks." I realize that in Dad's quest to industrialize, he had to forfeit things, one of them being a simple way of life. Tears often came to his eyes because as he sang it, he believed it.

My dad's appreciation for "plain folks" was always encouraged by the fact that Mom never lost sight of the important values of life. She schooled us in the basics so that our lives would be founded on Christ rather than our immediate circumstances. I realize now that Mom's beautiful humility was the result of prayer.

Humility and the fear of the Lord bring wealth and honor and life.

—PROVERBS 22:4

Thought . . . Do you envy the wealthy? Jesus said it's difficult for the rich to enter the kingdom of Heaven (Matthew 19:24). Share with rich folks the wealth you own in enjoying the simple pleasures of Christ.

Tales from the Innsbrook Woods

BY LYNN D. MORRISSEY

There is a pleasure in the pathless woods, / There is a rapture on the lonely shore / There is society, where none intrudes, / By the deep Sea, and Music in its roar: / I love not Man the less, but Nature more.

—LORD BYRON

I sought solitude in autumn woods,
but found fraternity.
Cicadas trilled. Locusts droned.
A lone heron sentineled the pond,
swelled with rain.
A skein of geese unraveled in the sky.
Winds stirred myriad maples,
loosening leaves like butterflies fluttering,
falling in mosaics on the lake.
The sun hung like an amulet,
gilding the riplets.
At water's edge, three deer leapt,
twining stars in their high-branched heads.
I left the woods unwillingly.
In the city, loneliness waits.

Then God said, "Let the land produce . . . trees . . . Let the water teem with living creatures, and let birds fly above the earth across the expanse of the sky . . . Let the land produce living creatures . . . that move along the ground . . . And God saw that it was good."

—GENESIS 1:11, 20, 24, 25

Thought . . . How can you cope with life's complexities? Occasionally "escape" urban and suburban life and head for the woods. Enjoy the simple pleasures of nature, and seeing God there at every turn.

Have a Nice Nap!

BY GRACE WITWER HOUSHOLDER

A nap is a time to cool down, recharge the batteries, and harmonize the mind.

—GERALD CELENTE

On the first day of school, I walked out on the front porch to wave good-bye to my youngest. We live only five blocks from school, and all four of our children have had the privilege of walking there. Just as he was about to break into a run (my daughters walked to school, Paul always *ran*), Paul turned and yelled loudly enough for the entire neighborhood to hear, "Bye, Mom! Have a nice nap!"

Had I been closer, I would have seen a twinkle in his eye. But at the time I felt silly. The whole neighborhood had heard that my son expected me to head back to bed. I had a house to clean, clothes to wash, meals to prepare, bills to pay, calls to make, and stories to write. I had enough work for two days, not one.

During the summer, with four kids at home, I didn't often get the opportunity to have a nap—a time of quiet that I really treasure and *need*. But with all four children in school now, I would be able to enjoy a time of blissful solitude and reflection. The truth is that when I "nap," I'm letting my mind stretch and wander. I pray. Sometimes I fall asleep. Sometimes I discover the perfect idea for a story or a meal. A day with a nap is simply a good day, a better day than a day of perpetual motion.

Thanks, Paul, for reminding me!

". . . Come to me, all you who are weary and burdened, and I will give you rest. . . ."

—MATTHEW 11:28

Thought . . . When did you last take a nap? Take one now. A **NAP** offers Nurture as you rest your body, Answers as you allow your mind to reflect, and Peace as you rest your soul. Every woman needs a nap!

Message in the Sand

BY LUCI SHAW

A man's true value consists in his likeness to God. . . .

—PAUL TOURNIER

For all of my life, the effortless, arbitrary beauty of seaside shells has signaled divine generosity. Shells and grains of sand remind me of the importance of the individual as well as of the collective.

I prefer to walk close to the wave edges. There the wet shells can be seen individually in their tangerine and pink and butter yellow and rainbow iridescence. Their shapes draw my eye to them, as they glint in the sheen of each receding wave. They seem to whisper, "Here I am, waiting just for you." I bend and touch and rinse clean and caress each one with my fingers before I store it in the bag I have brought along just for this. I carry it home with me, to the center of a continent where there are no saltwater beaches, no shells like these.

In my home I have shells in every room—in green glass bottles on mantels or windowsills where the light can touch them. Each of them seems to me to be a parable of personal choice and significance. I am amazed when I think of how God values us, bending down and raising us from among a million others, choosing us with an appreciative glint in His eye, wanting to take us home with Him. God searches us out—you and me!

O Lord, you have searched me and you know me.

—PSALM 139:1

Thought . . . Why has God chosen you? Even before the foundation of the world, He chose you to be holy (Ephesians 1:4) and to bear fruit (John 15:16). What a responsibility *and* privilege!

Memories

Taking Pictures with My Heart

BY VICKEY BANKS

Memory is the treasury and guardian of all things.

—CICERO

It was an extraordinary moment at the end of an otherwise ordinary day. And, where was my camera? Snug in its case, tucked away in a cabinet.

I was walking down the hallway of our home when I chanced upon the sweetest sight I had ever seen: my three-year-old son brushing his teeth. It wasn't the fact that Parker had taken the initiative to brush his teeth that was special; it was what he *looked* like at that moment. Even with the aid of his well-used footstool, he still had to stand on his tippy-toes to barely see the mirror. Clad only in his tiny white tee shirt and "big boy" underwear, the little muscles in his calves were clearly outlined. He looked so small, so innocent and pure.

I froze in place. Looking on, I realized someday that that same precious little boy would probably be bigger than I. He would be able to pick me up! So, I willed time to stand still for a few marvelous moments while I soaked up the memory of what he looked like up on his tiptoes.

I thought of going to get my camera to capture this memory on film, but I couldn't bear to turn away. Instead, I did what mothers have been doing for centuries. I took a picture with my heart.

But Mary treasured up all these things and pondered them in her heart.

—LUKE 2:19

Thought . . . Are your children growing up more quickly than you had anticipated? Take time to enjoy little moments with your child. Even so, you'll eventually lose the moments themselves, but you'll be making indelible memories.

The Thankful Heart

BY CATHERINE MARSHALL

What then is God? . . . Creator of minds to receive His own fulness, imparting to them life to be conscious of Him, prompting them to desire Him, enlarging them to receive Him, . . . enkindling them with zeal.

—BERNARD OF CLAIRVAUX

After dinner one evening my mother and I were comfortably settled in our living room. Through the room and around us flowed the music of a fine recording. As we listened, our hands were busy working on some table mats that were to be a gift. The singing, soaring melody was a delight to the emotions.

All at once it happened. My heart overflowed with praise. Silently, I lifted all of it to Him, aware now of His presence. . . . *This quiet room, the comforts and the peace of it. No bombs are falling outside. No Gestapo is going to pound on the door . . . By Your mercy and grace, Mother is still with us, the inimitable Christy, so gentle, yet so full of her own kind of ginger. You love her, too. Isn't it great that she and I have such rapport that often conversation isn't even necessary! . . . This music, so glorious. It must be pleasing You, too. Work for my hands to do, work that I enjoy. You know all about work with the hands. This moment—what delight—what an oasis—in the midst of busy life.*

The thankfulness bubbled up and up, and still I had not spoken.

Then I marveled that such a quiet, unassuming moment had meant so much. Why, I wondered?

The word "consciousness" is probably the key to the answer. The thankful heart raised in praise and adoration, verbal or silent, becomes the vessel to hold the sense impressions and the distilled essence of the presentness of life.

Everyone was amazed and gave praise to God. They were filled with awe and said, "We have seen remarkable things today."

—LUKE 5:26

Thought . . . Are you *fully aware* of God's presence? Thank Him for His "presents"—His blessings—and be "lifted up into the Heavenlies" with Him in praise.

Stuff Worth Keeping

BY TINA KRAUSE

The best things in life aren't things.

—ART BUCHWALD

Over the years, I have surveyed my attic and basement to rid myself of the "stuff" that has accumulated. Yet, I have often regretted eliminating the items that have monetary value today.

Who would have known that my son's 1979 Star Wars action figures would cause collectors to salivate in 1999? Instead, I kept the noncollectible toys like Lincoln logs and a set of miniature soldiers, complete with a tiny cannon. A pearl from my broken necklace served as a cannonball.

One day, as I anguished over my foolhardy choices, my twenty-eight-year-old son stopped by. "Hey, my toy soldiers!" he exclaimed when he noticed the unboxed toys. I left the room and when I returned, Jim was sprawled across the floor. He had lined the soldiers in a straight row, and fired the pearl cannonball. "Hey it still works!" he bellowed. After I had properly teased him, he insisted on storing the soldiers in tissue paper. Carefully, he boxed them in their safe, new living quarters and scrawled, "JIM'S SOLDIERS" in indelible ink on the box's exterior.

Suddenly, I remembered why I had kept them. These were collectibles swaddled in fond memories—valuable to the one who had once spent hours with them in child's play.

How similar, I thought, are the blessings of God. His forgiveness, joy, peace, and love have no monetary value, yet these treasures sustain me daily. And I realized that "God-stuff" is the only stuff worth keeping, stored safely within the inner sanctum of my heart.

Do not let them out of your sight, keep them within your heart.

—PROVERBS 4:21

Thought . . . Are you storing the Holy Spirit's fruit in the vault of your heart? The only way to receive His "deposit and seal" is to receive Christ as your Savior (Ephesians 1:11–14).

Memories

BY JONI EARECKSON TADA

Hope is wishing for things to come true; faith is believing that they will come true.

—NORMAN VINCENT PEALE

My sweetest memories are ones that inspire hope. Many of them are of life before my accident. I recall the grating sensation of a nail file against the tips of my fingers, and the sound of my nails tapping cool, ivory piano keys. I can still "feel" my fingers plucking the tight nylon strings of my old guitar, touching peach fuzz, digging under an orange skin and peeling it.

Many of my freshest memories have to do with my hands. I'm looking at my paralyzed hands right now. I love it when my husband, Ken, holds my hand. Sometimes when we're wheeling around a mall, I'll hold my arm out, a signal to him to grab my hand. I can't feel it, but I like seeing his hand covering mine.

Why would memories like these inspire hope? They remind me that one day soon I'll have new hands. Fingers that will work and feel again, touch and pluck and pick and scrub and dig. Hands that will embrace loved ones. The first thing I'm going to do is reach for Ken's new, glorified hand and give it a squeeze, just to see what it feels like. It'll happen! God promises me in Jeremiah 29:11, "I know the plans I have for you . . . They are plans for good and not for evil, to give you a future and a hope (The Living Bible)." My best memories help give shape to that hopeful future.

Let your memories be your handhold on Heaven.

But if we hope for what we do not yet have, we wait for it patiently.

—ROMANS 8:25

Thought . . . How do you overcome discouragement? Like David, look back to past victories of faith, and hope in the faithfulness of God (Psalm 42). Look forward to Heaven, where there is no pain.

The Morning Glory Club

BY JANE E. MAXWELL

What the heart has once owned, it shall never lose.

—HARRIET WARD BEECHER

My skin goose-bumped in the frosty morning air as I walked up the driveway to Willow Point Nursing Home. It was Friday. My Morning Glory Reminisce Club would be gathered around a table in the dining room. This delightful group of "old-timers," like morning glory flowers, rise early and cheerily, eager to share their adventures in living. Although Mary, Madeline, Susie, Joan, and Anna have physical disabilities, their joyful laughter abounds.

Over the last year, we have mind-traveled back to one-room schoolhouses, outdoor commodes, farmhouses, and county fairs. We've enjoyed singing favorite songs—"Moonlight and Roses," "If You Knew Susie," and "Let Me Call You Sweetheart." Home remedies have been freely shared: Colds can be cured by drinking sulfur and molasses or tying garlic around your neck; warts disappear when covered with a penny.

The Morning Glory members have traveled through the Depression and several wars. They have lost homes and loved ones, and have become disabled themselves. They have also thoroughly enjoyed happy times, choosing to release life's disappointments while calling up good memories. Their wisdom, humor, and faith in God are their sources of strength. Death is not frightening. As Anna always says, "When I die, I just want someone to put my favorite fork beside me, for I know the best is yet to come."

I feel immeasurably blessed to be a part of the lives of these ladies and will always treasure our time together. They are leaving their imprint on my heart forever. They are sharing the glory of God.

Praise the Lord, O my soul, and forget not all his benefits.

—PSALM 103:2

Thought . . . Do you treasure growing older? Your years have brought a gold mine of wisdom and wealth of memories. Your future holds the rich inheritance of Heaven.

Dad's Hands

BY JOYCE LANDORF HEATHERLEY

Now, God be prais'd, that to believing souls gives light in darkness,
comfort in despair!

—WILLIAM SHAKESPEARE

Sometimes after the winter was firmly set in, [my father and I]
walked to church across the river on ice. But my joyous jumping
up and down was instantly squashed the moment my dad and I
took our first sliding steps onto the ice. Dark rings of ice and
water surrounded the big ships on either side of the river and
the terrible blackness around those ships terrified me.

I would never have crossed the frozen path if my father, in
loving confidence, had not said, "Joyce, take my hand. Walk
with me. You'll be all right."

Hesitantly, I put my little mitten in his big glove and we began what looked to be a daring journey. But there was something so confident in my father's manner that almost immediately I lost my terror and the walk turned into a wonderful adventure. I remember doing a lot of sliding and twirling. How
joyous and free I acted—all because Daddy held my hand.

Today, I discovered something dark and forbidding in my
life. I understand that I need to reach up and take my Heavenly
Father's hand. The dark thing still scares me, but my hand is safe
inside a larger one.

My Heavenly Father is not discouraged—not afraid. He is to
be trusted. He will not shove me into the dark waters that are
over my head. God walks firmly, confidently, and so can I. I am
happy even in the presence of dark things, for my trembling
fingers are safely enclosed in His steady hand.

. . . God is light; in him there is no darkness at all.

—I JOHN 1:5

Thought . . . Do you fear the dark tunnel in which you
find yourself? Let God guide you. He promises that
though you might stumble, you won't fall because His
hand upholds you (Psalm 37:23–24).

The Chalkboard

BY SHIRLEY TERESA LANGLEY

We cannot extend unconditional love until we have experienced God's unconditional love.

—DEBRA WHITE-SMITH

In 1933, Daddy carried railroad ties for fifty cents a day. Though I remember my parents literally counting pennies, as the youngest of five, I was not fully aware of our troubled times. Yet Mother always seemed to find a way to save a little money for Christmas to purchase some small gift. One year, I received a beautiful, bright red comb and stored it among other treasures in a special drawer.

Our occasional trips to Mr. Latham's general store always found me in front of a chalkboard, practicing my alphabet. Oh! How I wanted that chalkboard! When Mr. Latham told me it would cost one hundred twenty-nine pennies, I knew it would never be mine.

Christmas morning arrived! I ran into the room, anticipating the usual small trinket. My family laughed and whispered as Mother drew me into her embrace. Then Daddy proudly set the new chalkboard before me. I couldn't contain my excitement as I hopped from one foot to the other, repeatedly hugging everyone. Suddenly, I realized no one else had received a single present. Quickly, I ran to my special drawer. Grabbing my prized possession, I entered the room, holding it out before me, and said, "Someone can have my red comb!"

I was only five when the Lord used my family to show me the powerful gift of giving and receiving. My real treasure that Christmas wouldn't fit into my special drawer, but the love I received and gave still fits perfectly in my heart.

Be devoted to one another in brotherly love. Honor one another above yourselves.

—ROMANS 12:10

Thought . . . What is the best gift you have received because it required someone's sacrifice? This Christmas, forego family gift-giving to give to a family in need. You will treasure their gratitude forever.

Sweet Potato Memories

BY SUSAN DUKE

There is no friend like an old friend who has shared our morning days, no greeting like his welcome, no homage like his praise.

—OLIVER WENDELL HOLMES

Everything always smelled so good at Betty's and Pickitt's. I especially remember the sweet potatoes. It seemed like every time I went next door for a visit, sweet potatoes, baking in an old wood stove, were almost ready to eat. Betty always said, "Sugar, you're just in time for some mighty good vittles."

The fact that Betty and Pickitt were Black and I was White never entered my little four-year-old mind. I loved them like most kids loved grandparents and felt safe and welcome at their house. Sometimes Betty read me stories from her well-worn Bible.

Although the friendship between a White child and an elderly Black couple was an unlikely combination, it bridged a gap in an all too prejudiced society and taught me lessons I'd treasure forever.

Tucked away inside this grown-up heart is a childhood smile that makes its way to my lips whenever I remember my special friends. One of the first things that I think I'll do when I get to heaven is to look up Betty and Pickitt. I have a feeling that their mansion will be easy to find. I'll just look for the smoke curling from their chimney and follow my nose to their door, where I know, inside, sweet potatoes will be cooking in an old wood stove. I expect that a kind and gentle face will greet me and say, "Why Miss Suzie, we've been waitin' for you, Sugar. Come on in and let me fix you a plate."

There is neither Jew nor Greek, slave nor free, male nor female, for you are all one in Christ Jesus.

—GALATIANS 3:28

Thought . . . Have you encouraged your children to have friends of different nationalities and races—from different economic and denominational backgrounds? Prejudice must be learned. What are you teaching your children by the friends that you keep?

Shelter from the Storm

BY JILL BRISCOE

The Lord's our rock, in Him we hide, a shelter in the time of storm.

—VERNON J. CHARLESWORTH

Barely six, I remember sitting by a roaring fire on a Sunday during the Second World War. Our family had fled the bombs, chasing us away to the English Lake District. This area of Britain kept poets in business, and John Keats' "season of mists and mellow fruitfulness" became part of my heritage.

This day was different. The mists were gone and a storm had broken over our heads. The rain slashed against the windowpane, and thunder grumbled. I didn't like storms.

I was old enough to understand that a bigger storm was raging—involving the entire world. But at that moment it seemed far away.

The fire was warm. My father, reading the paper, was sitting in his chair. Aware I needed reassurance, he put down his paper. "Come here, little girl," he said. I was safe in his arms, feeling the beat of his heart. What a grand place to be!

I have realized how my Heavenly Father shelters me from storms of life. When torrents of sorrow swamped me at my mother's funeral, when floods of fear rose as I waited for the results of frightening tests, I sensed my Heavenly Father saying, "Come here, little girl." I climbed into His arms, and murmured, "This *is* a grand place to be!"

As I rest in that safe place, knowing that my Father is bigger than any storm of life, I can watch the rain and listen to the thunder and know that everything is all right. Here I can feel the beat of my Father's heart!

". . . There is no Rock like our God. . . ."

—I SAMUEL 2:2

Thought . . . When "storms" of life threaten your peace, where do you turn? God doesn't always stop the storm, but can calm you in the midst of it!

Old Sassy

BY PAT DEVINE

The groves were God's first temples, ere man learned to hew the shaft . . .

—WILLIAM CULLEN BRYANT

We were sad to see that sometime over this past winter the sassafras tree had died. No leaves appeared on her branches, nary a flower nor berry to announce spring. The hollow, hidden by a big piece of loose bark that had been a hiding place for the special golden egg at Easter, had grown large enough over the years to hold two or three toddlers playing hide and seek.

Although we had planned the end, we were unprepared for the actual undertaking. As each branch fell to the ground, it rocked and rolled like a downed elephant on the African veldt. Two big men hustled it away to a shredder before we could make note of its passing.

We settled, Joe and I, for holding hands and recalling its halcyon days when grandchildren played in and around it. "A ghost tree." "An owl's nest." "I bet rats are in there—Ugh!" No imagination could rival the reality of its value.

Its strong branches had provided support for leafy nests built by gray squirrels. Pokey opossums and nocturnal raccoons taught their babies to climb its gnarled trunk. Its generous shade sheltered summer suppers, and its tender shoots provided sassafras tea for the adventurous.

We sighed our good-bye to this backyard treasure as the surgeons looped a yellow rope around her upper trunk, braced their feet on the grassy slope at her roots and yelled, "Timber!"

Softly we echoed . . . "Timber."

Then God said, "Let the land produce vegetation: seed-bearing plants and trees on the land that bear fruit with seed in it, according to their various kinds." And it was so.

—GENESIS 1:11

Thought . . . Have you heard people say, "Trees are my friends"? That may be loving nature in the extreme. Yet, God has created it for our enjoyment. Sit under your favorite shade tree, worshiping the Lord for His beautiful creation. You'll feel close to Him there.

Early Morning Whispers

BY GUYLA GREENLY COOPER

God designed you to be a unique, distinct, significant person unlike any other individual on the face of the earth, throughout the vast expanse of time. The mold was broken, never to be used again, once you entered the flow of mankind.

—CHARLES R. SWINDOLL

Early in the morning, before anyone else was up, Grandpa Walt would lean over the sofa bed and whisper, "Guyla, wanna have pancakes with Grandpa?" My feet were on the floor before my eyes ever opened. Grandpa would brew himself a pot of coffee and whip up a batch of his famous pancakes. The first pancake or two would go to the dog because, as all great pancake chefs know, it takes a few passes with the batter to properly season the griddle.

Two golden, fluffy pancakes smothered in butter and Mrs. Buttersworth later, I knew that I was the most important child on the planet, maybe even the universe. I come from a long line of twins. Of five grandchildren, I am the "odd man out." But I never *felt* that way. I always told people that I was the special one because I was the only "singleton."

My grandpa had a major role in shaping my attitude. Now that I'm an adult, early each morning, my Lord whispers, "Guyla, wanna spend time with Me?" So often I blink and roll over or jump up and rush into the day's activities. However, when I do read His Word, especially a psalm or proverb, I feel that I am the most important person in the universe. God loves me more than my grandpa did. He loves me so much that He sent His only Son to die a brutal death on the Cross, and He would do it all over again—even were I the only "singleton" in the world.

> Let the morning bring me word of your unfailing love, for I have put my trust in you. Show me the way I should go, for to you I lift up my soul.
>
> —PSALM 143:8

Thought . . . Do you know how much God treasures you? "Seeing" is believing. Read God's "love letter" to you, the Bible. Record in a notebook every verse that pertains to God's love. Ponder these truths often.

You Are His Treasured Possession

BY LIZ CURTIS HIGGS

The human soul is God's treasury, out of which He coins unspeakable riches, thoughts and feelings, desires and yearnings, faith and hope—these are the most precious things which God finds in us.

—HENRY WARD BEECHER

Suppose that you wake up tomorrow morning to find your house engulfed in a raging fire. You and your family are safely headed for the door, but you have time to grab one cherished item on your way out, your most treasured possession. What would you take?

If I could only take one thing, I'd probably yank from the wall a precious old family quilt done in the crazy quilt style. I wouldn't take it because of its market value, but rather because of its emotional value. It was passed down through the family. Through my single years, I treated it with kid gloves, but time began to take its toll on the delicate silk border. I should have put my *kids* in gloves when they came along, because they slid their tiny fingers in the torn places and the fabric gave way even more. Still, this doesn't lessen its value one bit to me; if anything, it adds another layer of memories when I look at that quilt on the wall.

This passage from Deuteronomy [below] suggests that if an unquenchable fire were burning—and it is—the Lord would pull you out of the fire as His most treasured possession—and He did.

None of us is in "mint condition" either. Our lives are tattered and torn with poor choices and painful failures. But God looks at us, crazy quilts one and all, and lovingly embroiders His name on our hearts. You are His most treasured possession, saved by grace from that certain, unquenchable fire.

> . . . Out of all the peoples on the face of the earth, the Lord has chosen you to be his treasured possession.
>
> —DEUTERONOMY 14:2

Thought . . . Do you feel inadequate because your life is torn apart? Because Jesus died for you, your life has great value. He'll also mend the torn places.

Daddy Said Grace

BY DORIS C. CRANDALL

There are times in a man's life when, regardless of the attitude of the body, the soul is on its knees in prayer.

—VICTOR HUGO

"Today's Thanksgiving, isn't it?" Daddy asked from his hospital bed, his voice weakened from heart disease.

"Yes," I replied, "and it's starting to snow."

As I drew the covers snugly around him, he reached out and pushed the button that signaled the nurse. "Bring my daughter a tray, please." It was the most he had spoken all day.

Thinking of Thanksgivings past, I remembered the entire family, gathered at the farmhouse. What a feast Mama put on the table! And Mama, never Daddy, said grace. "Why is that, Mama?" I questioned when I was a child. Mama wrinkled her brow. "I don't think he feels comfortable with words. He didn't get to go to school much because he had to work in the fields. But understand this, Honey, prayer requires more of the heart than of the tongue."

Today, with only Daddy and I to eat Thanksgiving dinner together, I didn't expect him to say grace. I began to compose a special Thanksgiving prayer in my mind. The nurse brought the trays. I moved close to Daddy to help him with his knife and fork. Bowing my head, hesitating a moment to wipe away my tears, I heard Daddy say, "Thank you, Lord, that my daughter is here with me today." The spiritual treasure Daddy's prayer gave me that day can never be erased from my heart. I thank God for it.

The Lord has heard my cry for mercy; the Lord accepts my prayer.

—PSALM 6:9

Thought . . . Do you know people who find it terribly difficult to pray? Offer a one-sentence prayer, suggesting they try the same. "Ping pong" back and forth to the Lord. Prayers are just individual, heartfelt sentences strung together in love and sincerity.

The Last of the Firsts

BY MELISSA HUDSON-BERRY

Wisdom begins in wonder.

—SOCRATES

"Well, that should do it," the hairdresser assures, clipping the last curl from Jonathan's head. She removes the blue bib designed to catch falling tendrils. Jonathan scoots for the toy box. My husband, David, did not agree that Jonathan was ready for his first haircut. Now I realize that *I* am the one who wasn't ready.

As I watch Jonathan play, it seems like a lifetime ago that I held him, skin to skin, when he was hours old. Before his first birthday, I never thought past his first year or placed significance on *any* of his "firsts." But today, I feel a change; I understand the wonder of it all.

The hairdresser hands me a plastic bag containing blonde curls and a certificate to signify his first haircut. Jonathan is no longer a baby, but a little boy—a vibrant treasure contained in a small, constantly moving body, too active for cuddling. Today's event evokes in me an unexplained sadness—a moment come and gone too quickly.

A mom treasures the "firsts." Baby books dedicate an entire page to "firsts"—first step, first word, first tooth, first shoes, first haircut. Firsts are important. With the blink of an eye, we have experienced the last of our *baby's* "firsts" today. Now I must embrace the next phase of his life.

"Ready to go?" David asks. "Yes," I reply, smiling. Our handsome son reaches up a tiny hand for mine. I gladly accept his invitation, for all too soon I will have to let him go.

. . . But his mother treasured all these things in her heart.

—LUKE 2:51

Thought . . . How do you commemorate your child's "firsts"? One way is by having the last word about them. Record each precious memory in a journal. Then the "firsts" become lasting treasure.

Memories of God's Goodness

BY SHERI BERGER

As it is in nature, so it is in God's kingdom. From the winds and rains of adversity comes abundant growth and a beautiful life worth painting.

—LAURA LEWIS LANIER

As the helicopter ambulance lifted my children up in the air, all I could think of was how precious they were to me and how precious they were to God. The sound of a siren blaring from the distance brought my mind back to the present. We had just been in a serious car accident. Smoke and commotion were everywhere. As the siren stopped and I was lifted into the ambulance, my mind returned to constant prayer. *Would my son survive a broken back? Would my daughter be able to walk again? Would my husband lose his eyesight?* I agonized.

All day long I lay in the intensive care wing praying for my family. I often thought about the many scrapbook photo albums that I had completed which chronicled our family memories. How thankful I was to have created a visual and written documentation of our times together. *Would there be more memories to add in the future?* I wondered.

Six months later, my son is out riding his bike, my daughter is jumping rope, and my husband is working on the computer. I am busy completing yet another scrapbook page and writing the story of our accident, detailing God's protection and love. How thankful I am for these albums, for they contain the memories that make our family who we are. They contain our trials, our triumphs, our heartaches, our happiness, our struggles, our blessings. They contain the treasures of my heart.

I will remember the deeds of the Lord; yes, I will remember your miracles of long ago. I will meditate on all your works and consider all your mighty deeds.

—PSALM 77:11–12

Thought . . . How do you preserve family memories? If a picture is worth a thousand words, why not record the story behind the picture? Journaling greatly enhances scrapbooking.

Washtub Sled

BY MARY ELLEN WRIGHT

The supreme happiness in life is the conviction that we are loved.

—VICTOR HUGO

One of my favorite childhood memories took place when I was four and my sister was two. Zipped tightly in heavily padded wool snowsuits, our feet scrunched into rubber boots, we sat nose to nose in Mom's big stainless steel washtub. It scraped and screeched over the icy street as Daddy pulled the tub by a rope secured to the handle. How we loved washtub sledding down the steep hill of our Seattle suburb home.

Winter was full of delights. We made snowmen, punctuating their white faces with eyes and mouths of coal. We plunged into snowball fights, though we were too small to throw very far. And while we envied older children who were allowed to sled down our hill alone, we enjoyed a greater sport. With Daddy's ingenuity and help, we took frightful, snow-blowing, speed-gathering, cheek-reddening, tub-spinning rides in Mom's wash-tub. Daddy never seemed to tire of our pleas for "just one more time." He gave us so much. Endless times he trudged up the hill to release the rope and watch his two elfin marshmallow chil-dren careen, squealing, down the snow and ice. With every tub-over-toe dump in the snow, he repeatedly picked us up, dried our tears, and gave us confidence to try again.

Freely Daddy gave us time and utter all-out fun. He loved us and he showed it by *being* with us. I will always treasure my memo-ries of washtub sledding and my father's love.

... Let us not love with words or tongue but with actions and in truth.

—I JOHN 3:18

Thought . . . How much time do you give your children? Ultimately, they won't treasure the trinkets you gave, but the time you spent. And their memories of you will increase in value over the years.

Secret Language of the Heart

BY BRENDA WAGGONER

And now, here is my secret. A very simple secret. It is only with the heart that one can see rightly. What is essential is invisible to the eye.

—ANTOINE DE SAINT-EXUPÉRY

Have you ever hiked on a mountain path and come upon a young fawn, barely distinguishable at a distance through the trees and undergrowth, as she silently lapped water from a glassy pond—or walked along the beach at sundown when sea foam, mixed with glints of brilliant sunlight, spilled mounds of liquid diamonds?

On a cold, clear winter evening, my husband and I often pull up chairs to gaze out our large atrium window, facing west. Like mesmerized moviegoers, mindlessly poking popcorn into their mouths, we share a snack and watch the sky turn bright yellow-orange just moments after the sun descends beyond the horizon. As orange darkens into pink, then deepens to purplish rose, we hold hands, spellbound by the majestic, hand-painted horizon.

It is our *hearts* that respond to God's wooing voice, rather than our intellects. The prophet, Elijah, learned this when he looked for God in a great wind, but He was not there. Nor was He found in the earthquake, nor the fire. It was in a soft, gentle whisper that Elijah heard the voice of God.

Like a lover whispering sweet intimacies into our ears, God speaks His love-messages through soothing sounds of poplar leaves shaking in caressing breezes or through brush-stroked sunsets. In the most natural, simple settings, a secret language of the heart is heard if we'll but listen.

I will give them a heart to know me, that I am the Lord. . . .
—JEREMIAH 24:7

Thought . . . Do you know God intellectually through His Word?—emotionally through your senses? Experiencing treasured intimacy with your Creator requires both. Listen for God's quiet love-whispers, especially in nature. Spend time discovering Him there.

On Our Knees

BY JAN FUGMAN

It's not easy to fix our eyes on what is unseen. But it's necessary.

—MAX LUCADO

The ground squished as I crawled forward on my hands and knees. The flashlight's beam cut through the darkness, revealing water droplets clinging to the short blades of grass. Dad had mowed the lawn that evening right before he watered. "Got to have the grass short, Janny, so it's easier to grab those critters when they stick their heads up out of their holes."

Night crawlers! How I loved to gather night crawlers with Dad for a fishing trip early the next morning. Looking back, I have to chuckle and wonder who really were the night crawlers—the fat worms we plucked from the ground and dropped into our bait pail, or Dad and I traversing the front lawn on all fours?

I learned a lot from those late-night excursions: there are some things better accomplished on our knees, and there are things you can't rush. Dad found joy in the journey and cultivated a cadence of contentment throughout his lifetime. The essence of his peace was in knowing there is a perfect rhythm for our lives, and that when we try to hurry the pace, we risk altering the destined plan.

Dad trusted in God's timing, knowing it is always perfect. And like Dad and I and the night crawlers, the victory is in knowing when to proceed and when to be still and wait on the Lord.

But I trust in you, O Lord; I say, "You are my God." My times are in your hands . . .

—PSALM 31:14–15

Thought . . . Is your life's rhythm frenzied? God is your Conductor. Focus on Him and follow His beat, whether it's allegro or adagio. And observe His rests in life's score. When you sing the song of life in God's timing, you sing it joyfully.

238

Surprises

Awakening

BY MARGARET BECKER

A single event can awaken within us a stranger totally unknown to us. To live is to be slowly born.

—ANTOINE DE SAINT-EXUPÉRY

I sit in the rattan chair, terry cloth robe bundled around me. It is daybreak. My feet and face are chilled by the crisp Gulf breeze flowing through the open French doors. It is the first moment of my awakening.

I stare into the sun as it lifts off the black-green ocean. I know it is too cold to sit like this, no coat or shoes, but I am chilled already in so many ways. It is familiar. I watch pelicans fall seaward, their beaks pointed like spears at their breakfast. Dolphins arc into the sky, slick gray fins flashing. I swallow deep breaths of icy air. These are long, luxurious, unhurried breaths, driving the present moment into my innermost recesses.

Tints and textures melt into a recognizable scene, a beautiful portrait coming into focus after a long sleep. I've been dormant for quite some time, derailed by the act of living itself. Frozen, encumbered. Gummed with goals. Paranoid with purpose.

I've come to this house to right myself in life, to wake up, to rest. I've come here because had I refused, I believe I might have blinked and missed another decade. It is my first day without the phone, the fax, the deadline, and the doorbell.

I sit in thick sweaters at the water's edge, soothed by endless combinations of folding surf. I keep a promise to myself to view every sunrise and every sunset. They become a personal art gallery, open all hours, glorious vistas offering insights into the Creator's soul.

. . . The hour has come for you to wake up from your slumber . . .

—ROMANS 13:11

Thought . . . Are you spiritually asleep, just going through the motions? Ask the Lord to give you "new eyes," to see life from His perspective. Every moment will become a surprise to treasure.

The Reminder

BY MARJORIE K. EVANS

The Lord my pasture shall prepare, and feed me with a shepherd's care; His presence shall my wants supply, and guard me with a watchful eye.

—JOSEPH ADDISON

It wasn't that I didn't enjoy Christmas, the joyous season celebrating the birth of Jesus Christ, but as my husband and I finished our shopping, I felt sad and lonely. Tears welled up in my eyes. I thought, *Christmas won't be the same with our son and his family thousands of miles across the ocean from us.*

In June, the Air Force had sent Charles to Taiwan. Then, after he found a suitable apartment, Diane and six-month-old Cody, our only grandchild, joined him. Long letters and cassette tapes to and from Taiwan helped alleviate my concern, but I knew how terribly homesick they were. And I longed to see them and to cuddle baby Cody again.

Now we trudged back to the car. As my husband put packages into the trunk, I stood there disconsolate, my head bowed down. Then, on the blacktop, I noticed a delicate butterfly pin made of tiny strips of blue and tan bamboo. Picking it up, I exclaimed in surprise, "Ed, look! Here's a butterfly pin for my collection." (Butterflies are special to me, for they symbolize new life in Christ.) Turning it over, I read, "Made in Taiwan."

Again, tears welled up in my eyes, but this time they were tears of joy. I breathed, "Thank You, dear Heavenly Father, for surprising me with this reminder of Your love and care. Not only are You watching over Charles, Diane, and Cody in Taiwan, but You are thinking about me constantly."

How precious to me are your thoughts, O God! How vast is the sum of them! Were I to count them, they would outnumber the grains of sand. . . .

—PSALM 139:17–18

Thought . . . Are you experiencing deep loneliness? Jesus, your Shepherd, is always near to comfort you. Aloneness fosters the treasure of fellowship with your Savior. You're not alone at all.

An Eternal Investment

BY TERESA ARSENEAU

There was never a person who did anything worth doing that he did not receive more than he gave.

— HENRY WARD BEECHER

One morning the phone rang in response to my ad. A man arrived an hour later and bought my entire porcelain doll collection without haggling the price. In addition to tithing from this sale, I felt the Lord wanted me to set aside an extra hundred dollars for an unknown cause.

To my surprise, another knock came at the door not an hour later. It was an unemployed man with a wife and three children. Desperately in need of food, he'd been going from house to house offering to do odd jobs. No one could or would help him. I told him about my dolls and how the Lord had instructed me to set aside a certain amount from the sale. He explained that he and his wife were Christians but, hurt and discouraged, they hadn't gone to church for a long time.

"Dan, I believe this is meant for you," I said, handing him a sealed envelope. He thanked me and left. Minutes later, another knock came. I opened the door to a man sobbing and broken with gratitude. Dan was overwhelmed by the contents of my envelope. Weeping myself, I hugged my newly discovered brother in Christ, promising to pray for him.

Since that time, other Christians have reached out in loving, practical ways to this family. They are still fearful, but slowly Dan and his wife are opening their hearts to the Lord and His people again. My little hundred dollar investment is already generating dividends that will last throughout eternity.

Command them to do good, to be rich in good deeds, and to be generous and willing to share. In this way they will lay up treasure for themselves as a firm foundation for the coming age, so that they may take hold of the life that is truly life.

—I TIMOTHY 6:18–19

Thought . . . Do you cling to money like treasure, or use it however the Lord wishes, whether tithing or giving to those in need? Your money belongs to God. In obedience lies great reward.

Coming Home

BY RUTH BELL GRAHAM

When we all get to Heaven, what a day of rejoicing that will be!

—ELIZA HEWITT

"I shall miss Mother this Christmas," the clerk in the store told me. Her mother had died recently. "I used to go home in the evenings, and we'd have such good times."

In the hospital, the doctor told the children to stay out of her room in order for her to rest. "So I stayed out," she continued, "waiting . . . listening. Finally I could stand it no longer, and I went in."

"'I thought you'd never come!' Mother said."

Blinking back tears, the clerk added, with a smile, "I'm thinking they'll be the first words she'll say when I get to Heaven!"

• • •

"Precious in the sight of the Lord is the death of his saints" (Psalm 116:15).

I've never understood this verse. Then this past spring, we were getting ready for visits from the children, culminating in a Bell Family Reunion. There were curtains to be replaced, pictures to hang, meals to plan. All the while, down deep inside there was a growing excitement. It has always been this way since the children left home—whether to boarding school or to marry—their return brought a joy they will understand only when their children grow up, leave, and come home again.

Then I realized I have been looking at death from my perspective, not from God's. Just as "there is joy in the presence of the angels of God over one sinner that repenteth," so too there is joy in Heaven over each child of God coming home. This is what my friend, the clerk, was saying.

"... In my Father's house are many rooms ... I am going there to prepare a place for you. ..."

—JOHN 14:2

Thought . . . Have you ever thought about death as a "homecoming"? When you do, it's surprisingly easier to give up earth's rental property for a permanent residence with your Heavenly Father.

243

Not Second-Rate

BY MARTHA B. YODER

My attitude determines whether grief causes a disease in me or a glorious everlasting reward.

—S. I. McMILLEN

"Handicapped persons are not second-rate!" I exclaimed excitedly to my husband. "Listen to this verse: 'Who gave man his mouth? Who makes him deaf or mute? Who gives him sight or makes him blind? Is it not I, the Lord?' That list could include neurofibromatosis, Melvin. It's all in God's perfect plan!"

What a surprising revelation this was to me. As I began to praise the Lord for this much-needed relief, a heavy load lifted that I had carried too long. Worrying over NF had brought much grief as we discovered that our two sons had inherited this disorder from their father, whose disease had resulted from a new mutation at his conception. Doctors who had told us that it was not hereditary were wrong.

My mother's heart ached because our sons were given the life sentence of disfigurement; yet despite this difficulty, our sons have become men of God. Each has found a brave, sweet wife with whom to share life's uncertainties and joys.

Now, years later, God had brought this insightful verse to me. Melvin and the boys were God's creations—treasured creations—not second-rate. Though His purposes defy our comprehension, His grace is sufficient for life's journey as we focus on Him and accept His plan. How blessed we are when we consider NF not as a tragedy, but as the treasured touch of an all-knowing God!

It was good for me to be afflicted so that I might learn your decrees.

—PSALM 119:71

Thought . . . Have you allowed God to transform your trials to treasure? When you entrust them to His divine purposes, which are always good, your attitude and your life are gloriously changed.

244

Artful Surprise

BY MARY ELLEN WRIGHT

> The Holy Spirit descended upon me in a manner that seemed to go through me, body and soul. I could feel the impression like a wave of electricity going through and through me. Indeed, it seemed to come in waves and waves of liquid love . . . like the very breath of God . . . it seemed to fan me like immense wings.
>
> —CHARLES G. FINNEY

My day had been stressful with demands far outweighing my coping skills. Breathing in the cool autumn air, I walked with determined steps down our graveled road, pouring out my soul: "Lord, please help me to be more like You. I get overwhelmed so easily. Lord, I need Your peace. Forgive me for my impatience and critical heart today."

Rounding the corner, I began to sing, my mood lifting as I felt the companionship of His nearness. It was dusk now as the sun slowly slipped into the western horizon. There before me was a feast of color—incredible truly blue skies were brush-stroked with sweeping splashes of strawberry pink. My gaze dropped to the tree line, intensified by the deep forest green of maples, oaks, and ash. The trees stood sentinel around huge fields of ripened soybeans, colored rich mahogany.

Observing the "brush strokes" more closely, I was struck with the image displayed before me. There, many miles wide, was the outline of the biggest Holy Spirit dove I had ever seen. His head was pointed earthward, and His outstretched wings arched upward. Standing alone, surrounded with this treasure of nature's splendor, I raised my hands and voice in praise to my Father. He had surprised me with His love. I was reminded that He knows who we are, where we are, what we need, and how best to meet our need. I had asked for peace, and He showed me His symbol of peace, a dove. Hope flooded my soul.

> The heavens declare the glory of God; the skies proclaim the work of his hands.
>
> —PSALM 19:1

Thought . . . Does peace elude you? When you receive Christ as your Savior, the indwelling Holy Spirit will "grow" the fruit of peace in the ripened "field" of your heart (Galatians 5:22).

A Divine Appointment

BY DIANA L. JAMES

Want to see a miracle? Plant a word of love heart-deep in a person's life. Nurture it with a smile and a prayer, and watch what happens.

—MAX LUCADO

That Sunday morning, mine was the last car leaving the church parking lot. My husband, Max, had left earlier and was probably wondering what was keeping me. I zipped along the deserted rural road, hardly noticing the forlorn figure of a young woman carrying a backpack, suitcase, and carry-on bag.

She was trudging in my same direction and, after I passed her, I looked in the rearview mirror. She was crying. God must have been steering my car, not I, because it made a quick U-turn. I don't usually pick up strangers, but this was surprisingly *different*. God clearly was directing me to stop.

With some hesitation, the young woman got into the car, and introduced herself as Peggy. Peggy's story was pitiful and her life, a mess. She had nowhere to turn, and was planning suicide by walking off into the mountain wilderness.

I took her home and she lived with us for several months. Max and I helped her get a job. At first she frowned at anything "religious," but we prayed for her anyway. Today she is married, has a wonderful job and, best of all, she is a devoted Christian, serving the Lord. How can we ever doubt that God makes divine appointments for us?

That day God entrusted me with a most important assignment. One of His sheep was lost, and He needed someone to lead her out of danger and despair. I got the call, and for that I will be eternally grateful.

Trust in the Lord with all your heart and lean not on your own understanding; in all your ways acknowledge him, and he will make your paths straight.

—PROVERBS 3:5–6

Thought . . . Do you follow God's divine "nudges" to reach out to others? Don't be a "no-show." Keep His appointments. Someone's eternal future may depend upon it.

God's Treasure Hunt

BY DEBBI TAYLOR

Keep your life so constantly in touch with God that His surprising power can break through at any point. Live in a constant state of expectancy, and leave room for God to come in as He decides.

—OSWALD CHAMBERS

My husband and I began our family with a commitment that I would not go back to work until our children began school. Knowing how essential a child's early development is, we longed to instill godly character whatever the cost. The Lord blessed us with three sons in four years.

Committed to being a stay-at-home mom gave me the gift of time with my boys . . . time to explore hundreds of wonderful books, time to play at the park, and time to intercede for them. Hearing their very first words and watching them take their first steps—these were treasures of inestimable value! However, the financial pressure of living on one income created frequent opportunities for God to manifest His faithful provision.

Lacking the necessary $569.48 to pay our property taxes one April, we prayerfully committed this need to our loving Father. We were hosting a home Bible study group and, as I was cleaning up afterward, I was surprised to find a twenty dollar bill under a pillow. Just then my husband shouted, "Come here!" He had discovered another twenty dollar bill wrapped around the toothpaste! Like excited children on a treasure hunt, we discovered five, ten, and twenty dollar bills hidden throughout our home. Within ten minutes, we had collected five hundred and seventy dollars, cash—just enough to pay the taxes, including postage!

My heart was overwhelmed with the realization that I serve a personal God Who is my provider. There is no limit to His creativity.

And my God will meet all your needs according to his glorious riches in Christ Jesus.

—PHILIPPIANS 4:19

Thought . . . Has God asked you to make a financial sacrifice? He promises to supply all your needs, not *wants*. As He provides your needs, the greatest treasure you'll receive is trust.

Choosing to Grow

BY NANCIE CARMICHAEL

My business is not to remain myself, but to make the absolute best of what God made.

—ROBERT BROWNING

I was a mother of two now, a wife of a minister. It was so unlike what I thought it would be, to be married. I wondered what my all-fired hurry was to be married. And while I wasn't sorry I married early, I was learning that family life was incredibly hard. A crucible.

Where did I go from here? It was what I had always wanted— to build a life of significance, of service. But life was requiring something more; indeed, there seemed to be much ahead, much that I did not know and was not equipped to handle.

It was a moment of epiphany. I made a promise: "Whatever happens in my life, I promise that I will keep growing—never stop learning as long as I live." I said it almost as a prayer, but I have never forgotten. I knew I needed to frame my life with a choice to grow, to learn.

I know now that as I chose to grow, each challenge became like another room added to my life, making it bigger, more productive. Steps of growth come at moments I would most like to avoid—often the places of my weakness and fears, but these offer a place to grow a larger life. Learning never stops—and with learning comes new choices.

This greediness to learn, to grow, must be tempered by submitting our will to the will of God, or it can be a dangerous choice, taking me to harmful things. The heart can betray me if it is not submitted to God.

But grow in the grace and knowledge of our Lord and Savior Jesus Christ.

—II PETER 3:18A

Thought . . . How are you growing? Learning worldly facts is ultimately futile. Keep learning about Christ, "in whom are hidden the treasures of wisdom and knowledge (Colossians 2:3)."

A Treasure Almost Overlooked

BY CINDI MCMENAMIN

How blind we are to Heaven's gifts!

—LUCAN

I was confused . . . and a little bit scared. Why would God with-hold another baby from us? Wasn't He pleased with the way that we had parented the child we already had? Did He have something else in mind for us?

It had been two years since my husband and I had decided that we wanted another child. And still, *nothing*. Since I became pregnant with my first child almost immediately, we couldn't imagine what was going wrong now. As the months progressed, we began to pray fervently for a second child, and to undergo tests for secondary infertility. Finally, the doctor called with the results of our tests.

"You know that miracle baby you've been praying for?" he asked. "Well, you already had her three years ago." The doctor explained that there was fertility incompatibility between my husband and me and, medically speaking, we shouldn't have been able to have any children at all!

As I hung up the phone, I sunk to my knees in gratitude to the Lord for the surprising miracle we had already received, with-out even realizing it. By concentrating so fully on what I didn't have, I had lost focus of the blessing that I already had—a happy, healthy three-year-old who, without God's intervention, wouldn't have been here at all. I realized then that one of my greatest treasures in life was someone whom I had almost taken for granted.

Every good and perfect gift is from above. . . .

—JAMES 1:17

Thought . . . Do you truly treasure your children, consid-ering them a gift and reward (Psalm 127:3)? If you do, your entire attitude will change in how you treat them. You won't take one precious moment for granted.

A Mother's Hope

BY DIANN G. MILLS

The Christian life is gloriously difficult, but the difficulty of it does not make us faint and cave in, it rouses us up to overcome.

—OSWALD CHAMBERS

I remember the bleak day I realized I had only enough food for two more days. I had no money and no job. How would I take care of my four young sons? I tried to pray, but fear hung suspended in my mind. I wanted to cry, but knew that once I started, the tears might never end.

Swallowing my pride, I phoned my parents in another state. Perhaps they'd take the boys until I got on my feet. The thought of parting with them made me physically ill. They had already dealt with abandonment issues from their father's recent departure, and I knew being separated from me would increase their insecurities—and mine.

After the phone call, I painted a smile on my face and began preparing dinner. The doorbell rang, interrupting my silent prayer for faith. A middle-aged woman stood there, looking somewhat perplexed and nervous.

"Can I help you?" I asked.

She nodded and gave me a faint smile. "I think so. God told me that the family living here needs food. I have my station wagon full of groceries."

God had sent an angel to feed my family! The food in those grocery bags fed us for a long time. Every item was something I would have purchased. This blessing marked the beginning of many. Within a week I found a job directing a day care center, and my children never went hungry. The true treasure was the provision of our faithful God which ensured that our family never had to be separated.

I lift up my eyes to the hills—where does my help come from? My help comes from the Lord, the Maker of heaven and earth.

—PSALM 121:1–2

Thought . . . When you can't seem to pray, what do you do? Just pray for faith to believe. You don't need to know how God will solve impossible situations, just that He will! He'll surprise you with His creativity.

The Art of Worship

BY CLAIRE CLONINGER

God wants worshipers before workers; indeed the only acceptable workers are those who have learned the lost art of worship.

—A. W. TOZER

I had been feeling down on myself for weeks, struggling with writer's block. The day before I had received another book written by an extremely prolific author-friend. Feeling more like pouting than praying, there was not much worship rising in my spirit.

Suddenly my eye caught a little spider jumping along the floorboards of the porch. He seemed so spunky and pleased with himself! Near the spider, ambling slowly, one thread-like leg at a time, was a huge daddy longlegs.

I watched those two spiders without thinking anything. As a soft breeze stirred, I lifted my eyes. I found myself looking at dozens of different trees. Oaks. Pines. Pecans. Each had a different kind of bark. A different leaf or needle. I was surrounded by a symphony of bird songs, and gliding out across the river, like an angel, was a snowy egret.

"Lord, what are you saying?" I asked.

"Claire," I seemed to hear, "I delight in the diversity of my creation. In spiders, trees, birds, people. I delight in you just as you are. When you are critical and impatient with yourself, when you compare yourself with others, you hurt me, for you are criticizing my design for your life. Learn to agree with me about who you are—my child—a priceless work of art!"

I let His words sink in. I wrote in my Bible, "I praise You, for I am Your work of art." Though I had not sung a single song or lifted my hands, I knew that I had worshiped.

Then God said, "Let us make man in our image, in our likeness . . ."

—GENESIS 1:26

Thought . . . Does feeling inadequate prevent you from worshiping God? Focus on Him, and not on yourself. Lost in the surprise and wonder of His magnificence, you'll be lost in worship!

Touching Treasure

BY ARMENÉ HUMBER

O Lord my God, when I in awesome wonder consider all the worlds
Thy hands have made, I see the stars, I hear the rolling thunder, Thy
power throughout the universe displayed!

—STUART K. HINE

She spoke sharply to our two young sons. "Please stay on the
protective carpet. We're trying to preserve the Castle's beauty."
In a moment of curiosity, they had leaned over the roping to
peek around the adults blocking their view. I quickly nudged
them back into line, and the docent resumed our tour through
Hearst Castle, pointing out the priceless artwork and treasures
collected by William Randolph Hearst in his monumental
castle-home.

An hour later, I was relieved to be back in the car, headed
toward the ranch that was our lodging for the night. As the tiny
road meandered through acres of almond orchards, and the sky
darkened into solid blackness, we strained to find the entrance.
Finally, we spotted a small weathered sign and turned into the
ranch. Opening the car, we peered through the darkness as a
man emerged from a doorway. "Hey," he called, "we're about to
go on a hayride! You're just in time if you want to come along."
What an unexpected treat! Our boys raced toward the hay
wagon.

As we slowly swayed over rutted roads between mountain
silhouettes, I relaxed against the sweet-smelling hay and looked
up through untouched darkness at the million fluorescent stars
surrounding the moon. Suddenly overcome by the majesty and
holiness of this enormous outdoor sanctuary, I sat reverently
still. From His heavenly altar, God whispered, "Today you toured
the works and treasures of man. I brought you here tonight to
show you mine. No ropes, no restrictions. Enjoy my surprises,
dear child."

The heavens praise your wonders, O Lord, your faithfulness too, in the assembly of the holy ones.

—PSALM 89:5

Thought . . . Have you opened the treasure chest in your
own backyard? Enjoy a moonlit stroll or pick a garden
bouquet—God's free gifts for the taking.

God's Loving Presence

BY AMY CARMICHAEL

Whether or not you avail yourself of the opportunities which God's presence offers, is dependent entirely upon whether or not you have learned the lesson of drawing on His strength.

—CHARLES S. PRICE

There was a year a long time ago when I had to be left alone because illness had forced fellow missionaries to go home. That year began when I stood on the verandah of our bungalow, listening to the wheels of the bullock cart as it turned on the gravel and drove unwillingly away. The cry of a child in delirium seemed to fill the house (a little girl I was nursing was very ill). There was no one else in the house.

I was not lonely. There was something new in the "feel" of the house, and that sense of a light in a dim place, and an infinitely loving Presence near ("near" is too distant a word) was an abiding strength. It is the fact of His presence that is our strength. When there is not any feeling we rest on His bare word, "Lo, I am with you always, all the days, and all day long." And we are content.

The bright flowers of the edelweiss waiting to be gathered among the rough rocks of difficult circumstances—we may call the consolations of God what we will—who are we that we should find such comforts anywhere? Love led us to these enchanting discoveries. A child cannot bear to enjoy delight alone; it turns to its nearest friend with joy and shares its treasures. Turn so to thy Nearest soul, beloved. Speak thy quick thanks and share thy joy. Offer not the discourtesy of remembering thy Unseen Companion only when nettles sting, and thy feet are cut on the stones.

You have made known to me the path of life; you will fill me with joy in your presence . . .

—PSALM 16:11

Thought . . . Do you thank God for His presence in good times and bad? You can when you realize it's surprising that He desires our presence at all!

Chosen Treasure

BY LAURA SABIN RILEY

Relying on God has to begin all over again every day as if nothing had yet been done.

—C. S. LEWIS

Do you perceive your children as little nuggets of treasure from God? Your answer probably depends upon the day, right?! Yet, despite good days and bad, that is *exactly* how God views them: as a heritage of invaluable treasure.

When my firstborn was a toddler, he had a myriad of health problems. His all-night bouts with croup, ear infections, and asthma attacks wore me out! After one nightlong session of croup, I received a card in the mail the next day from a friend who wrote, "God must have known Seth would need very sensitive, loving parents when He chose Jimmy and you to be his caretakers."

Her words not only uplifted me, but surprisingly changed the way I saw myself. God had *chosen* me to be Seth's mom! That realization brought new value to my role as a mother. God knew that I would be the mom Seth needed. This fresh way of thinking bolstered my exhausted attitude. I had been growing weary of caring for my precious treasure! After reviewing my friend's thoughts, I began to consider even those twilight hours in the rocking chair, holding a wheezing toddler, as a special assignment from God.

The time we have with our children is like precious treasure, growing more valuable with each passing year. Just as silver requires much time to polish to maintain its luster, so our children require much time to nurture. If we neglect these tiny nuggets the Father has entrusted to our care, they will become dull and lifeless.

"I am the Lord's servant," Mary answered. "May it be to me as you have said." Then the angel left her.

—LUKE 1:38

Thought . . . As a mother, are you "on assignment" from God? Because motherhood is a high calling from God, you can show up for work, ready, willing, and able— *able* because it is *God* Who enables you to do whatever He requires.

Telltale Marks

BY KAREN BURTON MAINS

Thirst must be quenched! If our desires are not met by God, we will
quickly find something else to alleviate our thirst.

—ERWIN W. LUTZER

"Jo-el Da-vid!" I called. Two small figures came bounding joy-
ously from the backyard, plastered with mud—my son and his
pal Georgie. "What have you been doing in my house? There's
mud from front to back!" Innocently, both boys checked their
boots. On all four were clods of clay. "Georgie/just/wanted/a/
glass/of/water." Each word was pronounced in a distinct tone.
"Well," I replied, being deliberately distinct, "tell him to/get/it/
in/his/own/house." Having had the last word, I dismissed them.

Within minutes, I erased the telltale evidences. Grabbing my
Bible, a little hurriedly I whispered, "Here I am, Lord. It's Karen.
What have You to teach me today?" I continued my study of the
Gospels. "If, as my representatives, you give even a cup of cold
water to a little child, you will surely be rewarded . . . " and
"Anyone who takes care of a little child is caring for God." Shame
flooded me. *Georgie just wanted a glass of water.* I prayed, "Father,
forgive me for caring more for clean floors than for two little
boys."

Suddenly I remembered a voice from the past—Linda's. "Does
your mother always sing around the house like that?" Linda
looked at me and with envy said, "You're so lucky!"

The world is full of Georgies just wanting a drink, and of
Lindas, wishing they had mothers who sang. Many of them are
our children's friends. We who know the One Who is Living
Water, this same One Who creates new songs in hearts—have
no choice but to open our homes and lives to those who leave
their telltale marks.

. . . if he is thirsty, give him water to drink.

—PROVERBS 25:21

Thought . . . Is Living Water flowing in your house?
Become, yourself, the conduit through which Christ's
love can flow to a lost world by practicing open hospitality. God will surprise you with the results.

Morning Song

BY RUTH BELL GRAHAM

When we affirm through praise the truth about God, then we
ourselves live with confidence.

—DR. GEORGE O. WOOD

I had been getting up early, fixing myself a cup of coffee, and
then sitting in the rocker on the front porch while I prayed for
each of our children, and for each of theirs.

One morning I awoke earlier than usual. It was five o'clock,
with dawn just breaking over the mountains. I collected my cup
of coffee and settled into the old rocker. Suddenly, I realized a
symphony of birdsong was literally surrounding me. The air was
liquid with music, as if the whole creation were praising God at
the beginning of a new day. I chuckled to hear the old turkey
gobbler, that had recently joined our family, gobbling away down
in the woods at the top of his voice as if he were a song sparrow!

And I learned a lesson. I had been beginning my days with
petitions, and I should have been beginning them with praise.

When the disciples asked our Lord to teach them how to
pray, He gave them what we commonly know as the Lord's
Prayer. The very first line is one of praise: "Hallowed be Thy
name."

In the seventeenth century, John Trapp wrote: "He lets out
His mercies to us for the rent of our praise, and is content that
we may have the benefit of them so He may have the glory."

Great is the Lord and most worthy of praise; his greatness
no one can fathom.

—PSALM 145:3

Thought . . . So you're not a morning person? Begin your
day with praise. You will be so filled with gratitude at
God's glory, you'll want to rise early. You may even
wake the birds!

Growing Up

BY HELENE C. KUONI

We do not wish for friends to feed and clothe our bodies—neighbors are kind enough for that—but to do the like office for our spirits.

—HENRY DAVID THOREAU

After clothes shopping all day with my mom, we passed the jewelry counter and a sparkling ring caught my attention—a citrine surrounded by diamond chips. The salesman allowed me to try it on, but when he stated the price, I handed it back. Though I'd recently graduated from college, I still weighed expenditures like a "starving student." I spent money only when it was essential. Furthermore, I believed that jewelry should commemorate special occasions. This was just a shopping-mall Saturday. My mother, who never spent money recklessly, surprised me. "You are working now," she said. "You have a good job. You can treat yourself, you know."

I looked at the ring. I wanted it, but still I hesitated, and Mom asked, "Why don't you buy it?"

"It's too good for me," I said.

The salesman overheard my remark and, banging his palm on the counter for emphasis, blurted, "Nothing is too good for you." He was a stranger, a salesman who wanted to sell, and yet his tone of voice told me more. Genuine and caring, his reaction exposed to me a serious problem—my low self-esteem.

I bought the ring and treasure it for many reasons, mostly for the memories of shopping with my mom, and for her wise counsel, but also for the memories of how the Lord used a stranger to change my life. I treasure it because on that day, many years ago, I caught a startling glimpse of myself and started to grow.

. . . think of yourself with sober judgment, in accordance with the measure of faith God has given you.

—ROMANS 12:3

Thought . . . Do you often compliment strangers? In a world that grows increasingly cold, when even families are distant, yours may be the only kind word someone receives and certainly needs.

Forgiveness through Jesus

BY CORRIE TEN BOOM

EDITOR'S NOTE: Miss ten Boom and her sister, Betsie, both Dutch, were imprisoned in Nazi concentration camps during WWII for hiding Jews in their father's home.

Forgiveness is a funny thing; it warms the heart and cools the sting.

—WILLIAM ARTHUR WARD

It was at a church service that I saw the former S.S. man who had stood guard at the shower room at Ravensbruck. Suddenly it was all there—the roomful of mocking men, the heaps of clothing, Betsie's pain-blanched face. He came to me, beaming. "How grateful I am for your message, Fraulein," he said. "To think that, as you say, [God] has washed my sins away!"

His hand was thrust out to shake mine. I, who had preached so often to the people in Bloemendaal the need to forgive, kept my hand at my side. As the angry, vengeful thoughts boiled through me, I saw the sin of them. Jesus had died for this man; was I going to ask for more? *Lord*, I prayed, *forgive me and help me to forgive him*. I tried to smile, I struggled to raise my hand. I could not. I felt nothing, not the slightest spark of warmth or charity. Again I breathed a silent prayer. *Jesus, I cannot forgive him. Give me Your forgiveness.*

As I took his hand the most incredible thing happened. From my shoulder along my arm and through my hand a current seemed to pass from me to him, while into my heart sprang a love for this stranger that almost overwhelmed me. I discovered that it is not on our forgiveness any more than on our goodness that the world's healing hinges, but on His. When He tells us to love our enemies, He gives, along with the command, the love itself.

" . . . Forgive us our sins, for we also forgive everyone who sins against us. . . ."

—LUKE 11:4

Thought . . . Do you struggle to forgive? Tell Jesus you *want* to obey His command to forgive and ask for His strength. You'll be surprised when He replaces His love for your hate.

Dreams Realized

Treasure in a Toolbox

BY JULIE EVANS

Children must be valued as our most priceless possession.

—JAMES C. DOBSON

One wonderful thing about children is that some of their dreams are just small enough that we, as parents, can actually make them come true.

At a recent family trip to K-Mart, we were moseying through the tool section. Suddenly, our son, Matthew, stopped in his tracks. He had discovered a small crowbar. "Wow! Cool!" he exclaimed, "I've wanted a crowbar all my life!" Six years he has waited.

This wasn't a case of the "gimmees." No, it was more like kiddie rapture. In my mind, the scene replays in slow motion with the theme song from *Home Improvement* playing in the background. Matthew sees the crowbar, does a double take, then eagerly grabs it and runs to show me his treasure. These are the kind of moments I treasure in my heart. Well, of course, my "mommy-heart" just melted at the sight of his innocent delight. *I've always wanted to make my kid's dream come true*, I thought to myself. So I bought the cute crowbar.

It's been precious to see what a six-year-old can find to do with a crowbar. The other day we received a box via UPS. Matt was ecstatic. "Please, Mama, don't open it yet!" he pleaded as he raced to his bedroom. He returned, breathless, with his crowbar in tow, and proceeded to pry open the package. "There you go, Mama," he said proudly when finally triumphant. It was another one of those moments for me—this time, with the theme song from *Rocky* resounding victoriously.

[The Lord] satisfies your desires with good things so that your youth is renewed like the eagle's.

—PSALM 103:5

Thought . . . Do you realize that even children have dreams? Help them discover their God-given talents and spiritual gifts. Assist them now to achieve their life purpose later. It's the greatest treasure you can bestow.

The Richest Lady in Town

BY JOYCE LANDORF HEATHERLEY

[She] is richest who is content with the least.

—SOCRATES

I never suspected until I was older that I lived with a woman who was extraordinarily rich and who planted the seeds in my heart of taking what I had, thanking God, and turning it into something of value.

Mother showed no sign of hysteria when I said I would have to have a long formal for graduation. She had me take her shopping to all the fancy stores. We didn't buy because, as she explained to salesclerks, "We're just looking."

I dreamed of a beautiful, but unobtainable dress. Later, when I walked into our living room, Mother was sitting at her sewing machine merrily stitching away. Flowing from her fingers was a long, white organdy, full-skirted dress. When I noticed the marvelous quality of the organdy, I blurted out, "Where did you get this beautiful stuff?" Mother smiled. "Oh, it's just some material I had," she said. Suddenly, the truth dawned on me. "Mother," I was almost yelling, "this organdy is the beautiful curtains we used to have in those windows!"

"Mmmm, yes." She went on, never missing a stitch. Without even wincing, my mother had cut up her treasured organdy curtains. No regrets, no martyr complex, no "poor me," no lecture on how long she had saved to buy them on sale; just a simple mental process, "Let's see, I need a long formal for Joyce . . . the organdy dining room curtains will do nicely." Snip, snip.

The dress now [is] in a cedar chest my parents gave me for my sixteenth birthday. It's a wonderful reminder of what treasures being poor can bring.

You have granted him the desire of his heart and have not withheld the request of his lips.

—PSALM 21:2

Thought . . . Do you wish you were wealthy? Do you have the Lord? Then you have more than the richest woman who doesn't know Him. Why not share *your* wealth with her?

A Child's Prayer

BY BODIE THOENE

EDITOR'S NOTE: Despite her dyslexia, Bodie Thoene has become a prolific, best-selling novelist. She writes in partnership with her husband, Brock.

Prayer does not change God, but changes him who prays.

—SØREN AABYE KIERKEGAARD

Is it possible that the course of a child's life can be set early? As a successful writer looking back over the years, nothing is as significant as when Mama took us to Sunday school. Children's Church was packed with kids. A grim-faced woman led the songs. I was having difficulty learning to read, so I could not read the words in the songbook. The teacher demanded I read the words aloud. When I could not, she ridiculed me and I left in tears.

I ran to the basement. I waited until Mama would come. In the corner, covered by a tarp, was an altar. A cross poked out from the tarp, and I was drawn to that visual sign of God's love. I felt I needed to tell God that I was sorry I was not good enough to join the kids singing!

"You, up there . . .," I whispered, feeling as if I had come into a holy presence, "I am Bodie. Mama said I should be in Sunday school, but I ran away and I'm sorry. I don't want to go back unless I can read." I paused for a long time. "I want to read like the other kids more than anything. If only you would help me, I would do anything you want. I would read the words from the songbook out loud. Maybe I would even write something just for You and read it out loud." That was the bargain I made with God. He heard the desire of my heart. And He began to answer . . .

I call on you, O God, for you will answer me; give ear to me and hear my prayer.

—PSALM 17:6

Thought . . . Do you encourage your children to pray for their dreams, no matter how seemingly impossible? God well could have initiated these desires, but requires prayer for their fulfillment.

Land Mines to Gold Mines

BY LOIS HUDSON

Rich the treasure, sweet the pleasure—sweet is pleasure after pain.

—JOHN DRYDEN

Effervescent laughter surfed down the hall seconds before he burst into the room, riding some unseen energy force like the crest of a wave, sun-on-water eyes sparkling, right hand already extended. "Hi, I'm Bennie, your physical therapist!" As Bennie took my medical history, he matter-of-factly shared some of his own. "If I miss something you say, just get my attention," he said, pointing to hearing aids in both ears. "I left most of my hearing in Vietnam." He had been too close to shellfire that ended his service career. Hospitalized for eighteen months, there was question as to whether he would ever walk again.

"I was so impressed with the rehab they gave me, I decided that that was what I wanted to do when I got out."

There was no question in Bennie's mind that he would walk again. Indeed, he fairly danced about his work. "I got the feeling," he continued, "that maybe He (pointing Heavenward) was trying to get my attention over there—I might have wished He'd found another way to do it, but then maybe I wouldn't have gotten the message any other way."

Bennie went on to fulfill his dream of establishing three successful rehab centers in Texas before a purchase offer he couldn't refuse eased him into early retirement with the urge to explore California. There a chance encounter with the director of a rehab program persuaded him out of retirement. His "merry heart" and skill have been working "good medicine" ever since.

Though I walk in the midst of trouble, you preserve my life; you stretch out your hand against the anger of my foes, with your right hand you save me. The Lord will fulfill his purpose for me . . .

—PSALM 138:7–8

Thought . . . Are you having difficulty overcoming adversity? Ask the Lord for a cheerful heart. Like no other medicine, it heals depression and a "crushed spirit" (Proverbs 17:22).

The Desire of Your Heart

BY JENNIFER KENNEDY DEAN

There is such a thing as coming into such a sweet relation to the will of God that we are fused into oneness with it.

—G. GRANGER FLEMING

A person cannot know the desire of her heart unless she knows the heart of her desire. Usually, what we think we desire is really the way we have imagined that the true desire will be met.

My son, Kennedy, played on the freshman football team, which often had games on Wednesday nights. One Wednesday evening each quarter, our church has a youth baptism. One Wednesday, two boys whom Kennedy had led to Christ were to be baptized, but Kennedy had a football game that night. So, Kennedy and I prayed that God would let it rain out the game. It wasn't that we really desired rain; it was that we wanted Kennedy to see his friends baptized. But we couldn't think of anything less than rain that would cancel a freshman football game.

It didn't rain. God had another plan. The game started and it became dark. The field lights malfunctioned and the game had to be called. Kennedy arrived at the church in plenty of time to see and to celebrate his friends' baptisms.

Our prayer was that it would rain, but our *desire* was that Kennedy would attend the baptism. Someday I will learn, once and for all, that God does not need my suggestions, just my prayers. But, while I'm learning, he is always saying "yes" to my heart's desire.

Delight yourself in the Lord and he will give you the desires of your heart.

—PSALM 37:4

Thought . . . What do you desire? Delight first in God, and His desires for you will become your own. Commit your way to God, trust Him, and He will do this (Psalm 37:5).

Secret Grace

BY LOIS WALFRID JOHNSON

Grace is not sought nor bought nor wrought. It is a free gift of
Almighty God to needy mankind.

—BILLY GRAHAM

On a day when I was nine and a half, I was very naughty, and my
mother needed to decide how to discipline me. She couldn't
spank me. I was too tender and had an older sister who always
said, "Spank me quick so I can run back out and play."

Nor could my mother send me to my room. I would simply
read a book, and that would not be punishment. So she asked
me to clean the leaves out of the barberry bushes in front of our
house.

It was a prickly job, scratching my hands and trying my patience. As I sat down on a sidewalk warmed by spring sunlight,
a nearby church bell began to ring. I knew that someone had
died, and counted the long tolls echoing across the countryside
. . . eighty-nine, ninety, ninety-one. Then they stopped.

What a long time to live, I thought. *I wonder what that person left
behind?* In that moment I knew there was one thing that I wanted
to leave behind. If I could ever possibly write a book, that's what
it would be. I wanted that book to tell others what I believed
about Jesus Christ.

That very night I started writing my first novel. Twenty-nine
published books later, I still treasure the same dream—wanting
to tell others about Christ. But now I know two secrets: the grace
of being called to a life's work while being disciplined for doing
something wrong, and that without Him I can do nothing.

". . . I am the vine; you are the branches. If a man remains
in me and I in him, he will bear much fruit; apart from me
you can do nothing. . . ."

—JOHN 15:5

Thought . . . When death's bell tolls for you, will you be
ready? Will you have completed the work God gave
you to do? It's never too late. Abide in Him. With Him,
all things are possible!

265

Mother's Mystery Birds

BY KATHLEEN DALE WRIGHT

Nothing is too small for the Creator's attention and activity!

—ANNE GRAHAM LOTZ

My mother loved birds. She fed them, carried a bird guide with her wherever she went, and loved to take walks with her binoculars to discover new birds. A few months before she died, mother developed a serious illness and had to spend most of her time in bed. A large bay window spread across the south end of her bedroom, and now her greatest pleasure was to watch the birds that came to drink from the birdbath just outside this window.

One afternoon, when I was visiting with Mother, I noticed a flurry of activity outside. I helped Mother to the bay window, and we watched as wave after wave of beautiful gold-crested birds covered the birdbath, the ground, and tree limbs nearby. She gasped with pleasure and said, "Those are cedar waxwings. I've always dreamed of seeing them, but one seldom does. That's why they're called 'mystery birds.'"

We watched until the last bird had continued its flight. Then I helped her back to bed. She talked about the birds for weeks, and marveled at the miracle of seeing this large flock of mystery birds just outside her window. A short time after Christmas, Mother mysteriously winged her own flight—from this realm to the next.

I'm so grateful that the Creator, Who made the birds and guides them through the pathless air, saw fit to send a special flock by the window of one of His needy children. Sharing her great pleasure that special day is a memory I'll always treasure.

". . . your Father knows what you need before you ask him. . . ."

—MATTHEW 6:8

Thought . . . Like a bird-watcher with binoculars, are you on constant "lookout" for God? He longs to delight you with His presence and comfort in the most unexpected places. Treasure His surprises!

God's Abundance

BY DARLENE DEIBLER ROSE

EDITOR'S NOTE: Mrs. Rose was a WWII missionary and POW in Japan. A woman prisoner had smuggled bananas past the guards. Mrs. Rose, deathly ill, dreamed of having just one banana.

Trustfulness is based on confidence in God, Whose ways I do not understand. If I did, there would be no need for trust.

—OSWALD CHAMBERS

A living skeleton, I lay emaciated in my cell, weakened from dysentery, exhausted from grueling interrogations. As women prisoners exercised in the courtyard under a guard's severe scrutiny, I hoisted myself to the window. Whenever the sentry turned away, one woman furtively inched towards a fence draped thickly with vines. Suddenly, a hand thrust through tangled creepers, bearing a bunch of bananas! The woman grabbed the fruit, stashing it under her sarong. I marveled at this secret operation, but was more amazed at the thought of eating a plump, delicious banana! "Please, Lord," I pleaded, "just *one* banana?" It was hopeless. How could God possibly deliver bananas through impenetrable prison walls?

The dreaded click of officers' boots outside my cell was the prelude to more horrific questions. I was filled with terror. As the door opened, I was stunned to see the smiling eyes of the camp commander, Mr. Yamaji. Tears filled his eyes. "You're very ill." "Yes, sir." "I'm going back to camp," he said, and left.

Oh, Lord, I didn't bow! This infraction guaranteed a beating. As the guard returned, I struggled to rise, knowing my fate. He opened the door and, with a sweeping gesture, laid at my feet *ninety-two* bananas from Mr. Yamaji. I was so ashamed! I hadn't trusted my Lord for even *one* banana, and He'd provided nearly a hundredfold! In the dark cell, God's words shone like jewels in my heart: "I delight to do the exceeding abundant above anything you ask."

[God's compassions] are new every morning; great is your faithfulness.

—LAMENTATIONS 3:23

Thought . . . Are you hopeless? Trust God to fulfill your dream. *All* things are possible to Him!

Sweet Dreams

BY JEANETTE CLIFT GEORGE

The painter will produce pictures of little merit if he takes the works of others as his standard.

—LEONARDO DA VINCI

My mother was a gifted pianist. Even though she gave up a concert career, she loved to play the piano and thought I would feel the same. I practiced obediently, if not skillfully. I was not a gifted student.

One afternoon I was laboring joylessly over The Happy Farmer, and Mother called from the yard, "No, it's F-sharp, honey!" I struck every note my two hands could reach and began to cry. Mother hurried in to me. "What's the matter?" she asked. "How did you know it was wrong?" I cried. Mother looked at me in dismay. She had not intended to discourage me. "Besides," I said, still spattering tears upon the keyboard, "I'm only doing this to please you."

My mother stared at me in astonishment. Never had she imagined that anyone did not want to play the piano. All her dreams of handing down the joy of music to her daughter melted in the glare of my outburst. And in one instant, she accepted the painful revelation. She came to me, smiling, and hugged me. She brushed away my tears and said, "Well, honey, you don't have to do it. We'll find something that pleases you."

I think back to that moment in awed awareness of my mother's love for me—a love so personalized that I did not have to live out her dream. She freed me to pursue my own dream: theater. No matter how demanding the role, my mother would always say, "Sugar, you can do it. I know you can." Something in me believed her.

Train a child in the way he should go . . .

—PROVERBS 22:6

Thought . . . Do you train your children in the way *they* should go? You can when you relinquish them to God, helping them to develop the gifts He's given *them*, and not you!

Russian Wild Strawberries

BY FERN AYERS MORRISSEY

Interest does not tie nations together; it sometimes separates them.
But sympathy and understanding does unite them.

—WOODROW WILSON

Across nine time zones, via versts and air miles, from ancient
Vladimir, Anastasia's letter arrived in St. Louis one late-Septem-
ber day. I was surprised to find tucked inside, countless tiny seeds.
Russian wild strawberries, incognito in a letter, had transferred
through sundry postal hands, bypassed customs, disregarded
postal regulations, and left their Mother Russia earth forever.
How could these native berries thrive in foreign mid-American
soil? Discouraged, I put the seeds aside.

Finally, in March, against all odds, I potted the seeds. To my
utter amazement, slender seedlings appeared in a week! Although
they continued to grow, I had misgivings about transplanting
them in the yard. They came from dissimilar soils and climates!

By July, I could wait no longer because the seedlings had out-
grown the pot. On an intensely hot day, I finally planted them
along the fence. Miraculously, they endured alien soil and fierce
Missouri heat. By fall, they spread out, then bloomed, celebrating survival! By the next spring, they propagated further, bloomed
abundantly, and yielded a multitude of red tart-sweet berries!

The real abundance, however, is the relationship this fruit
symbolizes—a dream fulfilled. After my trip to Russia during
the Cold War, Anastasia planted friendship seeds in a letter. More
than twenty years and countless letters later, crossing impossible cultural miles, our love has survived the odds. Though "enemies," we were able to share Christ with each other. The treasured fruit is the celebration of our salvation.

. . . All over the world this gospel is bearing fruit and growing, just as it has been doing among you since the day you
heard it. . . .

—COLOSSIANS 1:6

Thought . . . Do you share the Gospel with those you
consider least likely to receive it? Never avoid God's
nudge. Salvation is His responsibility. But you need to
plant the seeds.

Small Prayers

BY RUTH BELL GRAHAM

Heaven is full of answers to prayers for which no one ever bothered to ask.

—BILLY GRAHAM

". . . and please pray I'll catch a lizard."

Alone in the kitchen, catching up on the mail, I came across this very serious request to The Samaritan's Purse from a very serious four-year-old supporter. I laughed aloud. I loved it! Only the day before I read this four-year-old's prayer request, we had been in Paris where I had been with Bill for Mission France. Much prayer had gone up all over France on behalf of those who might be unfulfilled spiritually and stifled materially. And here was a small boy praying for a lizard! And God, our Father, Who so graciously answered prayer in France, cared also for the concern of one small four-year-old.

I wondered how God not only puts up with, but welcomes our prayers, considering *all* He has on Him. Not once has He ever said, "Don't bother Me. Don't you see I'm busy?" And He so well could—with a world in its present condition. No. Each person is special to Him, Who calls every star by name, Who has the hairs of our heads numbered, and Who knows the number of grains of sand on the ocean shores.

So even a small boy's desire for a lizard would be duly noted. In fact, I imagine the angels themselves enjoyed that small request—with, perhaps, angelic chuckles.

". . . His eyes are on the ways of men; he sees their every step. . . ."

—JOB 34:21

Thought . . . Do you teach your children to pray for "small dreams?" By teaching them to take every little request to God, you show them that He cares about their concerns in a big way.

To Really Know Him

There is only one thing more painful than learning from experience and that is not learning from experience.

—ARCHIBALD MCLEISH

Our son, Justin, had returned from college. Although he'd transferred closer to home, he was no closer in his relationship to God. I'd been praying for Justin for years, ever since his heart wandered from Christ in the ninth grade—dreaming he'd return to the Lord. Several girlfriends had passed through his life and he hadn't attended church or Bible study. Life had changed with a flurry of activities, but no spiritual changes had occurred—not until he came home to find a summer job.

One night as we drove across town, Justin shared his frustration about a soured dating relationship, and his difficulty in finding a good job. In a moment of vulnerability, he said, "Mom, I feel so empty—so far from God. I know that God hasn't moved—I have. I want more than anything to have an intimate relationship with Christ—to *really know* Him." My heart leapt in praise to God. I wanted to jump from the car and dance in joy!

Justin never looked back. His music, priorities, and habits changed. His view of girls changed, and he eventually married a precious Christian. God never wastes anything. Because of his struggles as a teen, Justin received from God a special compassion and understanding of the situations and temptations which young men face. And God continues to give me a heart to encourage moms never to stop praying—to know that the Lord will "keep that which we've committed to Him against that day!" It's this truth that I will always treasure.

> It has given me great joy to find some of your children walking in the truth, just as the Father commanded us.
>
> —II JOHN 4

Thought . . . Are you burdened by your children's struggles? Entrust them to God. Don't stop praying. And realize that God can ultimately turn their problems into His platform for ministry.

God's One Foundation

BY DONNA MESLER NORMAN

If I believe in God, I can be assured that all will be well, that He can draw light out of darkness, and make crooked things straight.

—THOMAS ERSKINE

The "church's foundation" was a work-in-progress on our wedding day. People had timidly questioned for weeks, "Won't it bother you if the sanctuary isn't completed in time?" No. After waiting almost forty years to fulfill my dream for an earthly lord and husband, my happiness knew no boundaries. We had joined *this* church and, whatever its physical features, here we would marry.

The late-January day dawned dazzling and cold. No nerves for this bride, until the stark reality of an unfinished vestibule engulfed me two hours before the ceremony. Scaffolding arched achingly tall, workmen shouted frantic last-minute instructions, and dust and dirt flirted menacingly around the folds of my gown. Panic flooded my heart and weeks of stoic resolve vanished like puffs of winter steam. It *did* matter! My fairy tale hour was lost in a cacophony of splintered madness!

No, this would not happen! I determined. Urgently seeking God, I pleaded, "Father, the sure foundation of this moment is our love for You, the treasure that we have in each other. I need You right now! Help me focus, to forget the paint-splattered floor. Strengthen me with Your cleansing peace!"

His forceful response took my breath away! Suddenly, the church building no longer mattered. And yet, a miracle occurred as gleaming woodwork mirrored the radiance of a blazing sunset, tools and shavings were hastily whisked into hidden recesses, and scuff-marked folding tables were transformed under crisply starched linens. Candles twinkled in the darkened sanctuary, as the eloquence of harp and violin called forth the procession. God's one foundation had proven sufficient after all!

For no one can lay any foundation other than the one already laid, which is Jesus Christ.

—I CORINTHIANS 3:11

Thought . . . Is some foundation in your life crumbling? Cling to your Rock, Jesus Christ, and the sure promises of His Word, which never change. You cannot be shaken (Psalm 62:6).

The Pixie Dust Extravaganza

BY DOTTIE McDOWELL

When we take time to dream, we discover the many windows to our soul.

—ISABELA BARANI

When I was a little girl, Peter Pan was my hero. Each time I heard about the boy who could fly, I felt inspired and energized. The story took my breath away, and I spent much time living and reliving each scene. I couldn't get enough of it.

I remember the day I wandered down into our basement when I was about five years old. Near my mother's washing machine, I spotted a large box of Ivory Snow. In my well-developed imagination, each beautiful flake looked like the pixie dust Tinkerbell used to sprinkle on Wendy, Michael, and John to enable them to fly.

Overcome with excitement, I knew that I could relive Tinkerbell's scene. I'll never forget the exhilaration I felt as I took handfuls of pixie dust and sprinkled them generously throughout the entire basement. It was magical.

When I was done, everything was covered with soap. When my mom discovered what I had done, she lovingly listened to my childish fantasy and dreams and recognized how much the experience meant to me. Instead of getting angry or frustrated, she laughed with me and encouraged me to repeat the whole story of Peter Pan to her. Later, lightheartedly, we cleaned up the enormous mess together.

From that day to this, the memory of my "pixie dust extravaganza" reminds me that my mom dreamed my dreams. I was important to her. She unselfishly chose to support and encourage my dreams—even childish ones—over her own interests or convenience.

Do not let any unwholesome talk come out of your mouths, but only what is helpful for building others up . . .

—EPHESIANS 4:29

Thought . . . Do you encourage your children's dreams even when they make mistakes? Even Tinkerbell had to learn to fly! Let your children try their wings.

Go Hard after God

BY ANNE ORTLUND

EDITOR'S NOTE: After meeting Anne Ortlund, as I was wrestling with my dream of becoming a writer, I sent her writing samples for critique. Her response is a letter I treasure above all others. I believe that her advice is important for *anyone*, writer or not, who desires to serve God whole-heartedly. I pray that it blesses you as much as it has me.

If you had any idea how much inward peace you would gain for yourself, and how much joy you would bring to others, by devoting yourself single-heartedly to God, you would certainly pay more attention to your spiritual progress.

—THOMAS À KEMPIS

Dear Lynn,

Thank you so much for letting me see your writings. You have a wonderful gift—for poetry and for poetry-flavored prose.

I have only one suggestion; otherwise, keep writing and writing and ask God to open publishing doors as He will. The suggestion: just *live*. Steep yourself in the Word and prayer; walk with God. The vehicle is excellent, but the world is full of clever words. The *message*, with bedrock truth and conviction, will be uniquely yours and full of life-changing power, as you go *hard* after God and write from that deep, gut-level—not to describe or display your-self, but to cleanse and motivate others. God bless you!!

Love,
Anne Ortlund

". . . Let your heart therefore be wholly devoted to the Lord our God, to walk in his statutes and to keep his command-ments, as at this day.

—I KINGS 8:61 (NASB)

Thought . . . Are you devoted to God above your gift, your ministry? Go hard after God, putting Him first. As you serve Him, you will have His perspective, pu-rity, power, and purpose to serve others.

Doorways

BY KAREN L. RILEY

Because eternity was closeted in time, He is my open door to forever.

—LUCI SHAW

I was twenty-seven years old when I finally made the trek across the Atlantic to visit Norway. As long as I can remember, I had dreamed of visiting this historic place which held great personal significance. For this was the place of my father's birth and the home of my mother's relatives.

I couldn't believe that I was finally standing on the doorstep of the home where my father was born, or visiting the sawmill of my great-grandparents. While it may have seemed an unusual thing to do, while touring each of these edifices, I photographed their doors. Each door represented the unique beauty of its building—the hand-crocheted lace curtains adorning the penchant door's window—a millstone propped against the old barn door.

Creating a framed collection of these treasured door photographs, I was reminded that doorways are important in our biblical heritage, as well. These entryways into our houses illustrate more than a framed structure—they are gateways into our families and, ultimately, into our hearts. As the last plague in Egypt raged on, the Israelites were instructed to spread lamb's blood on the doorframes of their houses as a protection from the destroyer. What a picture of sacrifice and love that was.

The most beautiful door I can imagine is the door Jesus offers to us when He entreats us to knock on the door to eternal life. He has promised to be there to answer. This is the door to our spiritual heritage—the most important door through which we will ever walk.

"... Knock and the door will be opened to you. For everyone who asks receives; he who seeks finds; and to him who knocks, the door will be opened."

—MATTHEW 7:7–8

Thought . . . Is Jesus "knocking on the door of your heart?" When you receive Him as your Savior, He promises to "come in," and to dine—to fellowship with you (Revelation 3:20).

Box of Broken Dreams

BY FLORENCE LITTAUER

How many people stop because so few say, "Go!"

—CHARLES R. SWINDOLL

As I wrote my first book, I remembered the treasured cigar box filled with Dad's broken dreams—his published newspaper articles and one magazine article, published posthumously. Wanting to be a writer, but receiving no encouragement, Dad had "buried" this treasure for thirty years behind the old upright piano.

When I had returned home during college vacation, my father took me quietly aside, showing me the secret box. As an English major I was amazed to discover Dad's articles, published in different Boston newspapers.

"You didn't tell me you could write!" I exclaimed incredulously. "I didn't want your mother to know. She felt I shouldn't write because of my limited education. So whenever something was published, I'd hide it in this box. I won't be leaving you my money—just this box of broken dreams."

I was impressed—my father—a *published* writer! I noticed his moist eyes. "This time, I tried for something too big." He'd submitted an article to our denominational magazine, but it hadn't been published. That was the last time we spoke. The next day he died of a heart attack.

As I opened sympathy cards, the church magazine emerged among the mail. *Oh, Lord, could father's article be here?* I burst into tears as I read Dad's published piece.

Though Father left no money and had no degree, he gave me the treasure of encouragement and the ability to write. That treasure has multiplied, as I have mentored writers and speakers through CLASS (Christian Leaders, Authors, & Speakers Seminar), encouraging them to "dare to dream"—to develop the "treasure" within, refusing to allow their talents to remain buried for a lifetime.

Therefore encourage one another and build each other up . . .

—I THESSALONIANS 5:11

Thought . . . Has your dream died because no one has ever encouraged you? God wants you to fulfill the purpose for which He has created you. He promises to make up for years "eaten by locusts (Joel 2:25)."

The Afterglow

BY MARJORIE HOLMES

If I can put one touch of rosy sunset into the life of any man or woman, I shall feel that I have worked with God.

—GEORGE MACDONALD

My mother always savored sunsets until the last lingering glow had faded. "Just look at that sunset now!" Mother was always urging us. "Your lessons can wait." We must stop whatever we were doing to follow her pleased gaze. "Isn't that the most beautiful sky you've ever seen?" Then after supper when the bright hues had melted into dusk and there was nothing left but a lasting stubborn band of burning rose, she would return to the porch a minute and stand there, arms wrapped in her apron against the chill and murmur: "The afterglow means hope."

What could hope mean to this middle-aged married woman whose dreams must surely all be behind her? I sensed her hopes but dimly: that the problems of her family would be resolved, wounds healed, frictions ceased, worries vanish . . . that a new company would be hiring soon, and that Dad would land a better job . . . there would at last be enough money to go around . . . her children's turbulent lives would get straightened out—the boys would find themselves. Hope? What did it mean to her? It spoke of her marvelous ingredient that keeps men going—something that is almost as vital to man as love—his God-given hope, his belief in tomorrow, his bright expectations that refuse to die. It was surely what the Lord Himself was talking about when He counseled His followers to be of good cheer, not to despair. My mother gave her children the gift of sunsets. But an even greater gift was her gift of the afterglow: the message she read in those remaining embers, burning like little fires of faith long after the sunset itself was gone, a lighted bridge across the coming darkness of the stars, "The afterglow means hope."

Thou dost make the dawn and the sunset shout for joy.

—PSALM 65:8B (NASB)

Thought . . . Are you downcast in the dark night of unmet dreams? Look to Jesus, the bright Morning Star of hope, Who rises above failure's sunset and lights the dawn of a new day and new dreams.

Contributors

Many gifted women contributed their stories to *Treasures of a Woman's Heart*. Below is some information about each contributor. The pages on which their stories can be found are listed in brackets at the end of each entry.

Charlotte Adelsperger, with her daughter, Karen Hayse, coauthored a new book for mothers, *Through the Generations*. She speaks to groups and has written for over seventy periodicals such as *Decision* and *Woman's World*. Contact: 11629 Riley, Overland Park, KS 66210-2254. [166]

Patricia A. J. Allen is thrilled to be graduating from college, enjoys her granddaughter, finds peace in looking at the mountains near her home, and finds joy in Jesus and His people. Contact: 1848 East NC 10, Newton, NC 28658. [98]

Teresa Arseneau is a freelance author of stories and plays. She is currently seeking to publish her first novella under the pseudonym, Teresa Tick'ell. Contact: 486 Wellington St., Sarnia, ON N7T 1H9. tnta@mnsi.net. [44, 242]

Esther Bandy accepted Christ when she was seven. She's married and has one son. She was a nurse, missionary, Spanish teacher, and CEF director. Now she enjoys writing. Contact: 51 E. Tregaron Ct., Shelton, WA 98584. Ebandy@juno.com. [82]

Vickey Banks is an inspirational speaker and author of *Love Letters to My Baby*. She is the happily married mother of two terrific children and truly treasures the relationships in her life. Vickey is represented by CLASServices, Inc. Contact: vbinokc@aol.com. [222]

Sheri Berger lives with her husband and two children in St. Louis, Missouri. She has enjoyed teaching scrapbooking classes and speaking to groups as a Creative Memories consultant for the past six years. (314) 391-7373. BergerPS@aol.com. [236]

Jan Brunette is the mother of four, stepmother of seven and grandmother of twenty. Besides freelance writing, she conducts retreats and remains active in her church with children's and women's ministries. Contact: 2711 Bayview, Eustis, FL 32726. (352) 357-7097. brunette@cde.com. [40]

Jan Clark Buckman is a deacon's wife, mother, and grandmother, she has led Precept Bible Studies since 1990, and serves as vice president to a St. Louis women's ministry, Gateway Women. Contact: 1604 Lake Shore Knolls, Lake St. Louis, MO 63367. bbuckman@nothnbut.net. [109]

Sandra J. Bunch and her husband, Rick, have two children through adoption, Aimee and Elisabeth. Sandra enjoys writing in her "spare" time and has been published by DaySpring Greeting Cards. Contact: Sandra J. Bunch, 10049 Ashbrook, St. Louis, MO 63137. (314) 388-1643. ApensPal@aol.com. [122]

Sandra Palmer Carr is a wife, mother, and grandmother, and a member of the Christian Writers' Fellowship of Orange County. She brings the hope of Jesus through poetry, stories, drama, and devotionals. Contact: 9421 Hyannis Port Drive, Huntington Beach, CA 92646-3515. (714) 962-0906. [142]

Ann Fox Chodakowski and **Susan Fox Wood** (the Tightwad Twins), and big sis, Charlotte Fox Messmer are authors of *Living on a Shoestring* and *Cookie Jar Riches* and *Hand-me-Down Wealth*, as well as seminar speakers for women. Contact: P.O. Box 1331, Brandon, FL 33509. (813) 689-0218. Foxtwin2@aol.com. [116]

Jeri Chrysong, poet/humorist, resides in Huntington Beach, California with teenaged sons, Luc and Sam, and pug, "Puddy." Her work has been featured in other Starburst devotional books and various periodicals. Jeri enjoys watching her kids play sports, especially football. [36, 145]

Penny J. Clark ministers through a Christian resource center, spends her salary on books, and writes because "I can't help it." Contact: 11833 Brookmont Drive, Maryland Heights, MO 63043. (314) 739-3963. [118, 173]

Joan Clayton has authored six books and has had over three hundred articles published. She and her husband, Emmitt, reside in Portales, New Mexico. Joan is currently the religion columnist for her local newspaper. [99]

Gayle Cloud is a mother of six, credentialed teacher, and education activist. She enjoys reading, quilting, writing, and speaking on issues of vital concern to growing families. Contact: 4237 Second Street, Riverside, CA 92501. (909) 788-9394. cloud9@pe.net. [79]

Guyla Greenly Cooper is a freelance writer living in the beautiful boonies of Tennessee. She serves as special feature chairman for the Jackson Christian Women's Club. Contact: 4010 Cash School Road, Enville, TN 38332. (901) 688-5370. guylac@centuryinter.net. [232]

Doris C. Crandall, an inspirational writer, lives in Amarillo, Texas. Cofounder of the Amarillo Chapter of Inspirational Writers Alive!, a group dedicated to Christian writing, Doris devotes much of her time to helping beginning writers hone their skills. [12, 234]

Barbara Curtis, mother of eleven, is author of two books and over three hundred articles in forty Christian magazines, including *Guideposts*, *Christian Parenting Today*, and *Focus on the Family*. She loves to speak at MOPS and women's retreats. Contact: barbaracurtis@home.com. [17]

Donella Davis taught junior high for six years. She lives in Oklahoma City with her husband, Dr. Mark Davis, and sons, Colten and Kyle. Currently, she homeschools both boys and is involved in Bible study and teaches senior high Sunday school. [112]

Jennifer Kennedy Dean is the author of several books, including *Heart's Cry: Principles of Prayer* and *He Restores My Soul: A Forty-Day Journey Toward Personal Renewal*. She leads in-depth conferences on prayer and the inner life. Contact: (888) 844-6647. jkdean@prayinglife.org. [80, 264]

Janey L. DeMéo is a pastor's wife, mother, writer, women's speaker, and founding director of Orphans First, a corporation for suffering children. Contact: 25 Ave. Robert de Joly, 30620 Uchaud, France. (33) 4.66.71.11.89. Fax: (33) 4.66.71.22.37. http://www.ggwo.org/orphansfirst/ or Orphansfirst@ggwo.org. [34]

Gayle DeSalles is a secretary at a private university in Nashville, Tennessee. She enjoys writing, reading, crafts, camping, hiking, and cycling. Contact: 300 Berkley Drive #E-9, Madison, TN 37115. (615) 865-2033. Gaylewrites@aol.com. [100]

Pat Devine is a published author and poet. She delights in husband, home, travel, grandchildren, and leading workshops to encourage others to explore their faith history and prayer journey through journal writing. Contact: 419 Argent Ave., Ferguson, MO 63135-2205. (314) 521-0419. jeanstone@excelonline.com. [9, 64, 135,231]

Celeste Duckworth, author and CLASSpeaker, delights in ministering in her hair salon. She is a popular, humorous speaker for seminars, conferences, and women's events. Contact: 630 N. Brierwood, Rialto, CA. 92376. (909) 820-6306. [78]

Susan Duke, best-selling author, inspirational speaker and singer. Books include best-selling *Courage For The Chicken-Hearted* series, *Heartlifters/Women*, *Heartlifters /Hope and Joy* and *God Things Come In Small Packages*. Contact: 6294 Brookfield, Quinlan, TX 75474. (903) 883-3355. suzieduke@juno.com. [229]

Sylvia Duncan teaches journal-keeping techniques and creative writing at Forest Park Community College. She is a professional storyteller and book reviewer. Contact: 6216 Potomac St., St. Louis, MO 63139. (314) 353-5815. sylvied@juno.com. [215]

Annette M. Eckart is the founder of *Bridge for Peace*. She is a spiritual director, an international retreat director and speaker. Contact: 8 Willow Ct., Medford, NY 11763. (516) 289-3880. bridge@fnol.net. [114, 132, 158]

Elisabeth Elliot is an internationally known best-selling author, speaker, and radio host for *Gateway to Joy*, aired on over two hundred radio stations nationally. Mrs. Elliot served eleven years as a missionary in Ecuador, South America, where her missionary husband, Jim Elliot, was martyred in 1956. [2, 191]

Julie Evans is a thirty-something wife and homeschool mom. Contact: davee@xuser.com. [138, 160, 260]

Marjorie K. Evans, a former teacher, is now a freelance writer. She enjoys grandparenting, church, reading, and her Welsh Corgi. She and Edgar have two grown sons and five grandchildren. Contact: 4162 Fireside Circle, Irvine, CA 92604-2216. (949) 551-5296. [241]

Becky Freeman is mother, wife, columnist, national speaker, and author of seven books, including *Real Magnolias, A View from the Porch Swing, Worms in My Tea*, and *Marriage 9-1-1*. Contact: Speak Up Services at (810) 982-0898 or speakupinc@aol.com. See also www.beckyfreeman.com. [22, 32]

Jan Fugman is a wife, mother of four, grandmother of ten, and a freelance writer. She works part-time at her church and leads a divorce recovery class. Contact: 2416 SW 23rd Circle, Troutdale, OR 97060. (503) 669-7598. jfugman@itiacess.com. [238]

Cheri Fuller is an inspirational speaker and author of over twenty-two books including best-selling *When Mothers Pray* and *When Children Pray*. She is a contributing editor for *Today's Christian Woman* and other publications. Contact: www.CheriFuller.com (has weekly Parent Tips and Encouragement for Moms). cheri@cander.net. [271]

Jeannette Clift George, stage and film actress, speaker, founder and artistic director of A.D. Players, a professional Christian Theater based in Houston, Texas with theaters for general audiences and children, and touring units, and Academy. Author of books, articles, and published plays. [268]

Donna Clark Goodrich, freelance writer, editor and proofreader, is a wife, mother of three, and grandmother of two. She teaches at Christian writers' seminars across the United States. Contact: 648 S. Pima, Mesa, AZ 85210. DGood648@aol.com. [76]

Sandi Gordon is married and has four children. Diagnosed with Parkinson's disease at age thirty, she has written two books that share her story and faith. Sandi also does motivational speaking. Contact: 677 Cranbrook, Kirkwood, MO 63122. (314) 821-4906. PSBOOKSINC@aol.com. [182]

Cristine Grimm is a singer, poet, writer, and painter. She manages a product design company and enjoys writing grant proposals for nonprofit organizations. Contact: Suite 124, 101 Washington St., Grand Haven, MI 49417. cgrimm@designmax.com. [208]

Kathleen Hagberg is married, the mother of three adult children, a human interest newspaper columnist, author of a book of children's verses and children's stories, and a director of Children's Ministries. Contact: 41 Bittersweet Trail, Wilton, CT 06897. (203) 762-0541. [33, 96]

Lydia E. Harris, M.A., is a wife, mother, and grandmother who writes book reviews, articles, devotionals, and a syndicated column. She presents workshops for writers and speaks on tea and hospitality. Contact: 4725 N.E. 193rd St., Seattle, WA 98155. Lmharris@foxcomm.net. [144]

Karen Hayse is a fifth-grade teacher, pastor's wife, mom, and writer. This year, she and her mother, Charlotte Adelsperger, coauthored *Through the Generations*, a gift-book for mothers. She also enjoys writing novels. Contact: Klvs2write@aol.com. [206]

Joyce Landorf Heatherley, author, speaker, musician. Over 7,000,000 books, audios, videos, and other products in circulation. Contact: P.O. Box 340079, Austin, TX 78734. (800) 777-7949. Joyce@balconypublishing.com. [117, 193, 227, 261]

Marilyn Willett Heavilin is a wife, mother, and grandmother. She has authored five books and speaks internationally on family life, prayer, biblical issues, and dealing with loss. Contact: P.O. Box 1612, Redlands, CA 92373. (909) 792-6358. Roses1nDec@aol.com. [5, 184]

Marjorie Holmes, For inspiration and hope, readers wordwide turn to Marjorie Holmes, best-selling author of *Who AM I, God? How Can I Find You, God?, Hold Me Up a Little Longer, Lord!, Two from Galilee*, and more than 30 other beloved books. [277]

Grace Witwer Housholder, award-winning journalist and author of *The Funny Things Kids Say Will Brighten Any Day*, says children and laughter are gifts from God. Enjoy! Contact: 816 Mott St., Kendallville, IN 46755. (219) 347-0738. www.funnykids.com. [218]

Michele Howe has published over three hundred articles and writes curriculum for Group Publishing and Christian Service Brigade and reviews for *Publishers Weekly*. Michele has also authored two books. Contact: 6154 South Otter Creek Road, LaSalle, MI 48145. jhowe@monroe.lib.mi.us. [21]

Valerie Howe is a wife, mother of five, author, and speaker. She enjoys speaking to women about the difference Christ can make in their lives and can include singing in her presentations. Contact: P.O. Box 141, Lebanon, MO 65536-0141. (417) 532-1009. vhowe@llion.org. [72]

Linda J. Huckabee is happily single with "furry" kids (animals)! She traveled around the world singing in a Christian rock group and enjoys sharing Christ through speaking, teaching, writing, acting, and directing. Contact: 11602 Bob White, Houston, TX 77035. [15]

Jo Huddleston is a speaker and author of three books and over two hundred stories and articles published in over fifty different publications, including *Guideposts* and *Decision*. Contact: P.O. Box 1683, Auburn, AL 36831-1683. johudd@earthlink.net. [74, 92]

Lois Hudson writes for and edits a daily devotional published monthly by her church, oversees small group ministries, writes curriculum, leads Bible study classes and workshops, and composes music. Contact: 17921 Romelle Ave., Santa Ana, CA 92705. (714) 532-4626. [263]

Melissa Hudson-Berry is a wife and mother of Jonathan and Andrew, children's minister at New Hope Christian Church, Lawrenceville, Georgia, and directs the Mother's Morning Out program. Contact: 2225 Toucan Court, Lawrenceville, GA 30044. (770) 822-0865. [235]

Betty Huff writes short devotionals, poems, and true stories. She has been published in *Catholic Digest*, three *God's Vitamin C for the Spirit* books, and miscellaneous publications. Contact: 10025 El Camino #25, Atascadero, CA, 93422. (805) 461-5619. bjhuff@thegrid.net. [110, 176]

Armené Humber is a freelance writer, instructor, and career counselor at the Women's Opportunities Center at UCI, whose passion is to capture and sculpt stories of God's work in today's world. Contact: 11166 McGee River Circle, Fountain Valley, CA 92708. (714) 775-6705. armhumber@aol.com. [171, 252]

June Hunt, author, singer, speaker, founder of *Hope for the Heart*, a nationwide radio ministry proclaiming biblical hope and practical help on approximately one hundred counseling topics. God's truths for today's problems! Contact: Box 7, Dallas, TX 75221. (214) 239-9999. www.hopefortheheart.org. [216]

Alison Joy Hutchins has spent her college years pursuing a writing career. She has interned with three companies and is published in several magazines, including *Profile* and *Christian Bride*. A native of Vermont, Alison has lived in Lancaster, Pennsylvania for two years. [203]

Kristen Johnson Ingram is author of fourteen Christian books and several hundred newspaper and magazine articles, short stories, and poetry. She lives at the edge of the woods in Springfield, Oregon. [90, 148]

Diana L. James, former radio/TV interview host, is a professional speaker and writer whose work has appeared in national magazines and in eight anthologies. She is the author/editor/compiler of two books: *Bounce Back* and *Bounce Back Too*. [75, 246]

Sandra Jensen is a writer and coeditor of *Beanie Baby Stories* (Starburst). She also writes for Christian broadcasting, missionary periodicals, and inspirational publications. Contact: 1411 Richman Knoll, Fullerton, CA 92835. RSJensen@earthlink.net. [120]

Jane Tod Jimenez lives with husband, Victor, and two teenagers in Tempe, Arizona. Appreciating life's variety, she has had careers in real estate, accounting, and teaching. When not working, she's either quilting, cooking, or gardening. Contact: jvjimenez@yahoo.com. [183]

Lois Walfrid Johnson is the author of *The Disappearing Stranger* and other *Adventures of the Northwoods*, children's novels with family values. For speaking contact: Jeanne Mikkelson, Bethany House, Bhpjeanne@aol.com. From forthcoming *Either Way, I Win: God's Hope for the Tough Times*. [35, 101, 265]

Rebecca Barlow Jordan is a writer, inspirational speaker, marriage leader, and author of three books, including the best-seller, *Courage for the Chicken Hearted* series, and over 1,500 greeting cards, poems, stories, etc. Contact: 318 Jamie Way, Greenville, TX 75402. rebecca@unicomp.net. [3, 19]

Ellie Kay, author of *Shop, Save and Share*, is an international speaker, local television personality, humorist, and "half-witted mother of five." Married to an Air Force fighter pilot, she's from "everywhere and nowhere." Contact: P.O. Box 202, Alamogordo, NM 88310. Halfwit5@juno.com. [58]

Norma Howard Kirkpatrick is a member of Oregon Christian Writers, with published devotionals, poems, articles, and photographs, and edited a newsletter for The American Lupus Society for six years. Married forty-seven years, she has three grown daughters and five granddaughters. [104, 137]

Tina Krause is a wife, mother of two adult sons, grandmother of Ian James, award-winning newspaper columnist, freelance writer of over seven hundred columns and magazine articles, and speaker. Contact: 223 Abington St., Valparaiso, IN 46385. tinak@netnitco.net. [224]

Lynn Worley Kuntz has written award-winning fiction and nonfiction for newspapers and magazines, is author of two children's books, and has cowritten screenplays for several award-winning children's productions and the movie, *Dakota*. Contact: lynnk@frontier.net. [4, 50, 129]

Helene C. Kuoni, cofounder/publicist for the fifty-voice interdenominational Hollwegs Choir, enjoys writing, doing needlework, and working on her church's communications task force. After many years in the oil industry, she now enjoys writing for the Christian market. Contact: jkuoni@erols.com. [31, 71, 257]

Shirley Teresa Langley is a gospel singer/songwriter with four hundred assignment songs accepted. Charter member: East Texas Inspirational Writers Alive; First Place Winner International Poetry. Contact: 423 E. Main, #23, Bullard, TX 75757. (903) 894-7923. GSSW3@aol.com. [228]

Florence Littauer is an internationally acclaimed speaker and author of thirty books. Her most popular is *Personality Plus*, selling a million copies and translated into twenty languages. Contact: 1611 S. Rancho Santa Fe F2, San Marcos, CA 92069. (760) 471-0233. CLASSSpkr@aol.com. [276]

Marita Littauer, professional speaker for over twenty years, author of nine books, president of CLASServices Inc., an organization that provides resources, training, and promotion for speakers and authors. P.O. Box 66810, Albuquerque, NM 87193. (800) 433-6633. www.classervices.com. [128]

Gail MacDonald has gladly spent thirty-eight years at her husband, Gordon's, side in pastoral ministry. Besides writing, and being a grandma, she also loves teaching from Scripture and sometimes travels to speak in seminary or conferences. Contact: P.O. Box 319, Belmont, NH 03220. [119, 164, 172]

Karen Burton Mains, a national prize-winning author, her experience in the communications industries—publishing, religious broadcasting and television—has prepared her to serve as codirector of The Chapel Ministries which enables churches to reach a "sight and sound" generation. [162, 255]

Gracie Malone coauthored best-selling *Courage for the Chicken Hearted* and *Eggstra Courage for the Chicken Hearted* and has written numerous magazine articles. She is a Bible study teacher, speaker, and mentor to women. Contact: 3008 Creekview, Grapevine, TX 76051. (817) 488-2317. gmalone@ix.netcom.com. [87]

Gail Gaymer Martin, college instructor and contributing editor for *The Christian Communicator*, is a speaker, novelist, and freelance writer with twelve books to her credit. Contact: members.aol.com/martinga/romance/index.htm, or martinga@aol.com. [48]

Sylvia A. LeFort Masi is a wife and mother, United Methodist pastor, author of over five hundred articles, and editor of and contributor to *Field Conditions*, a book of stories of first ministry experiences. Contact: 220 Long Swamp Rd., New Egypt, NJ 08533. (609) 758-9458. salefortm@yahoo.com. [85]

Jane E. Maxwell, R.N., is a mother of four adult children, and writer of inspirational and health articles and devotionals. Also involved in ministries for single parents, abused women, and the elderly. Contact: 1704 Pearl St., Vestal, NY 13850. (607) 785-3017. [226]

Carole Mayhall and her husband, Jack, live in Colorado Springs and have worked with The Navigators since 1956. Carole has written seven books and has cowritten two others with Jack. She also speaks frequently at women's retreats. [73, 169]

Ruth E. McDaniel, a full-time caregiver to her husband of thirty-eight years, is a freelance writer, coleader of the Christian Writers' Group, speaker, and entertainer. Contact: 15233 Country Ridge Dr., Chesterfield, MO 63017. (314) 532-7584. [107]

Dottie McDowell, thirty-plus-year staff member of Campus Crusade for Christ, is the wife of Josh McDowell and the mother of four children. Dottie has coauthored several children's books with her husband and works with him on numerous special projects. [273]

Marticia Burns McKinney is a wife and mother of one son. A former English teacher, she now specializes in writing for the Christian marketplace. Contact: 2100 Roswell Rd., 200C, Box 519, Marietta, GA 30062. (770) 423-1129. [134]

Cindi McMenamin is a pastor's wife, mother, and freelance writer who has authored the book *Finding True Love: Experiencing Intimacy with God*. Cindi speaks for women's retreats and conferences. Contact: 25653 Lola Court, Sun City, CA 92586. (909) 679-1174. Hcmcmen@pe.net. [249]

Liz Moore Meeks, wife of Bill for forty years, mother of three, and grandmother of six, is a Bible study leader, circle prayer chairman, speaker, and Sunday school teacher for disabled children. She recently completed a devotional book for her grandchildren. Contact: jwmmeks@swbell.net. [14]

Kathy Collard Miller is a wife, mother, author of over forty books, including *God's Abundance*, and a speaker. She has spoken in twenty-two states and three foreign countries. Contact: P.O. Box 1058, Placentia, CA 92871. (714) 993-2654. Kathyspeak@aol.com. [49]

DiAnn G. Mills is a wife, mother of four adult sons, and author of two books, short stories, articles, and devotionals. An active church member, she is a church librarian and sings in choir. Contact: 14410 Dracaena Court, Houston, TX 77070. millsdg@flash.net. [250]

LaSarah Montgomery is a missionary wife in Guadalajara, Mexico, an English and piano teacher, and has previously discipled and mentored teens. Contact: 3110 Prescott, Garland, TX 75041. (214) 278-8915. lasarahmex@hotmail.com. [157]

Fern Ayers Morrissey is a Christian mother of four, grandmother of eight, aspiring poet, diarist, premier pen pal with correspondents spanning seven countries/fifty years; loves literature, Russian language, classical music. Husband, Bill, says she can cook, too! Contact: 3836 Oak Ridge, St. Louis, MO 63121. [94, 269]

Lynn D. Morrissey is author of *Seasons of a Woman's Heart*; contributing author to *God's Abundance* series and *Teens Can Bounce Back*; an inspirational CLASSpeaker (prayer-journaling and women's topics); and vocalist. Contact: P.O. Box 50101, St. Louis, MO 63105. lynnswords@primary.net and members.primary.net/~lynnswords/ [163, 189, 217]

Amberly Neese is a passionate speaker and author. She encourages thousands annually with insightful stories and humor. Amberly and her husband, Scott, live in southern California where he is Pastor of Worship and she ministers to children. Contact: (714) 847-3573. [51, 200]

Donna Mesler Norman is a freelance writer, speaker, and soloist, who enjoys creating children's stories, classical music, and travel to anywhere. She and her husband, Phillip, reside in a lakefront chalet nestled deeply in the woods of eastern Missouri. Contact: (636) 745-7914. [204, 272]

Doris Hays Northstrom writes for national publications, teaches creative writing, and is an inspirational speaker. Other passions are juggling the joys of two families with her new husband, Ron, sharing biking, hiking, gardening, and tennis. Contact: 1308 N. Cascade, Tacoma, WA 98406. (253) 759-9829. [211]

Karen O'Connor is an award-winning author, CLASSpeaker, and Personality Plus trainer who specializes in encouraging people toward greater intimacy with God, themselves, and others. Contact: 2050 Pacific Beach Dr. #205, San Diego, CA 92109. (619) 483-3184. wordykaren@aol.com. [133, 197]

John-Eva B. Orsa is a wife, mother, and grandmother who recently turned fifty and plans to use the next fifty years sharing all she's learned up till now prayerfully to the glory of God! Contact: 668 Charles St., Moorpark, CA 93021. MyGuy50@aol.com. [174]

Susan Titus Osborn is a contributing editor of *The Christian Communicator*, director of the TCC Manuscript Critique Service, and an adjunct professor at HIU. She has authored nineteen books and numerous articles. Contact: 3133 Puente Street, Fullerton, CA 92835. Susanosb@aol.com. [149]

Donna Otto is the founder of Between Women of God (Mentors for Mothers), author of six books and numerous magazine articles, and a popular Bible teacher/speaker. She and her husband, David, live in Scottsdale, Arizona, and have a grown daughter, Anissa. [84]

Pat Palau, a popular speaker at a variety of events and author of numerous articles, is the wife of international evangelist Luis Palau and the mother of four grown sons. She and Luis live in Portland, Oregon. Contact: P.O. Box 1173, Portland, OR 97207. (503) 614-1500. lpea@palau.org. [153]

Nisel Pardo-McDonald has actively ministered to women for almost twenty-five years, and lives with her husband, William, in the beautiful San Bernardino Mountains of California. They have two grown daughters, Esther and Amanda. Contact: P.O. Box 2754, Crestline, CA 92325. niselm@yahoo.com. [127]

Jane Parrish is a wife and mother of two adult children. She is a Bible teacher and has taught a Precept study at St. James Bible College in the Ukraine. Contact: 837 Guenevere Dr., Ballwin, MO 63011. ljparr@swbell.net. [143]

Edwina Patterson, A Heart For The Home Ministry founder, author, radio personality, and conference speaker to women through the United States and Europe. Contact: 3101 Deep Valley Trail, Plano, TX 75075. (972) 599-2590. www.heart-for-home.org, ecwina7@aol.com. [56, 177]

Patricia Perry is a wife, mother, and grandmother. She is a writer of children's books, as well as articles on Christian marriage and family. Favorite activities are gardening and spending newly found time with her mother-in-law. Contact: patiperry@home.com. [86, 130]

Kathryn Thompson Presley, retired English professor, has published twenty-five short stories and poems in national magazines, journals, and anthologies. Kathryn speaks to women's groups. Contact: Route 1, Box 312, Somerville, TX 77879. kpresley@myriad.net. [60, 155]

Margaret Primrose, former missionary and teacher, is retired from Nazarene Publishing House. She has authored two children's books and many shorter pieces. Contact: 808 E. 100th Terrace, Kansas City, MO 64131. (816) 943-0119. [29]

Paquita Rawleigh, a bilingual poet-writer, has published her work in several books and anthologies, and has received several awards for her writings. Contact: 6318 Westview Dr., Riverside, CA 92506. (909) 780-9203. Paquitar@yahoo.com. [93]

Karen L. Riley is a wife, mother, and freelance writer. With a background in marketing, she writes, designs, and produces communication materials. Contact: 725 E. Illinois Street, Wheaton, IL 60187. [198, 275]

Laura Sabin Riley is a wife, mother, author, and a passionate speaker. Laura is the author of *All Mothers Are Working Mothers*, a devotional book for stay-at-home moms (Horizon Books), and numerous short stories. Contact: P.O. Box 1150, Yuma, AZ 85366. RileysRanch@juno.com. [210, 254]

Jean Rodgers is a writer of business promotional pieces, newspaper essays, ten-year newspaper column "We Women," and contributor to *Vitamin C for the Spirit of Women* and *Hurting Spirit*. Married forty-one years to John, with four adult children and six grandchildren. Contact: 2253 Elizabeth Drive, Broadview, IL 60153. [65]

Joyce Rogers is a devoted wife, mother, and grandmother, and conference speaker, author, and women's ministries leader. She and her husband, Adrian Rogers, live in Memphis, Tennessee, where he pastors Bellevue Baptist Church. Her books: *The Wise Woman* and *The Secret of a Woman's Influence*. [77]

Lucinda J. Rollings is a freelance writer whose treasures include two children, two granddaughters, and a wonderful husband. Lucinda and her husband serve with Awana, an international Christian youth organization, as event coordinators for central and southern Indiana. [97]

JoAnn L. Rosa-Hanes, working mother of three, teacher of Sunday school and VBS, writer and director of Christmas programs at church, enjoys family, piano, crocheting, singing, journaling, and sketching. Contact: 181 Lemay Ferry Road, St. Louis, MO 63125. [47]

Darlene Deibler Rose and her husband, Gerald, are missionaries among the cannibals of New Guinea, where they have witnessed many coming to the Lord. She thanks God for every trial and for His faithful provision of every need. The Roses have two sons and six grandchildren. Contact: P.O. Box 533, Creighton, NE 68729. [267]

Linda Roswit works in the challenging field of home health, a daily source of humorous situations as well as heartwarming stories of human survival. She enjoys the great outdoors with her husband, Bill, and her nieces and nephew. [213]

Suzy Ryan lives in Southern California with her husband and three small children. Her articles have appeared in *Today's Christian Woman*, *Woman's World*, *The American Enterprise*, and various newspapers. Contact: KenSuzyR@aol.com. [185]

Fran Caffey Sandin is a wife, mother of two young adults, a new grandmother, a registered nurse, and freelance writer who coauthored the recent best-selling book, *Courage for the Chicken Hearted*. Contact: 105 Edgewood Drive, Greenville, TX 75402-3415. [91]

Doris Schuchard is a wife and mother of two children. After living most of her life in the Midwest, she has recently moved to Atlanta, where she is enjoying exploring and writing in her new home. [147]

Luci Shaw is writer in residence at Regent College, Vancouver, a poet and lecturer, and author of seventeen books of poetry and prose including *Water My Soul*. Contact: 4909 Lewis Ave., Bellingham, WA 98226. (360) 650-1515. Shawbiz@aol.com. Used by permission of the author. [106, 136, 207, 220]

Evelyn Anderson Sheets is a retired grandmother and writer of published short stories and poems. She shepherds a church group and keeps a daily personal journal (nineteen years). Contact: 4341 Desert Aire Avenue, Palmdale, CA 93552. (661) 267-6712. [24, 209]

Linda Evans Shepherd is a national speaker and author of *Encouraging Hands—Encouraging Hearts*, as well as *Share Jesus Without Fear* with Bill Fay. She is the mother of two and married for twenty years. Contact: www.sheppro.com. [41]

Diane Shirley, author and speaker, is founder of RubyGlenn Ministries for single parents of handicapped or chronically ill children. Contact: P.O. Box 63021, Colorado Springs, CO 80962. [55]

Doris Smalling is a retired high school/college teacher, published author/poet, and speaker. She teaches an adult Sunday school class, and does volunteer tutoring. Contact: 1137 N. Harrison Ct., E. Wenatchee, WA 98802. (509) 884-5992. dpsmalling@aol.com. [88, 170, 196]

Annette Smith is the author of *Whispers of Angels, Stories to Touch Your Heart* and *Sweeter Than Honey, Stories to Feed Your Soul*. Contact: P.O. Box 1221, Groveton, TX 75845. ranann@inu.net. [180]

Rachel St. John-Gilbert is a professional laugher and freelance writer. Her work has been published in *Better Homes and Gardens*. Fun-loving husband, Scott, and seven-year-old son, Trevor, keep her equitably humbled and encouraged! [27, 168]

Patty Stump is a wife, mother of two, frequent speaker for retreats and special events, writer, Bible study teacher, and Christian counselor. She communicates biblical truths with humor, wisdom, and practical application. Contact: P.O. Box 5003, Glendale, AZ 85312. (602) 979-1441. [54, 165, 187]

Lea C. Tartanian, a medical secretary, writer, and a member of Toastmasters, has written for twenty-three publications. Her goals are to publish inspirational books, conduct journaling workshops, and be an inspirational speaker. Contact: 3012 Phyllis Street, Endwell, NY 13760. (607) 754-3671. [190]

Debbi Taylor is a wife, mother, teacher, school administrator, and writer. Contact: 7754 McGroarty Ave., Tujunga, CA 91042. (818) 352-4808. Debbi777@aol.com. [247]

Cynthia Carpenter Thomas writes and recites poetry, speaks at women's conferences, and teaches Bible studies. She lives on a ranch in the Texas hill country and enjoys raising Boer goats. Contact: P.O. Box 291569, Kerrville, TX 78029. [64]

Joyce E. Tomanek is a wife, mother, grandmother, ham radio operator, crafter, organic farmer, cancer survivor, author, and poet. She coordinates two email prayer fellowships. Contact: 549 Traves Cove Rd. NW, Clarkesville, GA 30523. (706) 754-5030. neh_8_10@stc.net. [125, 194]

Marcia Van't Land is a teacher, author, and speaker, whose latest book is *Living Well With Chronic Illness*. She leads a chronic illness support group. Contact: 12648 Ramona, Chino, CA 91710. (909) 627-2024. [38]

June L. Varnum is the author of articles and devotions and is an amateur photographer.

She has taught Sunday school, led Bible studies, prayer groups, and retreat workshops. Contact: P.O. Box 236, Loyalton, CA 96118-0236. jvarnum @psln.com. [205]

Ann M. Velia teaches Bible studies through her church and writes a devotional column for her local newspaper. She and her husband, Jim, recently celebrated their thirty-fourth anniversary. Contact: 4248 Mission Bell Avenue, Las Cruces, NM 88011. (505) 521-3460. [154]

Brenda Waggoner is a licensed professional counselor and author of *The Velveteen Woman*. She leads The Velveteen Woman Seminar on Becoming REAL Through God's Transforming Love. Contact: 16301 CR 558, Farmersville, TX 75442. (972) 782-7680. FBWaggoner@aol.com. [219]

Shirley Pope Waite has written for *Guideposts* and over 150 other magazines and twenty-two books. She teaches memoir writing, leads writers' workshops, and has a speaking ministry. Contact: 1604 Pleasant, Walla Walla, WA 99362. (509) 525-5592. kswaite@juno.com. [59]

Phyllis Wallace hosts the *Woman to Woman* radio talk show, produced by Lutheran Hour Ministries and aired on over 350 stations. Guests share hope in Christ through discussions of life-issues impacting women. Personal appearances: (314) 951-4140. LLLWALLACP@lhm.org. [111]

Susan M. Warren is a career missionary with SEND International in Far East Russia, married for ten years, mother of four homeschooled children. Author of a handful of magazine articles and one novel. Contact: SEND International, Box 536, Palmer, AK 99645. aswarren@iname.com. [105, 152, 192, 214]

Bonnie Watkins is a wife, mother of two boys, and a literature and creative writing teacher. Contact: 10102 Chukar Circle, Austin, TX 78758-5530. (512) 837-7094. dwatkins@austin.cc.tx.us. [11]

Mildred Wenger writes children's stories and devotional articles, and also gives piano and organ lessons. She and her husband, Daniel, enjoy their family of five grown children and grandchildren. Contact: 1325 Furnace Hill Road, Stevens, PA 17578. [26]

Mary Whelchel is founder and speaker of the radio program, *The Christian Working Woman*, heard on over 500 Christian stations. She has written ten books and has an active speaking ministry. Contact: (630) 462-0552. [26, 70]

Karen H. Whiting is a freelance author and mother of five. Her books include *The Beatitudes, Finger Puppet Mania,* and *Creative Girls I* and *II*. She enjoys creativity and inspiring others to tap into their creativity. Contact: 10936 SW 156 Pl., Miami, FL 33196. whiting@gate.net. [67]

Leslie Whitworth lives on a ranch in the Texas hill country. She is a bilingual kindergarten teacher and enjoys gardening, kayaking, and being with her children, Sophie and Ned. Contact: HC 16 Box 14, Castell, TX 76831. Lesw64@aol.com. [150]

Elizabeth M. Wilt is an enthusiastic wife, mother, pharmacist, speaker, and author! She has written four unpublished books: *Insights of the Invisible, Glimpses of Glory, Mirrors of Majesty,* and *Windows of Wonder*. Contact: 16708 George Franklyn Drive, Independence, MO 64055. (816) 373-2308. elizabeth_m.wilt@dupontpharma.com. [8]

Cassandra Woods is a management engineer, writer, and speaker. Her writing has been published in various publications, and she enjoys challenging others to reach their full potential. Contact: P.O. Box 13311, Birmingham, AL 35202. Cwjoy@aol.com. [69]

Kathleen Dale Wright is a wife, mother of three, grandmother of eight and great-grandmother of one. She sold her first article twenty years ago and is a CTM in Toastmasters International. Contact: 19122 N. Highway 71, Mountainburg, AR 72946. (501) 369-4286. bkwright@earthlink.net. [6, 42, 266]

Mary Ellen Wright is a wife, a mother of three adult children, and grandmother of four, author, inspirational writer, and teacher of how to live the Christian life. Contact: 13605 Scott Avenue, Kearney, MO 64060. (816) 628-5780. Yiya44@aol.com. [237, 245]

Martha B. Yoder, forced from nursing by post-polio problems, writes for Christian Light Publications, is published in books by Starburst Publishers, and has nine children's story tapes for Gospel Sunrise, Inc. Contact: 1501 VA Ave., Apt. 159, Harrisonburg, VA 22802. (540) 564-6560. [244]

Jeanne Zornes offers fresh, encouraging perspectives through Apple of His Eye Ministries. She is the author of six books (including *When I Felt Like Ragweed, God Saw a Rose*), hundreds of articles, and frequent conference speaker. Contact: 1025 Meeks, Wenatchee, WA 98801. [52]

Credits

Some stories in *Treasures of a Woman's Heart* come from other sources, which are credited below. The pages on which these stories can be found are listed in brackets at the end of each entry.

"A Few Good Hens" and "Sweet Potato Memories" adapted from *Courage for the Chicken Hearted*, Becky Freeman, Susan Duke, Rebecca Barlow Jordan, Gracie Malone, and Fran Caffey Sandin, Honor Books Publishing, Tulsa, OK, 1998. Used by permission. [3, 229]

"Taking Time for Friendship" from *Treasured Friends*, Ann Hibbard, Baker Book House Co., MI, 1997. Used by permission. [7]

"Jesus, My Friend" from *Diamonds In The Dust*, Joni Eareckson Tada, Zondervan Publishing House, MI, 1993. Used by permission. [10]

"Quality Time" from *A Mother's Heart*, Jean Fleming, NavPress, CO, 1982. Used by permission. All rights reserved. [13]

"Time to Waste" from *Shaping a Woman's Soul*, Judith Couchman, Zondervan Publishing House, MI, 1996. Used by permission. [16]

"Moments Like These" and "Choosing to Grow" from *Your Life, God's Home*, Nancie Carmichael, Good News Publishers/Crossway Books, IL, 1998. Used by permission. [18, 248]

"That's Worth Everything" and "Fully Alive" from *Because He Lives*, Gloria and William J. Gaither, Zondervan Publishing House, MI, 1997. Used by permission.[20, 25]

"Be Still and Know" from *His Imprint, My Expression*, Kay Arthur, Harvest House Publishers, OR, 1993. Used by permission. [28]

"Joy Beads," "It's Later Than You Think," "Cookies For Breakfast," and "Enough Is Enough" from *Joy Breaks*, Patsy Clairmont, Barbara Johnson, Marilyn Meberg, Luci Swindoll, Copyright by New Life Clinics, Zondervan Publishing House, MI, 1997. Used by permission. [30, 61, 131, 212]

"Restoration" from *More from Mitford Newsletter*, Jan Karon, Penguin Putnam Publishers, NY, Volume 2, Number 6, Fall, 1998. Used by permission. [37]

"Put a Song in Your Heart" from *Meditations for Mothers*, Elisa Morgan, Zondervan Publishing House, MI, 1999. Used by permission. [39]

"Dialogue with God" from *Let Faith Change Your Life*, Becky Tirabassi, Thomas Nelson Publishers, TN, 1997. Used by permission. [39]

The Chocolate-Covered Cherries from *Making a Christmas Memory*, Twila Paris, Proper Management, TN, 1990. Used by permission. [43]

"The Wedding Gift" adapted from *Through His Eyes*, Kathy Collard Miller, NavPress Publishing Group, CO, 1999. Used by permission of author. [46]

"No Solution in Sight" and "Just Like a Blanket" from *Detours, Tow Trucks, and Angels in Disguise*, Carol Kent, NavPress Publishing Group, CO, 1996. Used by permission. All rights reserved. [53, 195]

"Little Things" and "Timeless Treasures" from *Seasons of My Heart*, Barbara Peretti, J. Countryman, TN, 1998. Used by permission. [57, 66]

"The Treasury" from *Things Pondered*, Beth Moore, Mark S. Palmer, Publisher, TX, 1995. [68]

"Honey, Did We Shrink-Wrap the Kids?" from *OverJoyed!*, Patsy Clairmont, Barbara Johnson, Marilyn Meberg, Luci Swindoll, Sheila Walsh, Thelma Wells. Copyright by Women of Faith, Inc., Zondervan Publishing House, MI, 1999. Used by permission. [81]

"Big Mama's Cornbread" from *Living Simply in God's Abundance*, Suzanne Dale Ezell, Thomas Nelson Publishers, TN, 1998. Used by permission. [89]

"A Tea Party of Love" from *Decision Magazine*, Janette Oke, Billy Graham Evangelistic Association, MN, May 1994. Used by permission. All rights reserved. [95]

"No Shortcuts to Love" from *Home Life Magazine*, Joan Clayton, The Sunday School Board of the Southern Baptist Convention, September, 1988. Used by permission of the author. [99]

"I Was in Prison, but He Was With Me" from *Clippings From My Notebook*, Corrie ten Boom, Thomas Nelson Publishers, TN, 1984. Used by permission. [108]

"Autographed by the Author," "Coming Home," "Morning Song," and "Small Prayers" from *Legacy of a Pack Rat*, Ruth Bell Graham, Oliver Nelson, a Division of Thomas Nelson Publishers, TN, 1989. Used by permission. [113, 243, 256, 270]

"Full of Joy" from *The Autobiography of Madame Guyon*, Jeanne-Marie Guyon, Translated by Thomas Taylor Allen, Keats Publishing, Inc., CT, 1980. [115]

"Tending the Fire" from *High Call High Privilege*, Gail MacDonald, Hendrickson Publishers, Inc., MA, 1998. Used by permission. [119]

"God Works in Conflict" from *As Silver Refined*, Kay Arthur, WaterBrook Press, CO, 1997. Used by permission. All rights reserved. [121]

"Wedding Preparations" from *Vision of His Glory*, Anne Graham Lotz, Word Publishing, TN, 1996. Used by permission. All rights reserved. [124]

"He Is the Bridegroom" and "You Are His Treasured Possession" from *Reflecting His Image*, Liz Curtis Higgs, Thomas Nelson Publishers, TN, 1996. Used by permission. [126, 233]

"Repeated Sunrise" from *Gift from the Sea*, Anne Morrow Lindbergh, Pantheon Books, a Division of Random House, Inc., NY, 1955. [139]

"God's Jewels" from *Shower of Blessings*, Helen Steiner Rice, Fleming H. Revell Company, a Division of Baker Book House Co., MI, 1980. [146]

"A Record of Footprints" from *A Mother's Footprints of Faith*, Carol Kuykendall, Zondervan Publishing House, MI, 1997. Used by permission. [151]

"Letter from a Friend" from *Footprints*, Margaret Fishback Powers, HarperCollins Publishers Ltd., Canada, 1993. [156]

"It's Your Life, Lord" from *Becoming a Woman of Excellence*, Cynthia Heald, NavPress, CO, 1986. Used by permission. All rights reserved. [159]

"A Little Night Work" from *Beautiful in God's Eyes*, Elizabeth George, Harvest House Publishers, OR, 1998. Used by permission. [167]

"Consecration" from *The Christian's Secret of a Happy Life*, Hannah Whitall Smith, Fleming H. Revell Company, a division of Baker Book House, NJ, 1952. [175]

"Simple Acts of Love" from *That's What Love Is For*, Stormie Omartian, Harvest House Publishers, OR, 1998. [178]

"God's Greatest Gift" from *In My Own Words*, Mother Teresa, Gramercy Books, Division of Random House Value Publishing, Inc., NY, 1997. [181]

"Heaven-Sent" from *Roses in December*, Marilyn Heavilin, Harvest House, OR, 1997. Used by permission. [184]

"Priceless Gifts" from *Decision Magazine*, Annie Chapman, Billy Graham Evangelistic Association, MN, December, 1993. Used by permission. All rights reserved. [186]

"Looking Higher" from *Grow Something Besides Old*, Laurie Beth Jones, Simon and Schuster, NY, 1998. [188]

"You Can't Take It with You" from *Timeless Treasures*, Emilie Barnes, Harvest House Publishers, OR, 1996. Used by permission. [199]

"Simple Pleasures" from *Friends for the Journey*, Luci Shaw and Madeleine L'Engle, Servant Publications, MI, 1997. [202]

"The Thankful Heart" from *Something More*, Catherine Marshall, Fleming H. Revell Company, a division of Baker Book House, MI, 1974. Used by permission. [223]

"Give Yourself Away," "Memories," and "My Father's Crutches" from *More Precious Than Silver*, Joni Eareckson Tada, Zondervan Publishing House, MI, 1998. Used by permission. [225]

"Shelter from the Storm" from *Decision Magazine*, Jill Briscoe, Billy Graham Evangelistic Association, MN, July-August 1992. Used by permission. All rights reserved. [230]

"Awakening" from *With New Eyes*, Margaret Becker, Harvest House Publishers, OR, 1998. Used by permission. [240]

"The Art of Worship" from *Dear Abba*, Claire Cloninger, Word Publishing, TN, 1997. Used by permission. All rights reserved. [251]

"God's Loving Presence" from *Gold By Moonlight*, Amy Carmichael, Christian Literature Crusade, Inc., PA, 1935. Used by permission. [253]

"Forgiveness Through Jesus" from *The Hiding Place*, Corrie ten Boom with John and Elizabeth Sherrill, Chosen Books, Inc., NY, 1971. Used by permission. [258]

"A Child's Prayer" from *Writer to Writer*, Bodie and Brock Thoene, Bethany House Publishers, MN, 1990. Used by permission. [262]

Other Books by Starburst Publishers®

(partial listing—full list available on request)

Treasures of a Woman's Heart: A Daybook of Stories and Inspiration
Edited by Lynn D. Morrissey
> Join the best-selling editor of *Seasons of a Woman's Heart* in this touching sequel where she unlocks the treasures of women and glorifies God with scripture, reflection, and a compilation of stories. Explore heartfelt living with vignettes by Kay Arthur, Emilie Barnes, Claire Cloninger, and others.
> (cloth) ISBN 1-892016-25-7   **$18.95**

Seasons of a Woman's Heart: A Daybook of Stories and Inspiration
Edited by Lynn D. Morrissey
> A woman's heart is complex. This daybook of stories, quotes, scriptures, and daily reflections will inspire and refresh. Christian women share their heartfelt thoughts on Seasons of Faith, Growth, Guidance, Nurturing, and Victory. Includes Christian writers Kay Arthur, Emilie Barnes, Luci Swindoll, Jill Briscoe, and Florence Littauer.
> (cloth) ISBN 1-892016-03-6   **$18.95**

More of Him, Less of Me
Jan Christiansen
> Subtitled: *A Daybook of My Personal Insights, Inspirations & Meditations on the Weigh Down™ Diet.* The insight shared in this year-long daybook of inspiration will encourage you on your weight-loss journey, bring you to a deeper relationship with God, and help you improve any facet of your life. Each page includes an essay, scripture, and a tip-of-the-day that will encourage and uplift you as you trust God to help you achieve your proper weight. Perfect companion guide for anyone on the Weigh Down™ diet!
> (cloth) ISBN 1-892016-00-1   **$17.95**

Desert Morsels: A Journal with Encouraging Tidbits from My Journey on the Weigh Down™ Diet
Jan Christiansen
> When Jan Christiansen set out to lose weight on the Weigh Down™ Diet she got more than she bargained for! In addition to *losing* over 35 pounds and *gaining* a closer relationship with God, Jan discovered a gift—her ability to entertain and comfort fellow dieters! Jan's inspiring website led to the release of her best-selling first book, *More of Him, Less of Me.* Now, Jan serves another helping of *her* wit and *His* wisdom in this lovely companion journal. Includes inspiring scripture, insightful comments, stories from readers, room for the reader's personal reflection and *Plenty of **Attitude*** (p-attitude).
> (cloth) ISBN 1-892016-21-4   **$17.95**

More God's Abundance: Joyful Devotions for Every Season
Compiled by Kathy Collard Miller

Editor Kathy Collard Miller responds to the tremendous success of *God's Abundance* with a fresh collection of stories based on God's Word for a simpler life. Includes stories from our most beloved Christian writers such as: Liz Curtis Higgs and Patsy Clairmont that are combined with ideas, tips, quotes, and Scripture.

(cloth) ISBN 1-892016-13-3   **$19.95**

God's Abundance for Women: Devotions for a More Meaningful Life
Compiled by Kathy Collard Miller

Following the success of *God's Abundance*, this book will touch women of all ages as they seek a more meaningful life. Essays from our most beloved Christian authors exemplify how to gain the abundant life that Jesus promised through trusting Him to fulfill our every need. Each story is enhanced with Scripture, quotes, and practical tips providing brief, yet deeply spiritual reading.

(cloth) ISBN 1-892016-14-1   **$19.95**

The *God's Word for the Biblically-Inept*™ series is already a best-seller with over 100,000 books sold! Designed to make reading the Bible easy, educational, and fun! This series of verse-by-verse Bible studies, topical studies, and overviews mixes scholarly information from experts with helpful icons, illustrations, sidebars, and time lines. It's the Bible made easy!

The Bible—God's Word for the Biblically-Inept™
Larry Richards

An excellent book to start learning the entire Bible. Get the basics or the in-depth information you are seeking with this user-friendly overview. From Creation to Christ to the Millennium, learning the Bible has never been easier.

(trade paper) ISBN 0-914984-55-1   **$16.95**

Revelation—God's Word for the Biblically-Inept™
Daymond R. Duck

End-time Bible Prophecy expert Daymond R. Duck leads us verse by verse through one of the Bible's most confusing books. Follow the experts as they forge their way through the captivating prophecies of Revelation!

(trade paper) ISBN 0-914984-98-5   **$16.95**

Health & Nutrition—God's Word for the Biblically-Inept™
Kathleen O'Bannon Baldinger

The Bible is full of God's rules for good health! Baldinger reveals scientific evidence that proves the diet and health principles outlined in the Bible are the best for total health. Learn about the Bible Diet, the food pyramid, and fruits and vegetables from the Bible! Experts include Pamela Smith, Julian Whitaker, Kenneth Cooper, and T. D. Jakes.

(trade paper) ISBN 0-914984-05-5   **$16.95**

Women of the Bible—God's Word for the Biblically-Inept™
Kathy Collard Miller

Finally, a Bible perspective just for women! Gain valuable insight from the successes and struggles of such women as Eve, Esther, Mary, Sarah, and Rebekah. Interesting icons like "Get Close to God," "Build Your Spirit," and "Grow Your Marriage" will make it easy to incorporate God's Word into your daily life.

(trade paper) ISBN 0-914984-06-3   **$16.95**

Genesis—God's Word for the Biblically-Inept™
Joyce Gibson

Genesis is the seventh book in the exciting *God's Word for the Biblically-Inept™* series designed to make understanding and learning the Word of God simple and fun! Like the other books in this series, the author breaks the Bible down into bite-sized pieces making it easy to understand and incorporate into your life. Readers will learn about Creation, Adam and Eve, the Flood, Abraham and Isaac, and more. Includes chapter summaries, bullet points, definitions, and study questions.

(trade paper) ISBN 1-892016-12-5   **$16.95**

Prophecies of the Bible—God's Word for the Biblically-Inept™
Daymond R. Duck

God has a plan for this crazy planet and now, understanding it is easier than ever! Best-selling author and End-time prophecy expert Daymond R. Duck explains the complicated prophecies of the Bible in plain English. Read with wonder as Duck shows you all there is to know about the End of the Age, the New World Order, the Second Coming, and the Coming World Government. Includes useful commentary, expert quotes, icons, sidebars, chapter summaries, and study questions! Find out what prophecies have already been fulfilled and what's in store for the future! Over 100,000 sold in this series.

(trade paper) ISBN 1-892016-22-2   **$16.95**

What's in the Bible for . . .™ Women
Georgia Curtis Ling

What does the Bible have to say to women? Women of all ages will find biblical insight on topics that are meaningful to them in four sections: Wisdom for the Journey; Family Ties; Bread, Breadwinners, and Bread Makers; and Fellowship and Community Involvement. This book uses illustrations, bullet points, chapter summaries, and icons to make understanding God's Word easier than ever!

(trade paper) ISBN 1-892016-10-9   **$16.95**

What's in the Bible for . . .™ Mothers
Judy Bodmer

Is homeschooling a good idea? Is it okay to work? At what age should I start treating my children like responsible adults? What is the most important thing I can teach my children? If you are asking these questions and need help answering them, *What's in the Bible for . . . Mothers* is especially for you! Simple and user-friendly, this motherhood manual offers hope and instruction for today's mothers by jumping into the lives of mothers in the Bible (e.g., Naomi, Elizabeth, and Mary) and by exploring biblical principles that are essential to being a nurturing mother.

(paperback) ISBN 1-892016-26-5   **$16.95**

The Weekly Feeder: A Revolutionary Shopping, Cooking, and Meal-Planning System
Cori Kirkpatrick

A revolutionary meal-planning system, here is a way to make preparing home-cooked dinners more convenient than ever. At the beginning of each week, simply choose one of the eight preplanned menus, tear out the corresponding grocery list, do your shopping, and whip up each fantastic meal in less than 45 minutes! The author's household management tips, equipment checklists, and nutrition information make this system a must for any busy family. Included with every recipe is a personal anecdote from the author emphasizing the importance of good food, a healthy family, and a well-balanced life.

(trade paper) ISBN 1-892016-09-5   **$16.95**

God Stories: They're So Amazing, Only God Could Make Them Happen
Donna I. Douglas

Famous individuals share their personal, true-life experiences with God in this beautiful new book! Find out how God has touched the lives of top recording artists, professional athletes, and other newsmakers like Jessi Colter, Deana Carter, Ben Vereen, Stephanie Zimbalist, Cindy Morgan, Sheila E., Joe Jacoby, Cheryl Landon, Brett Butler, Clifton Taulbert, Babbie Mason, Michael Medved, Sandi Patty, Charlie Daniels, and more! Their stories are intimate, poignant, and sure to inspire and motivate you as you listen for God's message in your own life!

(cloth) ISBN 1-892016-11-7   **$18.95**

Since Life Isn't a Game, These Are God's Rules: Finding Joy & Fulfillment in God's Ten Commandments
Kathy Collard Miller

Life is often referred to as a game, but God didn't create us because he was short on game pieces. To succeed in life, you'll need to know God's rules. In this book, Kathy Collard Miller explains the meaning of each of the Ten Commandments with fresh application for today. Each chapter includes Scripture and quotes from some of our most beloved Christian authors including Billy Graham, Patsy Clairmont, Liz Curtis Higgs, and more! Sure to renew your understanding of God's rules.

(cloth) ISBN 1-892016-15-x   **$17.95**

The God Things Come in Small Packages Introducing a new series that combines the beauty of gift books with the depth of devotionals.

Readers will be drawn to a closer relationship with God through:

- Narrative vignettes detailing powerful moments of revelation

- Encouraging Scripture presented as personal letters from God

- Reflective thoughts for reader meditation. Join best-selling writers LeAnn Weiss, Susan Duke, Caron Loveless, and Judith Carden as they awaken your senses and open your mind to the "little" wonders of God in life's big picture!

God Things Come in Small Packages:
Celebrating the Little Things in Life
Susan Duke, LeAnn Weiss, Caron Loveless, and Judith Carden

God's generosity is limitless and His love can be revealed in many forms. From a single bloom in winter to a chance meeting on a busy street, readers will be encouraged to acknowledge God's generous hand in everyday life. Personalized Scripture is artfully combined with compelling stories and reflections.

(hard cover) ISBN 1-892016-28-1 **$12.95**

God Things Come in Small Packages for Moms: Rejoicing in the Simple Pleasures of Motherhood
Susan Duke, LeAnn Weiss, Caron Loveless, and Judith Carden

From life as a soccer mom to the first grandchild, most mothers spend their days taking care of others. Now, busy moms will be reminded that God is taking care of them through poignant stories recounting the everyday blessings of being a mother. Each story combines personalized Scripture with heartwarming vignettes and inspiring reflections.

(hard cover) ISBN 1-892016-29-x **$12.95**

Purchasing Information
www.starburstpublishers.com

Books are available from your favorite bookstore, either from current stock or special order. To assist bookstores in locating your selection, be sure to give title, author, and ISBN. If unable to purchase from a bookstore, you may order directly from STARBURST PUBLISHERS. When ordering please enclose full payment plus shipping and handling as follows:

Post Office (4th class)
$3.00 with a purchase of up to $20.00
$4.00 ($20.01–$50.00)
8% of purchase price for purchases
    of $50.01 and up

Canada
$5.00 (up to $35.00)
%15 ($35.01 and up)

United Parcel Service (UPS)
$4.50 (up to $20.00)
$6.00 ($20.01–$50.00)
12% ($50.01 and up)

Overseas
$5.00 (up to $25.00)
20% ($25.01 and up)

Payment in U.S. funds only. Please allow two to three weeks minimum (longer overseas) for delivery. Make checks payable to and mail to:

Starburst Publishers®
P.O. Box 4123
Lancaster, PA 17604

Credit card orders may be placed by calling 1-800-441-1456, Mon–Fri, 8:30 A.M. to 5:30 P.M. Eastern Standard Time. Prices are subject to change without notice. Catalogs are available for a 9 x 12 self-addressed envelope with four first-class stamps.